THE LOG OF ROWING
AT THE UNIVERSITY OF CALIFORNIA
BERKELEY 1870–1987

THE LOG OF ROWING

AT THE UNIVERSITY OF

1870-1987

CALIFORNIA BERKELEY

JIM LEMMON

VARSITY CREW COACH EMERITUS
UNIVERSITY OF CALIFORNIA BERKELEY

WESTERN HERITAGE PRESS
BERKELEY, CALIFORNIA

ACKNOWLEDGMENTS

The Publisher expresses special thanks to the following individuals whose splendid cooperation helped make this book possible. Howard Brodie of Carmel, California, generously gave us permission to use a selection of his sketches of Cal's crew teams that appeared in the San Francisco Chronicle's *Sporting Green*. These are reproduced on the endpapers, in the front matter, and on pages 112 and 132. Libby Ellis, now of Martha's Vineyard, Massachusetts, took special interest in the project from the outset and secured numerous rights and permissions for photographs. Jim Kantor worked tirelessly to locate and identify photographs and records in the archives of The Bancroft Library, Berkeley.

The Friends of California Crew extends its gratitude to the following patrons of this book: Bill Andersen, Rich Bartke, George Blair, Beau Breck, Jim Dieterich, Stan Freeborn, Jack Hoefer, Hans Jensen, Bob Livermore, Bill Loorz, Marty McNair, Tom Mulcahy, Ken Noack, Gary Rogers, Bernard Schulte, Tim Scofield, Porter Sesnon, Stan Shawl, Kirk Smith, Maynard Toll, Roger Thompson, and Allen Trant.

Published by Western Heritage Press
Box 5108 Elmwood Station, Berkeley, California 94705
Phone: (415) 845-8134

First Edition

Printed in the United States of America

Designed and produced by David Comstock, Comstock Bonanza Press

Edited by Robin Dellabough

Library of Congress Cataloging-in-Publication Data

Lemmon, Jim.
The log of rowing at the University of California, Berkeley 1870–1987.

Includes index
1. University of California, Berkeley—Rowing—History.
I. Title. II: Title: Log of rowing.
GV807.U53L46   1989   797.1'23'071179467   88-33945
ISBN 0-9621956-0-X

DEDICATION

THIS MODEST HISTORY OF ROWING at the University of California, Berkeley, is dedicated to the hundreds of crewmen who did *not* make the varsity boat and earn their Big C. They rowed the same endless miles, had the same sore tails, and raised the same crops of blisters; they missed out, however, on the accolades and glory achieved by their more physically blessed brethren. As a coach, I know only too well that without them to provide the necessary competition to push their varsities to the limit and beyond, those California victories never would have been recorded.

—JIM LEMMON

CONTENTS

//

Preface	viii
Foreword	ix
Introduction	xi
The Chronology:	
The Genesis 1870–1915	1
The Ben Wallis Era 1916–1923	10
The Ebright Years: Before World War II 1924–1943	18
The Ebright Years: After World War II 1946–1959	36
Post-Ebright 1960–1972	50
The Renaissance 1973–1983	64
The Hodges Period 1984–1987	78
Epilogue	83
Equipment Changes: The High-Tech Revolution	84
Transportation of Equipment	86
Recruitment of Crewmen	92
Conditioning: On and Off the Water	94
The Other Pacific Coast Crews	95
The Training Table	97
Small-Boat Rowing at California	99
The Scow and the Shell Barges	100
The Varsity Rowing Club	102
The Boatman/Rigger	103
The Managerial System	105
Interclass Races and Alumni Day	107
Swampings and Dunkings	108
The Freshmen Coach	110
Crew Finances	111
The National Team	113
Glossary	115
Appendixes:	
A. Annual Boating of California Crews	118
B. List of Coaches	132
C. List of Shells	133
D. List of Senior Managers	134
E. List of Trophy Award-Winners	135
F. List of IRA results	138
G. List of Washington, Stanford, and Wisconsin Dual Race Results	139
H. Mike Livingston's Remarks at the 1983 Awards Banquet, Faculty Club, Berkeley	141
Index	142

PREFACE

///

THIS BOOK IS THE PRODUCT of one man's dedication and perseverance. While our sport at the University is blessed with a whole host of high energy individuals pulling together for common objectives, no one has been more dedicated, and certainly no other living person today has been more intimately involved and active in California crew for more years than Jim Lemmon. Schoolboy rower, varsity Big C oarsman, assistant coach, varsity coach, molder of champions, friend and mentor to hundreds of crewmen, and now our historian, Jim's work on this book adds a whole new dimension to his already numerous and significant contributions to the on-going tradition that is crew at California.

Knowing this task had to be done, and strictly on a voluntary basis, Jim has spent two full years going through old records, scrapbooks, the remembrances of many individuals, old race logs of his and other coaches, and the archives at the Bancroft Library. Jim even managed to rediscover old files that had been considered lost forever—some of them in a little-used storeroom beneath Edwards Track and Field Stadium. Never suggesting he was a skilled writer, Jim has nevertheless produced a record of significant historical interest: significant to all Cal crewmen, their families and friends; significant to University of Californians; significant to long-time San Francisco Bay Area residents; and significant, finally, to anyone who has been involved, one way or another, in the great sport of rowing.

We are deeply grateful to you, Jim, for your authorship of this record and for seeing this whole project through to fruition. On behalf of all Cal crewmen, past, present, and future, we extend our heartfelt thanks.

THE FRIENDS OF CALIFORNIA CREW
February 1989

FOREWORD

///

IT WASNT HARD TO AGREE when the Friends of California Crew asked me to try to pull together a history of rowing at the University of California, Berkeley. After all, I've been involved for almost half of the 100-plus years of that history, starting my career in rowing fifty years ago. My exposure to the sport of rowing began during the 1932 Olympic Rowing Championships, when I just about lived at the Marine Stadium in Long Beach. I must have obtained autographs daily of the California crew that represented the U.S. in the eight-oared event. Because of the Olympic interest, a rowing program was started in Long Beach high schools in 1933. By 1937, I was on the Woodrow Wilson High School varsity crew that beat its crosstown rival, Poly High, for the first time ever. It was during this period that I came to know Ben Wallis, Ky Ebright's predecessor, because he was coaching at UCLA, then working out at the Long Beach Marine Stadium, where the high school crews rowed.

Little did I know how rowing would shape my life in the days to come. I didn't think that I actually could go to college (this was still the Depression), until my cousin's husband, a member of the Southern C's, a U.C. booster club, found out I had rowed in high school. Before I knew what had happened, I was recruited to row at California. Of course, in those days, crew recruitment consisted of a one-way ticket on a Greyhound bus. Still, I was able to go to college and find a job. Best of all I could row at the college level—at Cal and under Ky Ebright. I didn't know then that eventually I would coach with him and later succeed him.

During my years at Berkeley I have come to know many of Cal's crewmen, who together cover almost the full span of the sport. In 1961 I wrote a paper on much of the crew's history, using many of the same sources as for this book. I wrote to a number of the old-timers for their memoirs. Among those I talked with at length about their involvement in the Cal rowing program are Harry Beal Torrey '96, a member of the Board of Governors of the old Boating Association and an avid crew supporter right up to his death in the 1960s; Dean Witter '09, coach and leading patron of Cal's crew under both Ky's and my tenure; Ed Harbach '24, another Cal oarsman and patron who helped establish rowing in southern California; Ed Dodge, bow on the 1905 championship four; Ivan Ball, letterman in 1907 through 1909; Lou Penney '17, stroke oar in 1915 and #7 in 1916 and 1917; and Harold Pischel '19, stroke. All were men I came to know well and to admire.

The members of the 1928 and 1932 Olympic champion crews all have been quite helpful, especially Don Blessing '28, cox, and Duncan Gregg '32, #6. Jim Dieterich '40, cox of the 1939 Intercollegiate Rowing Association (IRA) champions, also has been most supportive. The 1948 Olympic champs were, and are, quite close to me, for I was an assistant coach while they were rowing to fame.

Not only did I get to know Ben Wallis, I rowed under Ky Ebright for four years, including the last four-mile race in the IRA. I coached under him for eleven years: five as an assistant coach, and six as his freshmen coach. I also worked closely with my former freshmen coach, Russ Nagler, as an assistant coach for five years. I was able to learn much from these men, not only about rowing but about myself. So I have had input about rowing at Cal from all of these men, as well as from many alumni I do not have the space to list. In this way I have gained an overview of the sport at Berkeley that in all likelihood has not been available to anyone else.

In order to write this history, I relied on many sources in addition to my own experiences. For the chronology I used the race log that Ky started and I continued. Thanks to Tim Hodges, varsity coach from 1984 to 1987, the old files of the crew office were made available. The University Archives at The Bancroft Library at Berkeley were a rich source of material. Both the present archivist, Bill Roberts, and the archivists emeriti, May Dornin and Jim Kantor, were most helpful—Dornin during my earlier historical searches, and Kantor for this project. In fact I doubt I could have pulled all this together without the latter's help.

An outstanding example of what is available in the University Archives is the daily journal kept by Ben Wallis from 1915 through 1923. Another source was *The Log,* an annual newsletter which Ky started and I continued. Mike Livingston, varsity coach from 1981 to 1983, reestablished it after a lapse of a few years, and Tim Hodges carried it on. The old *Blue and Golds* (the University yearbook) were quite informative. Former coaches McNair, Gladstone, Livingston, and Hodges all have been very helpful. The Oakland Public Library's Historical Unit microfilm was an excellent source. Old IRA programs provided regatta results from Poughkeepsie and Syracuse, New York and from Mariettta, Ohio.

In short, I can cite no single source for this history, nor have I depended upon my memory alone. I have lived a large portion of it, and I feel it is important to get it all down as a matter of record. To have been a part of this history is a blessing indeed. I have organized this volume by first presenting a chronology of what happened in the major races each year from the start of the program through the 1987 season. In addition, I have included short discussions of various highlights of the program that I felt would be of interest. Some chapters are updates on subjects such as equipment. Some relate what used to be. Finally, in the appendix, I have provided crew and coach rosters down through the years, along with a list of California's results in the major regattas.

I have not included the brief history of women's rowing at Cal or the Bears' lightweight program. These teams began after I left coaching in 1966, so I will leave their record to someone else.

A special acknowledgment goes to Willis Andersen Jr. '54. A member of the board of directors of the Friends of Cal Crew, Big Bill made the initial proposal for a history of rowing at Berkeley, and he headed the committee that oversaw the project. While I tried to organize the facts, Bill tended to the logistics. Without his efforts this history would never have made it. Others also contributed, especially Rich Bartke '58, president of the board of directors. Rich and Bill were most helpful in the final selection of the book's photographs and illustrations. In short, this was in no way a solo effort on my part, and to all who helped I am most grateful.

JIM LEMMON
Oakland, November 1988

INTRODUCTION

ROWING AS A SPORT AT THE University of California is at least 100 years old, although the exact birth date is unknown. We like to believe that it all began in 1870, as stated in the 1907 *Blue and Gold,* as a rowing club on Lake Merritt in Oakland for "pleasure and exercise." The club was forced to disband, however, when the University moved from downtown Oakland to its new Berkeley campus. Nevertheless, by 1875 there was an official University of California Boat Club, the beginning of a rowing program that eventually won worldwide competitions—a degree of success that was beyond the wildest dreams of its founders.

No one man, crew, or year can take credit for all of California's victories or defeats. All the thousands of men who have participated in University rowing since its modest start more than a century ago have contributed. There have been great leaders: Jewett, the first commodore of the Boating Association; Witter, captain, coach, and patron. There have been great coaches: Garnett, the first to train winning Cal crews; Wallis, the first to have an eight-oared Pacific Coast winner; and, of course, Ebright, coach of Olympic and national champions.

There have been legions of great crewmen, without question—a glance at the record is proof. But it is the essence of the sport itself that makes it most compelling.

Rowing has thrived and grown in stature throughout these many years because it is an experience and an education for each man who tries to make his crew award. With little opportunity for individual glory, rowing attracts those interested in teamwork. Teamwork, together with top physical conditioning and the most exciting competitive opportunities, create a sport that truly molds young lives. There is an almost mystical bond among crewmen, universally understood though rarely acknowledged.

At Ky Ebright's retirement banquet in May 1959, University President Clark Kerr described rowing as different than other sports. At first he thought crew was more fraternal by nature; as he came to know more about rowing, however, he realized rowing must be a religion! While President Kerr may have been in jest, those who have rowed know that he came pretty close to the reason for rowing's persistence—and why it will continue at Berkeley for at least another century.

ROWING ON SAN FRANCISCO BAY began, as it had earlier in England and on the East Coast, with oarsmen ferrying crews and passengers from larger ships to shore. Competition for fares was keen; trying to decide who was the best "waterman" was only human nature. So races were held, usually on holidays such as the Fourth of July. After a few years of this competition, between 1860 and 1870, the entire concept of rowing in the Bay Area was revolutionized by the introduction of the first standard single shell with a sliding seat. (Letter written by Malcolm Steel, University Archives at The Bancroft Library.) Many rowing clubs sprang up all along the Pacific Coast, using these boats designed specifically for racing rather than for passengers.

Rowing centered around San Diego, Vancouver-Seattle, Astoria-Portland, and San Francisco. The more prominent Bay Area groups included the San Francisco Rowing Club, the South End Club, the Dolphin Rowing Club, the Ariel Rowing Club, and the Alameda Rowing Club. (Several of these clubs, including South End and San Diego, still exist.) Club rowing during this period usually was restricted to the four with cox or the single scull—sufficient for many spirited regattas held during the late nineteenth century up and down the coast.

The oldest sport at the University of California, Berkeley, is rowing. According to the University Archives at The Bancroft Library, the University of California

1875 Plan for proposed boathouse, University of California Boat Club. (Courtesy of The Bancroft Library.)

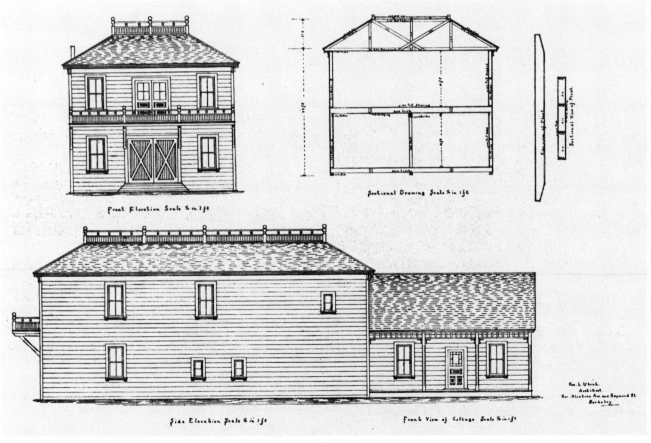

Boat Club began building a boathouse on San Antonio Creek (later named the Oakland Estuary) on October 25, 1875. Harry Tevis was elected president of the club and Charles Lee Tilden was vice-president. The secretary's book is in the University Archives, but there is no existing record of club activities such as racing.

Real competitive racing apparently did not begin until February 25, 1893 with the formation of the Boating Association of the University of California, the direct ancestor of our current rowing program. The Association's goals were "to give an opportunity to its members to enjoy the healthful sport of rowing, as well as to support a college crew for intercollegiate and inter-club races." Its first commodore was William D. Jewett; Stanley A. Easton was captain; and E. M. Garnett, Harvard '87, was coach. Professor C. L. Cory was vice-president; M. R. Gibbons was secretary; and W. G. Morrow was treasurer. The main organizer and chief financial donor

First page of minutes, October 15, 1875. This was the day the University of California Boat Club was formed and officers were elected. (Courtesy of The Bancroft Library.)

apparently was Jewett. He must have been an effective leader: by 1895, the Association was prospering, with a fine new boathouse on the estuary at Alameda Point, Sessions Basin, 75 life members, and 200 yearly members. (At that time, dues were $20 for a life membership and $2.50 annually.)

After several years of hotly contested interclass races, the Association's first outside competition was announced in a broadside: "The first appearance of a University crew upon the water will be a Four-Oar race with the Columbia Rowing Club of Oakland on Saturday April 27, 1895 at 3 p.m." Turning races were popular in those days; hence, the race course started in front of the boathouse, went one mile east up the estuary, turned, and finished at the starting point. Little did those pioneer crewmen realize, as they began California's competitive racing program, that their course would lead ultimately to national and Olympic championships. Or perhaps they did dream of such success—there is no record of who won that first race.

Unfortunately, the thrill of outside competition was short-lived. In May 1895 a fire completely destroyed the boathouse and most of the equipment, a loss of more than $5,000. Undeterred, the Association erected another, less extensive boathouse, which rose like a phoenix in 1896 and was used until 1906. By 1896 there were 112 life members and 177 yearly members.

Such a large group needed a concerned governing body, and the Association's Board of Governors provided men who were deeply interested in the sport of rowing. Not all of them were oarsmen, however. Harry Beal Torrey '96, for example, had been an outstanding University track team member. A marine biologist with a Ph.D., Torrey worked in a laboratory on the estuary, overlooking the Association's boathouse, a fortuitous twist of geography which led to a lifelong interest in rowing. In fact, he still attended California races in the late 1950s and early 1960s as an octogenarian.

Meanwhile, the Association faced several impediments to progress during its early years. The location of the boathouse seven miles away from the Berkeley campus, together with meager transportation, certainly was a handicap, one still faced today. Poor equipment and lack of experience also contributed difficulties. But the primary problem was the lack of intercollegiate competition.

When the Association was first formed, Stanford men had assured Cal that they too would start a rowing program, as had the University of Washington. But it wasn't until the 1900s that this movement materialized. So it was the Bay Area's rowing clubs, with men from all walks of life, that saved the day by providing stiff competition for the Association's fair-haired college boys. During the late nineteenth and early twentieth centuries,

Boating Association University of California.

Dear Sir:-

The first appearance of a University Crew upon the water will be in a Four Oar Race with the Columbia Rowing Club of Oakland, on Saturday April 27th., 1895. Program begins at 2:30 P. M. Four Oar Race at 3:00 P. M.

The course will be from in front of a Grand Stand erected on the point of land opposite the Boat House, easterly one mile, turn, and finish at starting point, total distance two miles.

Tickets to the Grand Stand 50 cents each, are now on sale at CLABROUGH GOUCHER & Co., under the Grand Hotel on Market St., San Francisco, at the Boat House and at Berkeley.

This being the first race since the organization of the Boating Association, the attendance of every one interested in University rowing is requested.

Take 1:30 P. M. Boat for Oakland; get off the Oakland train at Clinton Station.

THE BOARD OF DIRECTORS.

Left above: Handout announcing the first Outside Race for University of California Boating Association. (Courtesy of The Bancroft Library.) *Right above:* E. M. Garnett, Varsity Coach 1893–1896 and 1904–1908.

a number of races were held with understandably unsatisfactory results due to the Association's inexperience. In 1899 the University enjoyed its first recorded championship, the Feldenheimer Trophy for the Junior Championship at the annual Astoria Regatta. The winning crew was as follows:

4–Clifton H. Tracy	2–Roy Waggerhouser
3–Roy Fryer	1–Jimmy Hopper, Commodore of the Association
	Cox–Wilder

These men were the first in a long line of championship California crews.

1899 Crew, California's first Champions. They won the junior championship Feldenheimer Trophy at the Astoria Regatta. *Left to right:* coxswain Francis A. Wilder, #4 Clifton H. Tracy, #3 Roy Fryer, #2 Frank Waggerhouser, #1 Jimmy Hopper. (Courtesy of The Bancroft Library.)

Intercollegiate Competition Begins

Although club competition was good, often too good, the members of the Association looked forward to intercollegiate competition and hoped that their little group eventually would develop a college eight. Intercollegiate rowing in the East had begun in 1852, when Harvard and Yale met in what was the first intercollegiate athletic contest in the United States. The Cal Association wanted rowing on the Pacific Coast to play an equal role with the Eastern rowing establishment, with its prestigious annual championship at Poughkeepsie, New York dating back to 1895. At both Stanford and Washington, where rowing began in much the same way as at California, groups shared this goal. It was inevitable that these three schools would initiate intercollegiate racing on the Pacific Coast.

By the start of this century intercollegiate crews were competing. In 1901 W. B. Goodwin, Yale '90, offered to coach Cal's crew. (Garnett had resigned at the end of the 1896 season.) The Association ordered two coxless fours from Cornell, with plans to enter the Astoria Regatta in the fall and possibly a trip to Victoria, B.C. after that. Goodwin introduced a modified form of the classic Eastern style, as opposed to the club style the Bears had been using, which emphasized less body swing and quicker arm pull. In 1902 Cal hosted the first intercollegiate race on the estuary with Stanford in fours. Under good conditions and before a fair-sized crowd, the Bears pulled away convincingly from their Stanford rivals. Unfortunately, we lack further details of this race.

The following year, although Cal oarsmen again defeated Stanford, they lost to crews from Washington and the Portland Rowing Club in a separate regatta. This race was for the "T. S. Lippy Challenge Cup," symbol of the Pacific Coast championship and offered to the first crew to win it two successive times. Goodwin resigned after the 1903 season, and E. M. Garnett, the Association's original coach, returned. In 1904 the three Pacific Coast universities met for the first time, again for the Lippy Cup. Cal won, defeating Stanford and Washington on the latter's home course, thus becoming California's first Pacific Coast Intercollegiate championship crew. They rowed as follows:

4–Bunnell	2–Anloff
3–E. A. Bannister	1–Grindley
Cox–J. P. Loeb	

The 1905 California crew probably was the outstanding four-oared crew of its day, going undefeated against the best the Pacific Coast could offer. Again coached by Garnett, on April 15th they defeated Washington on the Oakland Estuary; Stanford did not race, having refused to row the course selected by the others. Cal defeated the Victoria Boat Club, the Northwest champions, on May 25th. On May 30th they defeated Washington by ten lengths and Stanford by eleven, for the Pacific Coast Intercollegiate championship and permanent possession of the Lippy Challenge Cup. On June 3rd they beat the Portland Rowing Club by four lengths to eliminate any doubt that they were champions of the Pacific Coast. The crew was as follows:

4–E. A. Bannister	2–D. E. Evans
3–George C. Jones	1–Edgar V. Dodge
Cox–J. P. Loeb	

Interestingly enough, Edgar Dodge, the bowman on this crew, lived in Berkeley until his death a few years ago, and he was the father of a champion oarsman, Larry Dodge '36, the #7 man on California's 1934 and 1935 IRA championship crews.

By 1906 facilities at the old boathouse were inadequate, and a plan was devised to build a new floating boathouse. A blueprint was drawn up as a prospectus with which subscriptions could be raised. This plan was unsuccessful, due in part no doubt to the 1906 earthquake, which put an end to any racing that year, including the triangular four-oared race between California, Stanford, and Washington scheduled for April 28th.

Still, 1906 was an important year in the history of rowing at Cal. First, the problem of a new boathouse had to be solved. The plans for building the floating boathouse were scrapped, and the former boathouse was taken over by its owner following the earthquake. Therefore the Associaton decided to purchase an old Southern Pacific ferry. Alfred J. Salisbury '07 led the drive to raise the required funds, which totaled $1,000. The *Amador* was moored at the Megnesite Brick Company dock in Sessions Basin on the Oakland Estuary in 1906 and was the home of California's crews until it sunk in 1913. A float and slip were added to the hull, the lower deck was used for housing the shells, and the staterooms above were dressing quarters. The *Amador* also became a social center; picnics and shows were not unusual events for the crewmen.

A second significant change in the rowing program occurred in 1906. The Associated Students, perhaps convinced by the success of the 1905 crew that rowing was here to stay, decided to take over the Boating Association and make it an official part of the athletic program. As reported in the *Blue and Gold,* this meant that varsity letters were awarded to crewmen.

The third important event of 1906 was the acquisition of three racing shells. A total of $1,100 was raised from solicitations and shows on the *Amador* to cover the cost and shipping of three secondhand eight-oared shells, Cornell University's varsity boats from 1899, 1904, and

1906 practice on the Estuary. In background is the *Amador,* a bay ferry used as Cal's boathouse from 1906 to 1913. (Courtesy of The Bancroft Library.)

1905 California Varsity, Four With Coxswain, Pacific Coast Champions. *Left to right, back row:* #1 Edgar V. Dodge, #2 D. E. Evans, #3 George C. Jones, #4 E. A. Bannister. *Left to right, sitting:* coxswain E. J. Loeb, coach E. M. Garnett. (Courtesy of The Bancroft Library.)

1906. Berkeley President Benjamin Ide Wheeler, a former Cornell professor and rowing enthusiast, helped arrange this crucial purchase. After considerable negotiations, the shells arrived on April 8, 1907. They were rigged on April 9th, and raced April 27th, according to a letter written by John Tyssowski, '08 crew manager, on November 30, 1954.

The Boating Association's fourteen-year-long struggle with interclass and club rowing, which necessitated four-oar equipment, finally had born fruit. Classic eight-oared competition on an intercollegiate basis was realized. Not only that, rowing had become one of the official University sports under the Associated Students. Rowing at California had arrived.

The Beginning of Racing Eights

The first triangular intercollegiate eight-oared contest on the Pacific Coast was held in the spring of 1907 and marked the beginning of the now historic series between California and Washington and California and Stanford. They chose a two-and-one half-mile course on Richardson Bay near Sausalito as a neutral site agreeable to all. The day of the race, April 27th, there were many spectators, numerous yachts, and an observation train carrying 600 people. Unfortunately, race organizers did not take into consideration the vagaries of San Francisco Bay, for the day was anything but tranquil. By the time the race started, the course was covered with whitecaps under a driving northwest wind. These adverse conditions be-

came even worse. Halfway down the course all three crews swamped. At the time Washington was in the lead with Stanford second, and California was third.

Washington had to leave that evening as its ship was departing for Seattle shortly after the race was supposed to end. Stanford and Cal raced in the morning a few days later. This time the water was ideal. California led in the beginning, but after a mile Stanford forged to the lead and won by six lengths.

Coach Garnett instituted fall practice in 1907, when he installed a sixteen-man rowing tank in a reservoir at Strawberry Canyon. The loss of the Golden Bears the previous spring might have inspired these plans. At any rate, the 1908 crew, with Dean Witter '09 as stroke and captain, defeated Stanford by five lengths, again on Richardson Bay under ideal conditions. Later in the spring this crew went to Seattle only to lose. The fact that examinations had intervened and one man was sick probably contributed to the defeat, for this crew was considered outstanding.

After the 1908 season, Coach Garnett left, and California rowing fell on hard times. The Stanford crew won in 1909 despite valiant efforts by Dean Witter to fill in as coach. In 1910 the *Blue and Gold* reported that "boating" at both Cal and Stanford was abolished as an intercollegiate sport; the two crews continued rowing, however. California, as the California Boat Club, and Stanford, as the Lagunitas Boat Club, raced in 1910, when Stanford won the freshmen four-oared event by four lengths. They

1908 California Varsity. Captain and stroke Dean Witter '09 rowing with crew on Lake Washington, Seattle.

1908 California Varsity. *Left to right, top row:* senior manager John Tyssowski, #5 Harold Ashley, #6 Oswald Robertson, #7 Tom Davidson, #2 Ivan Ball, #8 Dean Witter, coach Garnett. *Left to right, bottom row:* #1 H. H. Dignan, #4 Fred Ashley, coxswain Paul Myers, #3 W. H. Schroeder.

also won the varsity eight event by three lengths over a two-mile course.

In 1911 rowing was restored as an intercollegiate sport at both institutions, but the results for the Bears were no better. They lost again to Stanford and renewed the series with Washington, only to lose both the varsity and freshmen races. This was the first time the freshmen had gone north and the first race with Washington for the varsity since 1908. There is no doubt that the lack of an established coach following Garnett's departure after the 1908 season had a lot to do with this sorry turn of events.

Cal was not particularly successful from 1909 through 1915, and the honors went mostly to Washington and occasionally to Stanford. Finally California did place ahead of Stanford in the 1916 and 1917 triangular races, which were won by Washington. In 1918 there were no races due to World War I. When racing resumed in 1919, Stanford again trailed Washington and California in that order in the annual triangular regatta. In 1920 Cal defeated Stanford in a dual race, and that apparently was

enough to push Stanford into dropping the sport in 1921, not to be resumed until just before World War II.

Washington's record was impressive, coming in ahead of California in every contest through 1920. (No races were held between the two schools in 1909, 1910, and 1918.) The period 1909 through 1920, then, was a lean one for the Golden Bears, who most of that time could rate no better than third among the three universities rowing on the Pacific Coast.

In 1909 a significant step occurred in the University's athletic program that had a direct bearing on the future of rowing as a sport. At the Sigma Nu fraternity house on February 12, the Big C Society was formed, consisting of baseball, crew, football, tennis, and track. These charter members were designated as the major sports conducted at the University, with appropriate letter awards and privileges. Thus rowing achieved recognition as being one of the primary athletic endeavors of the University.

Appropriately enough, among the charter members of the Big C Society was Dean Witter. Dean never lost his

Left: Dean Witter '09. He was varsity stroke in 1907, varsity stroke and captain in 1908, and varsity coach in 1909. He also served as referee and starter for the Cal-Washington races on the estuary from 1917 to 1964—in addition to becoming the West's best-known stockbroker. *Left below:* Tom A. Davidson, Varsity Coach in 1912 and #7 1908–1911. *Right below:* Charles Stevenson, Varsity Coach 1914–1915.

interest in the sport, and early in his business career he became its leading patron. He also was the chief official and referee for Cal's home races from about 1913 into the 1960s. In 1962 he established the first of Berkeley's crew endowment funds.

There were several reasons for Cal's lack of success during the early period of eight-oared rowing on the Pacific Coast. The distance the crewmen had to travel from campus to the boathouse in the days of not-very-rapid-transit and the resulting loss of time had a great deal to do with it. Today this still is a problem. Without a doubt, the major factor was a constant turnover in coaches—in some years even the lack of a coach. The crews apparently were coached by each year's captain from 1897 through 1900 and from 1910 until 1912—at best not a satisfactory situation, with little continuity in style and leadership. In 1912 T. A. Davidson, varsity #7 from 1908 through 1911, attempted to fill the breach; he could do it only for one year though, so again the crew was coachless.

The Associated Students, now known as the ASUC, recognized the problem and in 1914 hired the first professional coach, Charles Stevenson. Stevenson introduced a standardized Eastern style that emphasized more body swing, and he used Lake Merritt for fall workouts. Although matters improved somewhat, and Stevenson's crews, stroked by California greats such as Ralph E. Merritt and Lou Penney, did considerably better, they still were defeated by the Indians and Huskies. By the end of the 1915 season Stevenson gave up, and again Cal was without a coach.

During this period a remarkable group of Californians rowed for the Blue and Gold, forming the nucleus of the California crew alumni, which has been most active ever since on behalf of rowing at the University, loyal through defeat and exultant in victory. This solid core of interested and understanding alumni has grown over the years. At present the crew alumni are the closest and most loyal of any athletic alumni group at the University. They were supportive and patient through the disappointments and defeats of those early years, knowing what it would take for Cal's crew to reach the pinnacle of success.

The *Blue and Golds* of 1913 and 1914 reported several interesting items. Although Cal was defeated by Washington and Stanford on the estuary in 1913, it was not without support. The races were followed by a thirty-two-car observation train, plus several hundred more spectators along the banks and in boats. Then in 1914 at Seattle, the varsity event was complicated by the fact that as the crews got underway, another race was started at the opposite end of the course. Near chaos resulted as the two flotillas, including racing shells, judges, launches, and following tugs, met around the one-and-one-half-mile mark of the three-mile race. Somehow all crews got through the churning water safely, and Washington won this somewhat bizarre event.

THE BEN WALLIS ERA 1916–1923

//

THE 1916 SEASON MARKED THE BEGINNING of a rise in the fortunes of rowing at the University, although the climb was slow and took another five years. The South End Rowing Club of San Francisco recommended to the ASUC a coach who would kick California rowing into high gear. The man was Ben Wallis, Yale '10, who had settled in San Francisco and was a claims adjuster for the Market Street Railway. Ben was an ardent crewman, having rowed in prep school under Jim Ten Eyck, one of the legendary Ten Eyck brothers who were all professional scullers. Ben stroked for the Yale crew for three years. He had joined the South End Club and was considered technically sound in his theories. Following a luncheon meeting with Dean Witter, Ben decided to try coaching Cal.

He reported for coaching duty on November 11, 1915, the start of crew's first period of continuity. A patient, understanding, somewhat gentle individual, Ben left his mark at Cal, where he remained through 1923. He worked as hard as his oarsmen, fighting to bring to the California crew the fame it had not enjoyed since shortly after the turn of the century.

During his years at Cal Ben was a volunteer and received little in the way of expenses. He would leave his job in San Francisco by ferry at 3:40 p.m., arrive in Oakland for workouts at 4:10 p.m., finish anywhere from 6 to 7 p.m., grab some dinner, and then finish his regular job in the evenings. (Source: Speech by Harold Pischel '19 at the 1942 Crew Banquet.)

The first thing Ben did as coach was to assemble the squad and explain his philosophy. He then observed the men on the battery of rowing machines that were located in the old Harmon Gym. He quickly learned their style was not even close to what he felt was the most productive system of rowing. After several days, he began to establish the basis for the long smooth stroke he had learned over the years. The changeover was difficult for the veterans, and success took its time, but the long hours and hard work put in by Ben and his squads paid off. By January 1916 he had ten crews, including freshmen, on the water. On March 21, 1916, he established the first varsity training table at the Sigma Chi fraternity. (Source: Ben Wallis journal, 1915–1923.)

Another change Ben made was moving the shed, or what they called a boathouse, from the Alameda side, where it had been for years, to the more convenient Oakland side, at the foot of Washington Street next to the Creek Route ferry terminal. This made for some interesting landings for the crews when a ferry also happened to be docking. What passed for a boathouse was perched high on pilings, with one big dressing room with cracks in the floor for ventilation, a pot-bellied stove for an illusion of heat, and cold water showers outside.

In the fall of 1916, Ben moved the rowing machines out of Harmon Gym to under the track stands. Success didn't happen immediately, but the younger crews and the freshmen began to win some races. As noted earlier, there was no racing in 1918 due to the war, but rowing resumed in 1919, despite the fact that the ASUC seriously considered dropping the sport. After lengthy negotiations with Bert Houston '19 and Harold Pischel '19, the ASUC agreed to let the crew use the equipment provided they would raise $1,000 during the season. The crew had to display a bank book that proved they had raised $500 by the end of the first month and $250 at the end of the next two months.

The team not only raised the money, they had a fine season. By this time Ben Wallis was president and general manager of an insurance company, with considerable responsibilities, but he agreed to come over at least four days a week. The varsity raced with Washington on the estuary, and the finish was so close neither crew knew who had won. It was finally given to Washington, although the next day movies showed otherwise. California had not yet beaten Washington, although they did defeat Stanford in 1919 and 1920.

Boathouse in 1920, Sessions Basin at foot of Washington Street, Oakland. (Courtesy of The Bancroft Library.)

1921 Varsity practicing on the Oakland Estuary. (Courtesy of The Bancroft Library.)

Start of Three-Mile Triangular Race on Oakland Estuary, April
1919. *Foreground:* second-place California varsity. *Middle:*
first-place Washington varsity. *Background:* third-place Stanford
varsity. (Courtesy of Cal stroke Harold Pischel '19.)

Above: Early 1920s on the Oakland
Estuary. (Courtesy of The Bancroft
Library.) *Right:* Captain Lou Penney
'17 meets with Coach Ben Wallis.
Below: 1920 Cal-Washington Race,
Lake Washington, Seattle. The
Huskies defeat the Bears by six feet at
the finish of the three-mile varsity
race. (Courtesy of The Bancroft
Library.)

Ben's efforts culminated in his great crew of 1921. For the first time since eight-oared competition had started in the West, Cal came out on top as Pacific Coast champions, defeating Washington at Seattle. This crew then went back East as Cal's first foray into the stronghold of rowing in the United States. Stopping off at Princeton first, California broke the course record only to take second to a very fast Tiger crew. The Golden Bears then entered the historic IRA regatta at Poughkeepsie, New York to race the best crews of the East. Unrated and all but ignored, the Bears surprised everyone by coming in a solid second to a great Navy crew. Navy had won the Olympic gold medal the previous year and still had most of that crew in their boat, so it was a magnificent effort upon the part of the upstart Californians.

The trip East also was a financial gain. Senior Manager John Mage '21 ran such a tight ship, he was able to return money to the University after the journey. Without a doubt he was the first—and last—senior manager to accomplish this feat.

The first of many great Cal eights, this crew gave the rowing world notice that eight-oared rowing had come into its own at Berkeley. It was a great season for Ben Wallis and his men, but an even greater one for the many crews and coaches before him who had been working toward such a goal. The 1921 crew was as follows:

8–A. E. Larson	4–T. J. Kemp
7–F. G. Mehan	3–L. A. Brown
6–Dan A. McMillan Jr.	2–E. F. Marquardson
5–R. C. Downs	1–J. M. Rogers
Cox–K. H. Repath	

Dan McMillan #6 also was an outstanding tackle on Andy Smith's Wonder Team in football.

Ben Wallis, Varsity Coach 1916–1923.

1921 California Varsity. They were the first Cal crew to go East to the IRA regatta at Poughkeepsie, New York, and they placed second to the Naval Academy varsity. *Left to right, standing:* #8 A. E. Larson, #7 F. G. Mehan, #6 Dan A. McMillan Jr., #5 R. C. Downs, #4 T. J. Kemp, #3 L. A. Brown, #2 E. F. Marquardson, #1 J. M. Rogers. *Seated:* coxswain K. H. Repath. (Courtesy of The Bancroft Library.)

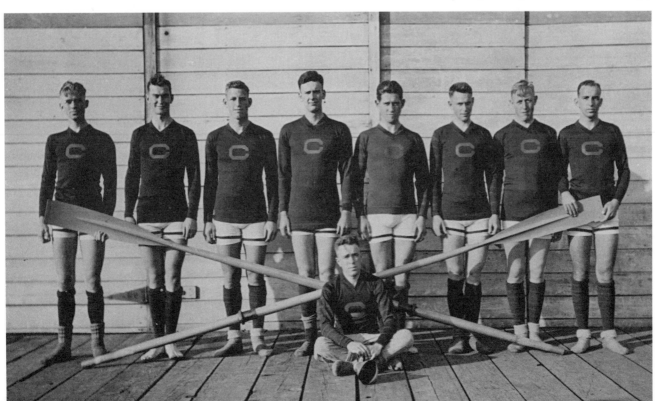

1921 Varsity race finish, Oakland Estuary. California Bears win three mile race defeating the Huskies by five feet to give California its first Pacific Coast eight-oared championship. (Courtesy John C. Rogers, son of captain and bowman John M. Rogers.)

Following the success of 1921, California's fortunes took a slight dip. Just before the Washington race, Ben was quite ill and Dan McMillan, who had taken over the stroke seat, was injured. Washington got full revenge for its 1921 loss by winning on the estuary by a solid ten lengths. The Husky crew proved this was no fluke by placing second in the 1922 IRA regatta, just as Cal had done the year before.

They lost again in 1923 to the Huskies, who that year became the first Western crew to win the IRA. Even so, everyone realized Cal rowing could compete with any of the major crews, so there was considerable discussion among various alumni about how to further strengthen the program. Up to this point the rowing team had been something of a stepchild, operating out of inadequate facilities at Sessions Basin and guided by the part-time, albeit heroic, efforts of Ben Wallis, an amateur (unpaid) coach. It was clear that if California rowing was to continue as a sport truly representative of the University, then a full-time coaching staff had to be provided for the oarsmen and adequate facilities had to be made available at a more logical location on the estuary.

The first problem was to select a full-time coach and an assistant. Ben could not be expected, nor could he afford, to give up an ongoing business and a successful career to turn to full-time coaching. Those who knew him well, however, realized that he was tempted more than most people suspected. He had built a good foundation, and who knows what he might have achieved with proper facilities and equipment. But he was committed to his insurance business, so the search for his replacement began.

Ben reappeared on the rowing scene ten years later, after he had moved his business to southern California. He took over the infant program at UCLA, which, following the 1932 Olympics, had started rowing in 1933 under Major Goodsell, a professional Australian sculler. Ben coached at UCLA for thirteen years, again building a firm foundation for what is now a well-established, nationally recognized rowing program. Ben Wallis certainly was a major contributor in securing the sport of rowing on the Pacific Coast and at the University of California. His role in this is all too often overlooked.

1921 Cal Varsity at Princeton before going on to the IRA at Poughkeepsie, New York. (Courtesy of John C. Rogers.)

THE CHRONOLOGY
THE EBRIGHT YEARS: BEFORE WORLD WAR II 1924–1943

//

A COMMITTEE, HEADED BY Dean Witter, was appointed to find Ben's successor. Also on the committee was ASUC president Bill Monahan '24. After considerable contact with members of the rowing fraternity, the committee chose Carroll M. "Ky" Ebright, Washington '17. Grandson of a Forty-Niner who later returned to Ohio, Ky was born in Chicago. In 1900 the family moved to Seattle, where Ky was raised. At the University of Washington, he was the last varsity coxswain under the legendary Hiram Conibear, who died in an accident the fall after Ky's graduation.

During World War I Ky served in the Army Signal Corps, the forerunner of the Army Air Force, as an instructor-pilot in Texas. Following his honorable discharge he worked for a large steel company in the Seattle area, planning to use his A.B. in business administration. He also was appointed to the Board of Stewards for the Washington crew and as a part-time assistant coach for Ed Leader, Conibear's successor, and then Rusty Callow, who took over after Leader left for Yale.

The Washington crew authorities were most cooperative with the Cal committee because of their concern that Cal might drop rowing as Stanford had done. This would leave the Huskies as the only collegiate crew on the Pacific Coast, and they then might be forced to quit. Fortunately for rowing at California, the committee convinced Ky to take a chance as head man. He accepted only because his former employer assured him that his job would be waiting for him if things did not work out. During his first few years, it's rumored that he gave this alternative considerable thought.

In the spring of 1924, the ASUC, headed by Bill Monahan, hired Ky Ebright as the first full-time professional coach of rowing at the University. Not only was this the start of a long and most successful career for Ky, unmatched in the coaching of crew, it heralded a golden period of Cal rowing. Ky selected Russ Nagler, Washing-

ton '21, who had been the varsity coxswain after Ky, as his assistant and freshmen coach. Thus began a partnership which lasted until 1951, when Russ resigned to go into real estate, a career cut short by his untimely death in 1952.

In addition to following the committee's recommendation for a coach, the ASUC also agreed to start construction of a new boathouse at a new location. The old boathouse had long been unsatisfactory, both structurally and geographically. The galvanized iron shed, built in 1914, had served almost two generations of college crewmen, but it never was adequate. Its occupants still can recall the wind whipping through the cracks in the floor, the lack of heat, and the cold water showers outside. The Sessions Basin location was poor, if not downright dangerous, due to the ferry boats docking nearby and competing with the crews trying to land at the boathouse float. Also the prevailing westerly winds could whip up whitecaps that a surfboat would have trouble handling, let alone a fragile eight-oared shell. Under such poor conditions, many workouts had to be canceled.

A new site was selected at the eastern end of the estuary above San Leandro Bay, which could be used when the rest of the estuary was too rough. The new boathouse, which cost $12,000, was completed in time for the 1925 season and has been occupied ever since. The majority of Cal's championship crews have used what was named the "Ky Ebright Boathouse," shortly before Ky retired. Just recently the inside of the boathouse was completely renovated, from the boat bays to the front door, through the generosity of Allen Trant, a Cal crew booster.

Ky's crews did not immediately take charge of rowing on the Pacific Coast, however; the first few years were hard, with more losses than wins. Still, Ebright and Nagler were building a foundation for future victory.

1924, Ky Ebright's first workout, Sessions Basin Boathouse. Ky is sitting in front row, sixth from left, wearing a sou'wester hat. Russ Nagler is in the front row, second from left, wearing a cap.

The first Crew Day, 1925. At the celebration, the new boathouse was opened and the shell *Berkeleyan* was launched.

Crews lined up on their stakeboats, Hudson River, Poughkeepsie, New York, June 1926.

Ky Ebright, Varsity Coach 1924–1959.
(Courtesy of Jim Lemmon.)

1928 California Varsity. They win the four-mile race on the Hudson River, Poughkeepsie, New York, breaking the twenty-seven-year-old record time.

The California Varsity defeats Yale to win the 1928 Olympic Trials.

The results of the Cal-Washington races demonstrate this progress. The 1924 race was a disaster, with the Huskies winning by ten lengths, in part perhaps because of Cal's loss of its stroke the day before the race. In 1925 this margin was cut to eight lengths, then down to five lengths in 1926. The Golden Bears returned to the IRA at Poughkeepsie in 1926 only to place sixth out of eight, with Washington winning. In 1927 the Bears finally beat Washington in the dual race by four lengths, and in the IRA, they came in a respectable third behind Columbia and Washington.

Some of Ky's early oarsmen said that he considered returning to his steel business in Washington following the 1926 season but decided to stay another year. As 1927 Pacific Coast champions and solid contenders in the IRA, Ky Ebright's Golden Bears were making themselves known in the crew world and were justifying the ASUC's decision of four years earlier.

Crewmen at Cal and elsewhere will long remember 1928, when the crew attained the very heights of rowing. Ky's system and his oarsmens' dedication paid off in an undefeated season. First they beat Washington by half a length, leading all the way, then they defeated the defending IRA champion, Columbia, by a length at Poughkeepsie, breaking the course record set in 1901. That was not all—for 1928 was an Olympic year.

The Olympic trials were held in Philadelphia on the Schuylkill River, which is quite narrow and requires Henley-style racing (two crews per heat). Coming from behind, the Bears first defeated Princeton. In the semi-final heat Cal led Columbia all the way and won by a half a length. In the finals California was up against the favored Yale crew, 1924 Olympic champs coached by Ky's old Washington teammate, Ed Leader. Cal blasted off the start and led all the way, despite Yale's closing at the end to 1.2 seconds.

Next, it was on to the Olympics at Amsterdam's Sloten Canal, where the narrow watercourse again required Henley-style racing. First Belgium and then Denmark were defeated by Berkeley without trouble. Then it was a high-stroking Italian crew that was beaten by two lengths. By the semi-finals the going got a bit rougher. Canada was a strong veteran crew, but the Bears held on to win by half a length. In the finals Great Britain

The California Varsity takes the Olympic Oath after winning the 1928 Olympic Trials.

Eight-Oared Finals, 1928 Olympics, Sloten Canal, Amsterdam. The United States, represented by Cal, defeats Great Britain by a half a length. (Courtesy of The Bancroft Library.)

roared out in front at the start, but the Bears caught them 500 meters from the finish and won by half a length, with coxswain Blessing waving his by now famous white towel in the final sprint. Little had those early pioneers, such as W.D. Jewett or Stanley Easton realized what they were starting to build in 1893. The members of this first California Olympic championship crew were:

8–Pete Donlon	4–Bill Thompson
7–Hub Caldwell	3–Fran Frederick
6–Jim Workman	2–Jack Brinck
5–Bill Dally	1–Marvin Stalder
Cox–Don Blessing	

The steamship *Roosevelt,* which carried the 1928 Olympic team and its equipment, also had two stow-aways aboard: Phil Condit, a reserve Cal oarsman, and Dick Van Loo, a Cal junior manager. The team fed them and helped conceal them during the trip over and back. General Douglas MacArthur was the head of the U.S. Olympic team. His aide suspected there were some extra crewmen on the ship, but he could never prove it until the return, two days out of New York. The two culprits were put to chipping rust for the rest of the trip. Ky told them it would do their souls good, although he was part of the conspiracy—one of the stowaways slept on the floor of Ky's stateroom. The other one slept on the floor of coxswain Don Blessing's room. Another footnote to this trip was that Ky's launch, *Oski III,* was taken along to use for training. The driver assigned to the launch de-cided to paint it red, white, and blue. Ky insisted that it be repainted its original blue and gold on the trip back.

In 1929 California had a powerful crew built around a number of the previous year's Olympic champions. The Bears won again in the dual race with Washington, making it three years in a row as Pacific Coast champs. Although a favorite for the 1929 IRA championship, Cal was one of five crews to swamp in the stormy waters of the Hudson River. The Huskies won the dual race in 1930 by less than a quarter length in spite of Cal leading right up to the finish. The Bears could only place fourth in the IRA; in the latter race the Huskies came in sixth behind California. Nineteen thirty-one was about the same; Washington won the dual race, and the Bears again

1928 Olympics, Sloten Canal, Amsterdam. The Cal varsity, representing the United States, receives the victors' wreath. (Courtesy of The Bancroft Library.) *Below:* 1928 Olympic Champions. *Left to right:* coxswain Don Blessing, #8 Pete Donlon, #7 Hub Caldwell, #6 Jim Workman, #5 Bill Dally, #4 Bill Thompson, #3 Fran Frederick, #2 Jack Brinck, #1 Marvin Stalder.

The Cornell, California, and Washington Boathouses along the Hudson River, Poughkeepsie, New York. (Courtesy of The Bancroft Library.)

1932 California Varsity, IRA Four-Mile Champions, Poughkeepsie, New York. They defeat Cornell. (Courtesy of The Bancroft Library.)

Finals, 1932 Olympic Trials, Lake Quinsigamond, Worcester, Massachusetts. Cal's varsity wins by .12 seconds over the Pennsylvania Athletic Club.

took fourth in the IRA. This time the Huskies came in ahead of Cal, in third place.

California and Ebright again made history in 1932, another Olympic year. Going undefeated during the regular racing season, Cal had beaten Washington in the dual race at Seattle by an unprecedented eighteen lengths and in rough water. The Ebright-designed single bar outrigger the crew used, which was quickly adopted by George Pocock and most other boatbuilders, no doubt helped. They then defeated Cornell by three-and-one-

half lengths, and Washington by another two lengths in the IRA at Poughkeepsie.

The Olympic trials were no different. The Bears rowed through the preliminary heats without difficulty, defeating first Princeton and then the Columbia crew, made up of crew veterans who felt they should have beaten Cal in the 1928 IRA. Their luck proved no better the second time around. The final in the trials was something else. The Bears' opponent was the Pennsylvania Athletic Club, a crew of excellent, mature oarsmen

Eight-Oared Finals, 1932 Olympics, Marine Stadium, Long Beach, California. The California varsity, representing the United States, defeats Italy by a boatdeck. Canada is third, and Great Britain fourth.

with considerable experience. They were easily the favorite to represent the U.S. in the 1932 Olympics, having won twenty-two races in a row, including the European crown in 1930. The race was eight-oared rowing at its best, with both crews all but even right down the course. First Cal had a slight lead, then Penn would nose in front. Shortly before the finish Penn seemed to lead, but the Bears put on a furious sprint to cross the line 0.12 seconds, or about two feet, in front.

"California's crew in California's Olympics" had been the rallying cry all season. Now it was true. The games were scheduled for Los Angeles, with rowing to be held on a specially constructed course in Long Beach. The Bears went through the preliminary heat without difficulty, defeating Canada, Germany, and New Zealand. The final heat was one of the most dramatic in the history of Olympic rowing. California drew the rough, wind-swept outside lane, and Italy, considered the fastest eight, drew the favored protected inside lane. Canada and Great Britain were in the two middle lanes. The race seemed a tossup all the way down the course. The Bears and Italy alternated nosing in front by a few feet at the most. A couple of boat lengths from the finish Italy appeared to have about a three-foot lead. The Golden Bears turned it on to fly across the line, winning by less than a second. The drama of this blue-ribbon event is indicated by the official picture of the finish in which all four crews appear with only a half a length from first to fourth. It was international, 2,000-meter racing at its very best.

Thus Ky established himself as one of the foremost coaches in the history of rowing, the first in the world to ever win two Olympic championships—in a row. Members of the 1932 California Olympic championship crew were:

8–Ed Salisbury	4–Burt Jastram
7–James Blair	3–Charlie Chandler
6–Duncan Gregg	2–Harold Tower
5–Dave Dunlap	1–Winslow Hall
	Cox–Norris Graham

Mike Murray, a reserve oarsman in 1932, did not make the Olympic squad, but he decided that he would be involved nevertheless. He became manager of the boathouse at Long Beach Stadium, the Olympic rowing site. He was present for the entire rowing program and collected several one-of-a-kind souvenirs that he has contributed to the California Sports Hall of Fame, including the Olympic flag that flew over the boathouse; the small American flag that was on the bow of the U.S. shell; and an oar blade with the signature of every crewman who participated in the 1932 Olympics. These are on display now in the Hall of Fame room in Memorial Stadium on the Berkeley campus.

During the fall of 1932, following the Olympic Games, the Lake Merritt Industrial League Whaleboat champions challenged the Cal crew to a race over a one-mile course on Lake Merritt in two of the league's whaleboats. The race was held one balmy afternoon, and the Industrial League champs won by lengths and

1932 Olympics, Marine Stadium, Long Beach, California. On August 13 Cal's varsity, representing the United States, defeated Italy by less than a second to win the gold medal. *Left to right, back row:* #3 Charlie Chandler, #7 James Blair, #1 Winslow Hall. *Standing behind:* coxswain Norris Graham, #5 Dave Dunlap, coach Ky Ebright. *Front row:* #2 Harold Tower, #4 Burt Jastram, #6 Duncan Gregg, #8 Ed Salisbury. (Courtesy of Duncan Gregg.)

1932 2,000-Meter Olympic Champions, Marine Stadium, Long Beach, California. *Left to right, standing:* #8 Ed Salisbury, #7 James Blair, #6 Duncan Gregg, #5 Dave Dunlap, #4 Burt Jastram, #3 Charles Chandler, #2 Harold Tower, #1 Winslow Hall. *Left to right, kneeling:* coxswain Norris Graham, starboard alternate Herm Holman, port alternate Hayes McLellan, coach Ky Ebright.

lengths of open water. Ky and the crestfallen crew went back to their boathouse in disgrace. The next day Ky got a call from the boatman at Lake Merritt asking that he stop by that afternoon. Curious, Ky went to the lake and found that the boatman had pulled the two whaleboats used in the race from the water to prepare them for winter storage. Pointing to the boat used by the Cal crew, he told Ky to check the keel. It was obvious at a glance why the Bears had had such a struggle. The enterprising Industrial Leaguers had nailed two open-ended five-gallon cans to the boat's keel, making very effective sea anchors. The boatman told Ky he didn't understand how the Bears could even move the boat, no less race for a mile. Such was the college crew's education in the wiles of Industrial League rowing.

In 1933 most of the Olympic crew graduated.

Washington won the dual race by a considerable margin to start a string of victories that would not be broken for the next six years. Because it was still the depths of the Depression, the IRA was canceled that year. Given the stimulation of the previous year's Olympics, however, a National Sprint Championship was established at the Long Beach course. Yale, Harvard, and Cornell were invited from the East, with Washington, California, and UCLA, which had just started rowing that year, representing the West. Washington won, with Yale, Cornell, Harvard, California, and UCLA placing in that order. The championship had been organized with the hope that rowing could be made into a gate sport; the Marine Stadium had been completely fenced in for the Olympics and admission could be charged. The sprint championships, unfortunately, did not have the attraction of an Olympics. In addition most rowing crowds were used to seeing races for free. Not a financial success, the sprint races were part of history after one more try two years later.

Ky had a predominately sophomore crew in 1934, so it was considered a building year. The dual race at Seattle proved otherwise when the junior varsity won by ten lengths, and the varsity fought the Huskies right down to the wire only to lose by a few feet. At the 1934 IRA Ky began a string of wins by Western crews that would continue right up to World War II. Only in 1938 did Navy slip in a win. During this period, which ended in 1941, Cal won four times, and Washington won the other four, all at the four-mile distance. This dominance by the West was undoubtedly the reason for the reduction of the varsity distance in the IRA to three miles when the race was revived after the war. California avenged its narrow defeat at Seattle in the 1934 IRA. Washington was second, with Navy leading the Eastern contingent, which trailed out behind. The 1934 IRA championship crew was as follows:

Coach Ky Ebright shows UC President Robert Gordon Sproul the Varsity Challenge Cup. Cal's 1935 defending championship varsity eight won the cup again at the IRA regatta, Poughkeepsie, New York.

8–Dick Burnley	4–Carroll Brigham
7–Larry Dodge	3–Evald Swanson
6–Ferd Elvin	2–Jack Yates
5–Ray Andresen	1–Frank Dunlap
Cox–Reg Watt	

1934 California Varsity, IRA Four-Mile Champions, Poughkeepsie, New York. *Left to right:* #1 Frank Dunlap, #2 Jack Yates, #3 Evald Swanson, #4 Carroll Brigham, #5 Ray Andresen, #6 Ferd Elvin, #7 Larry Dodge, #8 Dick Burnley. *Kneeling:* coxswain Reg Watt.

A veteran crew returned in 1935, but they took some time to get going. Most ended up in the junior varsity for the dual race. This made for a rather inexperienced varsity, but they rowed a fine race, leading Washington most of the way. At the finish the Huskies surged ahead to win by six feet. For the rematch at Poughkeepsie, Ky reshuffled the varsity and came up with a strong eight. The Bears won the IRA for the third successive time, beating out Cornell in second and Washington third, with Navy leading the rest of the East. Ky thus joined a select group of coaches whose crews had won three successive varsity races; one had to go back to the real old-timers to find an equal. Before, only Cornell coaches in the 1800s and the early 1900s had had such success. Since, only Rusty Callow, of Navy, and Stork Sanford, of Cornell, have joined this elite group.

In 1935 a final attempt was made to stage the National Sprint Championships at Long Beach. Syracuse, Pennsylvania, and Wisconsin represented the East; Cal, Washington, and UCLA were the Western entries. This time California won, with Washington second, Syracuse third, and Pennsylvania fourth. Under Ben Wallis, the Bears' old mentor, UCLA pleased the crowd by placing fifth, thus beating Wisconsin, a nationally ranked crew. The 1935 IRA championship crew was as follows:

8–Gene Berkenkamp	*4–Carroll Brigham*
7–Larry Dodge	*3–Evald Swanson*
6–Tevis Thompson	*2–Jack Yates*
5–Ray Andresen	*1–Harley Fremming*
	Cox–Reg Watt

1935 California Varsity, IRA Four-Mile Champions, Poughkeepsie, New York. *Left to right, standing:* #8 Gene Berkenkamp, #7 Larry Dodge, #6 Tevis Thompson, #5 Ray Andresen, #4 Carroll Brigham, #3 Evald Swanson, #2 Jack Yates, #1 Harley Fremming. *Left to right, kneeling:* trainer Bert Jones, varsity coach Ky Ebright, coxswain Reg Watt, freshmen coach Russ Nagler, senior manager Dale Kellogg.

The Bears' goal in 1936, another Olympic year, was to win their third gold medal in a row—a feat never yet achieved in Olympic eight-oared history. Ky felt he had the "horses" to do it. In fact, he thought the squad was so strong that he urged Ray Andresen, the #5 man the previous two years, to graduate even though he still had another year of eligibility. On Ky's recommendation, Ray became the first Cal oarsman elected to the Rowing Hall of Fame. But these were Depression days still, and Ray had a job waiting for him.

Washington also had been pointing for the Olympics and had a strong crew. In the dual race at Seattle, the Huskies won by open water over a two-and-one-half-mile course. Ky was not too concerned by this loss because he had been bringing the crew along slowly preparing for the long haul. By the time Cal was working out on the Hudson, he felt that all was in place for the assault ahead. The immediate goal was a fourth IRA win in a row, a feat only accomplished once years before by Cornell. Unfortunately, California came in second to Washington at the end of four miles, much to Ky's surprise and disappointment. He was certain he had the

better crew. When they returned to the California float, the reason for the loss became all too clear. Unknown to Ky, Al Daggatt, Andresen's replacement at #5, had been in a motorcycle accident just before coming East and had rowed the four-mile race with broken ribs. Obviously, he was lost for the Olympic trials a few weeks later. The squad's depth was unequal to this second loss of a key "power" oarsman. Although they won their heats handily, they were unable to quite match the Huskies' speed. Washington went on to win the gold medal at Berlin, so at least the American string of victories continued. Ky's dream retreated into the realm of "might have been."

The year 1937 was very much one of rebuilding, with all but the stroke from the 1936 crew graduated. Washington, which remained strong with good return of its Olympic champions, soundly defeated the Bears by five lengths on the estuary. At the IRA Washington defended its previous championship while the Bears were fifth out of seven. Cal would not stay down, however, and quickly rebounded in 1938. At Seattle Washington had to fight hard to win by a half a length of open water over the three-mile course. At Poughkeepsie California

1938 California Freshmen, IRA Two-Mile Champions, Poughkeepsie, New York. They were the first Cal freshmen to win this event. *Left to right:* #8 Bob Andresen, #7 Conrad Oberg, #6 Jack Klukkert, #5 George Talbott, #4 Dick Andrew, #3 Bill Blevins, #2 Dave Rice, #1 Earl Serdahl, coxswain Art Gassaway.

1939 California Varsity. They defeat the Washington varsity in the four-mile race on the Hudson River, Poughkeepsie, New York to win the IRA championship.

proved it had come back as a contender for national honors. The Bears and Huskies fought it out down the four-mile Hudson River course, with Cal sitting in front most of the way. The Bear crew was sure they had the race under control as they approached the finish line one half mile below the high railroad bridge. But they had failed to take into account a streaking Navy shell well over on the other side of the course. The Bears started to close on the Middie crew, but it was too little too late. Navy won, with California second, Washington third, and Columbia leading the rest of the Eastern crews.

The 1938 junior varsity matched the varsity by coming in second, although this time Washington won. It was the 1938 Cal freshmen who stole the show. Rowing a powerful two-mile race, the Bear Cubs came out on top over Washington in second place, followed by Syracuse, Columbia, and Cornell. This was the first time Cal freshmen had won a national championship, although they had placed second five times. The crew was as follows:

8–Bob Andresen	4–Dick Andrew
7–Conrad Oberg	3–Bill Blevins
6–Jack Klukkert	2–Dave Rice
5–George Talbott	1–Earl Serdahl
Cox–Art Gassaway	

By 1939 California was back on top with a vengeance. In the dual race on the Oakland Estuary the Golden Bears won by a resounding twelve lengths. In fact they had the effrontery to turn around and row back across

the finish line toward the landing float before the Huskies had even finished the race. Washington oarsmen were reminded of the insult for years thereafter. At Poughkeepsie Cal resolved not to overlook anyone. The crew started high and hard and just kept steaming down the Hudson as though pursued by more than Washington and the rest of the crews. Blasting across the finish line, California set the still existing four-mile record of 18 minutes 12.6 seconds. This record probably will never be broken as 1941 saw the last of the four-mile races on the Hudson, and the IRA is no longer held there. The 1939 crew that Ky said was one of his very best was as follows:

8–Kirk Smith	4–Linton Emerson
7–Chet Gibson	3–Dave de Varona
6–Stan Freeborn	2–Stan Backlund
5–Emil Berg	1–Benson Roe
Cox–Jim Dieterich	

Like Dan McMillan on the 1921 Cal crew, an outstanding football player also rowed in 1939 for the Bears. Dave de Varona #3 is the only athlete to row on a national championship crew and to play on a Rose Bowl championship football team. He was a starting tackle on the 1937 team that beat Alabama 13-0 on January 1, 1938. Sports ability apparently runs in his family; his daughter Donna, a member of the U.S. swim team, was the youngest competitor in the 1960 Olympic Games at Rome.

At Poughkeepsie in 1939 just prior to race day, the Cal, Washington, and Cornell crews were resting be-

1939 California Varsity, IRA Four-Mile Champions, Poughkeepsie, New York. *Left to right:* #8 Kirk Smith, #7 Chet Gibson, #6 Stan Freeborn, #5 Emil Berg, #4 Linton Emerson, #3 Dave de Varona, #2 Stan Backlund, #1 Benson Roe. *Kneeling:* coxswain Jim Dieterich. Their winning time of 18 minutes, 12.6 seconds is the record for the Hudson River course which the IRA used from 1895 through 1949.

tween workouts when they looked out on the river to see what was the most unique four-with-cox ever boated: Ky Ebright was cox; George Pocock, the builder of every shell in the IRA regatta, was at stroke; Walt Raney, Washington freshmen coach, was #3; Al Ulbrickson, Washington's varsity coach, was #2; and Norm Sonju, Cornell's freshmen coach, and later Wisconsin varsity coach, was at #1. This act was repeated in 1941 with Stork Sanford, Cornell varsity coach, replacing Walt Raney. All who witnessed these blue-ribbon crews agreed that they could really move. These were also the *only* two times Ulbrickson ever took directions from Ebright.

When the 1940 season came around, five of the 1939 champion oarsmen had graduated, so another cycle of rebuilding had to begin. The dual race was at Seattle and had the unique distinction of Ky switching his entire varsity and junior varsity crews the night before the race, much to the consternation of the sports scribes. The abrupt shakeup did not have its desired effect; the varsity lost by a length of open water and the JV by even more. The bright spot was that the freshmen won on Lake Washington for the first time since the series had begun in 1903—a sign of things to come.

I was a member of this 1940 freshmen squad. I had

graduated from high school two years earlier, but, feeling too immature to handle the college bit yet, I had joined the Civilian Conservation Corps in Sequoia National park. Two years later, I was ready for college—and crew. I really could not believe it when I first went down to the boathouse in the fall of 1939 to become a member of the California rowing team.

The 1940 IRA was something else. The week of the race had been calm and beautiful, but race day dawned windy and ugly. The freshmen race, which, in order to save money, Cal did not enter, went off without incident, but the junior varsity race was a disaster. All but two of the crews were swamped within the first half-mile of a three-mile race. The JV race was rescheduled for after the varsity race. It was doubtful the varsity crews could get underway, but finally at 8 p.m. it was decided they could make it. Starting conditions were foul, and California was anything but lined up on course when the starter's gun fired. Unable to recover, Cal came in fifth out of eight and was badly disappointed. Rowing into the wind and against the tide the crew was a full five minutes slower than their record the year before. The only slower race had been in 1929, when five, including Cal, of the nine crews swamped in rough water.

The junior varsity race was incredible. It was rowed in

Cal Freshmen defeat Washington for first time in 1940 on Lake Washington.

the dark after a floating start without stakeboats. Ky later said that to see those crews line up perfectly without anyone trying to take advantage by getting ahead was one of the finest acts of sportsmanship he had experienced. The race itself was a nightmare in which no one, including coxswains, officials, and coaches, could make out the crews. Somehow they all navigated the three-mile course without injury. In the end the official launch asked each coxswain where he had finished once a crew could be located on that Stygian stretch of the Hudson. Washington apparently had won because its crew could not find anyone in front of them even though they were on the opposite side of Cal from where they had started. The Bears were informed they were third when the coxswain told the official they came in a half a length

behind ". . . that boat over there," which was Navy in second place. Certainly the 1940 regatta was one that will be remembered by all who experienced its turmoil and travail.

World War II was beginning to shatter Europe in 1941, but the University's athletic program was not yet directly affected. In rowing the freshmen of 1940 were developing into a fast varsity crew comprised of at least five sophomores. They had rowed excellent times consistently in practice. In the dual race on the estuary, Cal broke the course record by some ten seconds. The problem, however, was that the Huskies also were fast; in fact, a bit faster, and they won by three-and-one-half lengths. The Bears, although shaken, went back to work in earnest, aiming toward what would be the last four-mile

1939 Coaches' Four with Coxswain, Poughkeepsie, New York. *Left to right:* coxswain Ky Ebright, Cal varsity coach, #4 George Pocock, shell builder, #3 Walt Raney, Washington freshmen coach, #2 Al Ulbrickson, Washington varsity coach, #1 Norm Sonju, Cornell freshmen coach. (Courtesy of A. Kirk Smith '39.)

1941 California Junior Varsity in near lane leads half mile from the finish and goes on to win IRA Championship. Washington in the middle lane placed second, and Cornell in the far lane was third in the three-mile race. (Courtesy of Frank Nicol.)

varsity race and the last IRA until after World War II.

The stage was set at Poughkeepsie when the Cal junior varsity won its first championship. Defeating Washington, Cornell, and Columbia, the junior Bears accomplished something that had eluded them since they had first entered the competition in 1926. There also was a behind the scenes drama in the junior varsity victory.

At the last minute before the crews left Berkeley to go East, sophomore Frank Nicol, a third-boat oarsman, was selected to replace the starboard alternate, a senior who had decided to take a job rather than go to the IRA. At the start of race week, Marshall Robinson, the JV #3 man, came down with the measles, and Frank replaced him in the crew. Winning the junior varsity event meant the crew had won Big C varsity letters. After accomplishing this, Frank made the varsity crew the next two

years and became a three-year Big C man with the treasured Blanket award. Marshall Robinson, a close friend and fraternity brother of Frank's, went on to row in the 1943 varsity. Members of the 1941 championship junior varsity crew were as follows:

8–Les Still	*4–Bill Lamoreaux*
7–Bob Olson	*3–Frank Nicol*
6–Howard Holmes	*2–Walt Casey*
5–George Misch	*1–Dave M. Turner*
	Cox–Bob Johnson	

The 1941 varsity race was a good one, with both California and Washington breaking fast. The Bears led by a small margin right up to the tall railroad bridge marking the three-and-one-half-mile mark, but the super-

1941 California Junior Varsity, IRA Three-Mile Champions, Poughkeepsie, New York. *Left to right:* coxswain Robert L. Johnson, #8 Les Still, #7 Bob Olson, #6 Howard Holmes, #5 George Misch, #4 Bill Lamoreaux, #3 Frank Nicol, #2 Walt Casey, #1 David M. Turner.

1941 California Varsity, Time Trial, Hudson River, Poughkeepsie, New York. *Left to right:* coxswain Art Gassaway, #8 Jack Kearns, #7 Jim Lemmon, #6 Harold Flesher, #5 Jim Moore, #4 John Friedrichsen, #3 Bill Blevins, #2 Bill Rawn, #1 Ray Mortensen. Cal placed second to Washington in the last of the four-mile IRA events. Following World War II the varsity race was shortened to three miles.

ior Husky strength began to take its toll. Gradually the Washington crew pulled ahead. Despite all the Bears' effort, Washington was a clear winner. The race had been rowed in what seemed two different divisions, as the *New York Times* sports section noted: "Washington wins IRA Regatta—Cornell wins Eastern Division." Clearly the two Western crews were standouts, and obvious protagonists in the future battle to represent the U.S. in the 1944 Olympics. Sadly, this was not to be. The 1940 Olympics already had been canceled due to the war in Europe. By 1944 all of these competitors would be in uniform fighting in Europe or the Pacific.

The IRA also was canceled in 1942 for the duration, but competition on a dual basis continued on both coasts

for two more years. At Seattle the Bears and the Huskies had it out with much the same crews as the previous year, with much the same results. Ky felt there was considerable potential in the Cal varsity and was frustrated that it didn't come out at Seattle.

The 1943 season was a fitting way for rowing at California to finish up before shutting down for the duration. The Bears proved their mastery over their northern rivals by winning the varsity decisively and losing the freshmen by only inches. For unknown reasons Washington felt it could not bring a JV crew. Following the 1943 season there was a two-and-one-half-year hiatus during which Cal's crewmen served their nation, some by giving their very lives.

THE CHRONOLOGY
THE EBRIGHT YEARS: AFTER WORLD WAR II 1946-1959

//

FOLLOWING VJ DAY IN AUGUST 1945, veterans, including myself, began to drift back to the Berkeley campus. The question of reinstating rowing as an intercollegiate sport became an issue in the ASUC executive committee, just as it had following World War I. The profit-oriented individuals wanted to eliminate rowing before it could start again. Plans were made to sell off the boathouse property and equipment. Fortunately, Don McNary, coxswain of the 1943 freshmen crew, was a member of the ASUC committee. A polio survivor, he had been unable to join the service and had continued as a student following the closing of the rowing program. He had shifted his interests to student politics and was the perfect person to lobby for rowing.

Don set up a meeting with Ky at his Regal Road home in Berkeley. I was one of the veterans Don had recruited and was more than pleased to be included. He explained that unless fast action took place crew might be dead at Berkeley. The boathouse, as well as all the equipment, would be sold. We all expressed our outrage and asked what we could do. We urged that Ky should come back to coach the crews. Ky was not that eager, indicating that perhaps crew's time was past. We would not accept this, and a discussion followed. Finally Ky's lovely wife, Kathryn, who had been sitting in the shadows, spoke up. "Ky," she said, "You are just like the old fire horse waiting for the bell to ring. Tell the boys you will come back." With that Ky grinned and said that Kathryn knew him better than he knew himself. He agreed to come back if the ASUC made an offer, and if an initial effort be made among the students on campus, using alumni pressure only at the last moment. This was a such a successful strategy that the rather powerful alumni were not necessary. After careful consideration and despite the urging of the gate-oriented factions, the ASUC unanimously decided to reinstate rowing immediately.

On March 5, 1946 Ky and Ernie Madson, the former crew bus driver, launch driver, and mechanic, went to work putting the boathouse back in shape. For six weeks Ky and Ernie worked long hard hours rebuilding the apron, the ramp, and the float. To get the shells in shape, a boatman/rigger, Jack Donnelly, was hired. It was truly a herculean effort. In order to satisfy the ASUC that rowing had started immediately, as mandated, several crews, made up of the few returned oarsmen from the pre-war years and a smattering of new candidates, were put in the water. The result was hardly Olympian. Workouts were not too demanding, and Ky's coaching launch was an underpowered outboard—even going all out it could not keep pace with the crews. Racing would not begin until after the fall.

That time frame suddenly changed when Washington decided to hold a national sprint regatta that June for all comers. The Eastern schools had kept up a fair rowing program during the war years, especially after VJ day. Late as it was Cal made a real effort. Four or five veterans of varying experience formed the nucleus of an undistinguished crew, which did its best to get in shape. The Seattle Invitational Sprint Championship was held on Lake Washington on a blustery June day amid a large gathering of local yachtsmen. Cornell, in a protected smoother inside lane, won. Cal was in the next to outside lane in almost surf-like water. After a full crab and a twisted outrigger, the rather tattered Bears finished seventh out of eight. To make matters worse, all of the crews swamped in the wakes of the departing pleasure boats and had to swim their shells into the adjoining beach. So it was that, as they were handing out diplomas in Berkeley in 1946, three seniors on the Cal crew, including myself, actually graduated up to their necks in Lake Washington.

Following the disaster at Seattle, Ky again expressed doubts about the rowing program. But in retrospect one can see that he was working hard to rebuild the team for the rebirth of Cal rowing in the fall of 1946. Indeed, all was ready to go by that fall. He rehired Russ Nagler as his assistant and freshmen coach, and the core of a very solid freshmen crew was formed. I became an assistant coach for Russ and Ky at this point. With the return of the veterans plus a number of new men, the varsity at Cal was ready to take water—Cal was on its way by the spring of 1947.

The race at Seattle in 1947 was remarkable. Both the junior varsity and the freshmen were destroyed, losing by lengths of open water. The varsity race started the same way, with Washington quickly going out to lead by several lengths. The last mile was a different matter. The Bears had been biding their time and had not panicked. Suddenly Washington began to struggle, and Cal gained stroke by stroke. By a quarter of a mile it was a question of whether or not the Bears had enough time left to catch them. As both crews bore down on the finish, Cal was flying and Washington was in trouble. Calfornia blew by about two lengths before the finish line, while Washington appeared to drift across. A most dramatic finish for the Californians, who again could call themselves Pacific Coast champions.

When they returned to Poughkeepsie for the first IRA regatta since 1941, the Bears were confident. They had defeated Wisconsin by five lengths on the Oakland Estu-

ary, and even more significant, the freshmen, eligible still under wartime rules, had raced the Wisconsin JV and won handily. For the IRA Ky took the stern five of the frosh and beefed them up with the three most qualified from the old JV to create a crew that could really move. By race day the junior varsity, young as it was, was considered a real contender. California reclaimed its IRA championship, which it had won back in 1941. Unfortunately, the varsity was fourth behind Navy, Cornell, and Washington. Members of the 1947 championship junior varsity crew were as follows:

8–Ian Turner	*4–Lloyd Butler*
7–Dave Brown	*3–John Goerl*
6–Darrell Welch	*2–Bill Scherer*
5–George Ahlgren	*1–Dave M. Turner*
	Cox–Bob White

Following the IRA at Poughkeepsie, all of the varsity crews came out to the Pacific Coast to participate in the National Sprint Championship sponsored by Seattle. Just as they had the previous year, the crews raced over a 2,000 meter course on Lake Washington. There were no heats, just one big twelve crew event. To the consternation of the IRA crews, the added guests, Harvard and Yale, came in first and second. Harvard was on top by a half a length. Host Washington came in a strong third,

1947 California Junior Varsity, IRA Three-Mile Champions, Poughkeepsie, New York. *Left to right:* #1 David M. Turner, #2 Bill Scherer, #3 John Goerl, #4 Lloyd Butler, #5 George Ahlgren, #6 Darrell Welch, #7 Dave Brown, #8 Ian Turner. *Kneeling:* coxswain Bob White.

Aerial view of site of National Sprint Championships, Lake Washington, Seattle, June 1947.

and California was a disappointing sixth. Certainly a different result for the Bears than their visit to the Northland earlier in the season. This is not the way they planned to wind up the 1947 season.

Ky faced a real challenge in 1948, the first post-war Olympic year. The California program had just started to get back on track. His varsity, with five sophomores, was young; there were really experienced oarsmen only at #7

Semi-finals, 2,000-meter Olympic trials, July 3, 1948, Princeton, New Jersey. California varsity leads all the way and wins by three feet over Washington.

and bow, and even the veterans had limited racing experience. The plus side was that even with two eighteen-year-olds holding down varsity seats, there was maturity among the war veterans who made up the rest of the boat. Coxswain Ralph Purchase, for example, was a thirty-two-year-old combat infantry man from the Pacific Theater. He became one of the more astute coxs Cal has ever had. There also was a unique stroke-seven combination in the Turner brothers, Ian and Dave.

Ky brought the crew along slowly, and the mileage increased during workouts. Even so, they were not ready by the time of the dual race, and Washington won by two-and-one-half lengths after three miles down the estuary. At Madison, Cal defeated Wisconsin by just under two lengths in a tuneup for the IRA. Despite the fact that Washington won the 1948 IRA, the varsity claimed they knew they could win the next time, having rowed much too low a pace at Poughkeepsie. They vowed to go all out at their next meeting.

By the start of the 1948 Olympic trials, Cal was ready to go for the gold an unbelievable third time. The Bears sailed through the initial heat, defeating Navy with ease, only to draw Washington for the semi-finals. It seemed clear that the victor of this race would become the U.S. representative. In an outstanding race Cal nipped the Huskies by three feet and went on to sweep past Harvard in the finals with relative ease.

At Henley, on a course shorted twenty meters from the usual 2,000 meters, they were never really pressed and won the third gold medal for the U.S. under Ky Ebright. This is a record that likely will stand forever. Many failed to realize how far Ky had brought a crew

that was quite inexperienced in time and technique. Film clips and movie loops of California working out for the Olympics on the upper reaches of the Thames were used for years later by the Cal coaching staff as examples of pure technical rowing. The crew had come a long way from the raw material put together in only January of that year. To have engineered an Olympic victory two short years after the horrendous startup of rowing in 1946 was truly an unparalleled coaching achievement.

This Olympic success had two footnotes. First, Cal's shell was the *George Blair*, at that time the only shell named after a person. In 1942 it had been three years since the crew had had a new shell, so George Blair '43, one of Ky's oarsmen, had contributed the price of a new shell when he left Berkeley for the Navy Air Force and fame as a fighter pilot.

After the final race was over, the Cal crew members rowed to a special float to receive their medals in a formal ceremony. For some reason the medals did not have the traditional ribbons, so the crew slipped them in their trunks as they rowed back to the landing float. There they shipped their oars and took the shell out of the water, placing it on the racks in the boathouse. As they were showering and dressing, someone asked Dave Brown, the #3 man, where his medal was. Brown, always the shy silent type, replied that it had fallen into the river. Consternation reigned, and everyone dashed back to the landing float. After determining where Brown had been standing, Hans Jensen, the starboard alternate, dove into the Thames, which was fifteen feet deep with a thick muddy bottom. After four exhausting dives, by some stroke of luck, Hans surfaced with the

Enroute to the 1948 Olympics in England. A dry practice session on board the *SS America*.

1948 Olympics, Henley-on-Thames, England. Coach Ky Ebright giving instructions to United States (California) eight prior to the race. (Courtesy of Lloyd Butler.)

Above: 1948 Olympics, Henley-on-Thames, England. Cal coxswain Ralph Purchase receives the traditional dunking following the United States victory over Great Britain. (Courtesy of The Bancroft Library.) *Below:* 1948 Olympics, Henley-on-Thames, England. The United States (California) eight standing at attention during the national anthem following their victory over Great Britain. *Left to right:* coxswain Ralph Purchase, #8 Ian Turner, #7 David L. Turner, #6 Jim Hardy, #5 George Ahlgren, #4 Lloyd Butler, #3 Dave Brown, #2 Justus Smith, #1 Jack Stack. (Courtesy of Lloyd Butler.)

1948 Olympic Champions. *Left to right:* coxswain Ralph Purchase, #8 Ian Turner, #7 David L. Turner, #6 Jim Hardy, #5 George Ahlgren, #4 Lloyd Butler, #3 Dave Brown, #2 Justus Smith, #1 Jack Stack. (Courtesy of Lloyd Butler.)

medal in his hand. As he broke the surface he looked up right into the eyes of an interested spectator—Grace Kelly, movie star and, later, Princess of Monaco. Hans said he almost dropped the medal right there.

The members of California's third Olympic championship crew were:

8–Ian Turner	*4–Lloyd Butler*
7–Dave L. Turner	*3–Dave Brown*
6–Jim Hardy	*2–Justus Smith*
5–George Ahlgren	*1–Jack Stack*
	Cox–Ralph Purchase

The 1949 season saw California riding the crest following its Olympic victory. With the now-seasoned veterans returning and some even stronger new faces, the Bears roared through undefeated. In the Washington dual race, the Huskies were bent on revenge; but the winning margin was ten feet in the Bears' favor. Wiscon-

sin was defeated by five lengths on the estuary, and the Bears went on to win the IRA over Washington, Cornell, Navy, and seven other crews in a memorable race. Conditions could best be called Wagnerian, for the black clouds rolled and the lightning flashed. One could almost see the Valkyries swooping over the Hudson looking for the souls of the favored heroes. Lightning even struck the high steel bridge at the three-and-one-half mile mark during the race.

It was also the last IRA to be raced at Poughkeepsie on the Hudson. Some said the reason for this move was dwindling community support; others said it was pressure from other communities to share this august event. The underlying reason probably was that the regatta had outgrown the course. Rowing was gaining popularity during the post-war period. Twelve crews entered the 1949 regatta, which meant the field was spread a long way across the river. The current varied considerably, depending on the distance a crew was away from shore.

During most of the pre-World War II days the field was not more than six, and this problem could be handled. As the number of crews kept increasing, some remedy had to be found. The regatta had to move to a less problematical site. It was the end of a grand tradition dating back to 1895, when Columbia had defeated Cornell and Pennsylvania. In the previous fifty-four years this premier event in college rowing had seen hundreds of crews and thousands of crewmen put to the test in topflight competition. Only a limited number came out winners, but all gained insight in how to establish their goals—and the price one must pay to accomplish them.

The 1949 IRA championship crew was:

8–Ian Turner	4–Lloyd Butler
7–Dave Draves	3–George Bauman
6–Bob Livermore	2–Justus Smith
5–Dick Larsen	1–Bob Spenger
Cox–Ralph Purchase	

In the California shell at #6 was Bob Livermore, whose great-uncle had introduced the first standard single scull with a sliding seat to the Bay Area.

For those remaining veterans of the 1948 Olympics, who had made such an impact starting in their freshmen year, 1950 was their last season. They were among the very few four-year varsity lettermen in Cal rowing, having earned varsity letters by winning the JV championship in the IRA as freshmen. The 1950 varsity gave a good account of itself. The dual race with Washington on the estuary was hotly contested, with the Huskies coming across the finish line at the Fruitvale Avenue Bridge three-quarter lengths in front.

The 1950 IRA, which had been moved to Marietta, Ohio on the Ohio River, was another story. The town of Marietta had really gone overboard to host this historic regatta. Usually placid, the river had seemed an ideal course. But on the day of the regatta it ended up in flood stage due to a series of storms at its headwaters. Trees, cows, and even parts of houses came roaring down the river. Should the races even be held? Finally, an attempt was made with nearly disastrous results. Shortened to a

1949 California Varsity, IRA Four-Mile Champions, Poughkeepsie, New York. *Left to right, standing:* #8 Ian Turner, #7 Dave Draves, #6 Bob Livermore, #5 Dick Larsen, #4 Lloyd Butler, #3 George Bauman, #2 Justus Smith, #1 Bob Spenger. *Kneeling:* coxswain Ralph Purchase.

mile and seven-eighths on the only remotely rowable stretch of water, the race was wild, better suited to the dories that run down the Grand Canyon. Washington won, with California right on its rudder; Wisconsin, Stanford, and MIT lead the rest of the pack. Somehow the field of twelve all finished without injury or incident. The junior varsity came in a strong second over a course shortened to two miles.

In the summer of 1950 Cal rowing had a new wrinkle: a regatta "down under." Ky had become close friends with Bob Stiles, a member of New Zealand's 1932 Olympic crew. Stiles soon became the George Pocock of New Zealand. At that time Pocock was building almost all the racing shells in the U.S., and Stiles was doing the same in New Zealand. As a tribute to Ky's magnificent record of three Olympic gold medals, the Bears were invited to the Christchurch Centennial Regatta and the New Zealand National Championships. Because of the season reversal, this meant the crews would have to row right through the fall and into winter. When darkness began to fall in the late afternoon as the crews worked out, flashlights were added to the bows of the shells, and finally Ky installed a powerful searchlight in the coaching launch. Oarsmen from those workouts tell of seeing the finger of bright light sweeping up and down the shells, with each man striving to be at his best when the beam fell on him. The coxswains had recurring nightmares of driftwood and rival shells appearing out of the gloom—it was an experience all remember with mixed emotions.

Departing December 17, 1950 for New Zealand, Ky and the varsity eight plus an alternate began a new adventure—competing internationally in a non-Olympic year. The single-alternate requirement had caused some concern because normally an oarsman rowed on either the port or the starboard side, never both. Race crews, therefore, utilized two alternates. Once the requirements of the invitation were announced, however, it was remarkable how fast the men learned to adapt to either side.

Meanwhile, I saw the crew off at the San Francisco airport and, against my will, was almost hijacked onto the plane. The fathers of crewmen Bill Loorz and Tom Adams had decided it would be a fine joke to smuggle me aboard for the flight—I was supposed to be married that

1951 California Varsity enroute to Australia and New Zealand. *Left to right, back row:* #6 Paul Henriksen, alternate Bill Durland, #2 Tom Adams, #7 Bill Hull, #1 Harry Gardiser, #5 Terry Grew. *Left to right, front row:* coach Ky Ebright, #8 Bill Loorz, #3 Dave Draves, coxswain Don Glusker, #4 Ken Cusick. (Courtesy of Ken Cusick.)

afternoon. Fortunately for Jean, my bride-to-be, and me, cooler heads prevailed, and I made the altar on time.

Once in Christchurch, the Bears had time for a few workouts to acclimatize themselves. They then successfully went through several heats, ending up in the finals of the Centennial Games on January 6, 1951. The other guest, Australia, won this event, with Cal just two seats back and the New Zealand boats trailing. A week later California entered the New Zealand National Championships at Akaroa Harbor. Again the Australian boat beat Cal, but only by about six inches, with three New Zealand boats a length and a quarter or more behind. It was a wonderful experience for the Bears and considering the different seasons and limited experience, they brought credit to Cal rowing. That there were several Phi Beta Kappas and Tau Bets among the oarsmen, plus an eventual Rhodes Scholar, was all in the crew's favor when they returned on a Sunday to face final exams that Monday. They had been invited for a month of racing in Australia, but studies took priority. The crew that made the trip "down under" was as follows:

8–Bill Loorz	*4–Ken Cusick*
7–Bill Hull	*3–Dave Draves*
6–Paul Henriksen	*2–Tom Adams*
5–Terry Grew	*1–Harry Gardiser*
Cox–Don Glusker	

The 1951 racing season began at the usual time. The added rowing for the Bears "down under" helped a mostly inexperienced varsity crew, with only one holdover from the previous varsity, and the remaining Olympic vets gone. The crew went north against what they knew was a strong Washington eight in a revival of the old triangular races of the early 1900s. For the first time since 1919, Stanford was entering the race. Its crew had been developing fast and had placed a very creditable fourth in the storm-shortened IRA at Marietta the year before. The race results were the same as in 1919: Washington was first, Cal was second by two lengths, and Stanford was third. The triangular revival was short-lived; 1951 was the last time the three schools raced together.

The 1951 IRA regatta was held at Marietta again with assurances that a repeat of the previous year's tumultuous events was out of the question and that the Ohio River would be its own calm self. The IRA officials were convinced and also felt that the town, which gave such excellent support to all the crews, should get a second chance. This time it was a tributary, the Muskingum River, that went wild, and again the race had to be shortened. Debris of all kinds floated down the swollen river. It took heroic measures to anchor stakeboats at the start and even greater courage to man them. The start of the race was a nightmare. In the junior varsity race the

Bears somehow survived and soon were roaring along in front. At the finish they led Washington and five of the Eastern crews headed by Columbia to notch their third IRA win. The 1951 JV champs were:

8–Ron Reuther	*4–Merritt Robinson*
7–Conway Peterson	*3–Al Lorenz*
6–Bill Durland	*2–Bill Schnack*
5–Fred Avilez	*1–John Lowe*
Cox–Don Glusker	

In the varsity races Wisconsin, swept off the stakeboat at the start, won this rodeo with Washington hard on their stern, followed by Princeton and then California. Seven more bedraggled crews trailed behind. Of all the schools, the Naval Academy suffered most, losing all three of its crews right at the start. So for the second time Marietta was a disaster, and a change of site was demanded for the safety of the crews.

The IRA searched for a new race course that could hold fourteen or more crews fairly in a community that would support such an event. After several places were considered, Syracuse's Lake Onondaga seemed the best bet, and the city fathers were eager to cooperate. The lake was wide and more than three miles long. The Syracuse boathouse was adequate as a headquarters, and there was plenty of room nearby in a park-like setting. Some Nisson huts (shades of World War II) could be erected as temporary boathouses for any number of crews if they doubled up. Just a couple of miles from the lake were the New York fairgrounds, where there was plenty of room to house and feed the crews. Buses could run a shuttle service to the lake to transport crews. There also was a railroad siding at the fairgrounds for shipping boats and equipment. In addition there was a park extending down the north side of the lake that provided excellent viewing for spectators for at least the last half of the course.

The IRA regatta has remained at Lake Onondaga ever since 1952. The town fathers are not as involved as they were in those early days; the coaches are no longer introduced at the prestigious Steward's Dinner at the Syracuse Hotel with its several hundred guests, nor are they furnished with courtesy cars. The crews now bunk down in dorms on the Syracuse University campus, a lot farther · from the lake but much more comfortable. Weather can be a problem, and it will be as long as the Board of Stewards insists on racing in the late afternoon (supposedly for the benefit of the New York papers). The regatta has lost some of its glamour, since Washington has declined to come in recent years, and Cal has done so only sporadically. The Eastern Sprint Championships also has detracted from the IRA, particularly since the distance raced is now the same. With the recent establishment of the National Championships at Cincinnati, it

1951 California Junior Varsity, IRA Three-Mile Champions, Marietta, Ohio. This race was shortened due to flood waters. *Left to right:* #8 Ronald Reuther, #7 Conway Peterson, #6 Bill Durland, #5 Fred Avilez, #4 Merritt Robinson, #3 Al Lorenz, #2 Bill Schnack, #1 John Lowe. *Kneeling:* coxswain Don Glusker. (Courtesy of Conway Peterson.)

may be that the glory is all but gone as the regatta approaches its 100th year. Be that as it may, the regatta saw some outstanding rowing over the years and until quite recently represented the hallmark of rowing in this country.

The 1952 season got underway with a more seasoned crew than the youngsters who had made the New Zealand trip. They trained hard and long for the dual race with Washington on the estuary. The freshmen started the day off by coming home in front for the first time since 1941. The junior varsity also came driving down the course in first place. It was up to the varsity to complete a first-ever Cal clean sweep in the many years of this series. The 1952 varsity would not be denied, and the broom signifying the clean sweep was hoisted over the boathouse. No one knew that this would be the last varsity dual race victory over Washington until nine years later.

One of those inevitable cycles in competition was about to swing toward the East. It began at Madison, Wisconsin when the Badgers beat California on Lake Mendota by two-and-one-half lengths. This was the first win for Wisconsin in the home and home series started in 1947. The stop-off at Wisconsin every other year on the way to the IRA had been an enjoyable experience for both crews and would continue on through 1960.

In the last twenty-one IRA regattas, Western schools had won fifteen (Washington nine and California six), while the East had only won six. First Navy, then Cornell, would be in the ascendancy during the next eight years. The 1952 IRA reflected this changing of the guard. Navy swept to a convincing win in the varsity event, with Cal back in fifth, and Washington even further back in seventh ahead of Stanford, Pennsylvania, MIT, and Syracuse. Navy went on to win the Olympic gold at Helsinki, Finland and became the second most successful U.S. eight-oared crew.

The pendulum swing for California continued in 1953, and the course was set for some of Ky's most unsuccessful years. Although the Bears won the first Newport Regatta, beating Stanford by three-and-three-fourths lengths, the dual race with Washington was a rout. The Huskies swept the lake at Seattle and won in the varsity by seven lengths. Wisconsin won on the estuary by four lengths. The IRA wasn't a bit better as Cal took an unremarkable sixth. Washington had rallied and took third.

The 1954 season saw some improvement, but it was limited and the only victory of any substance was over Stanford. In the varsity race with Washington, the Huskies won by six-and-one-half lengths. A new wrinkle was added to the Western Sprint Championships of the previous two years. They had been a form of "rowover" with Cal overwhelming the budding UCLA and USC crews. In 1954 Navy was invited to bring "The Great Eight" to the West. Still boating almost all of their Olympic crew, the Middies were formidable and defeated California by less than a boat length. Close isn't good enough to be a win as Cal rediscovered on Lake Mendota when it lost by half a second to Wisconsin. The IRA was equally unencouraging as the Bear varsity came in fifth. The junior varsity came in third, which helped a bit.

In 1955 the Bears were reeling. Nothing seemed to go right. Washington won the dual race by six-and-one-quarter lengths in the varsity. Wisconsin won by three lengths on the estuary. Navy returned to the Western Sprints to defeat a surprising Stanford boat, which was a quarter length ahead of Washington. Cal trailed the Huskies by a length. The next weekend Stanford won its first dual race with Cal since 1915; they came in two-and-one-half lengths in front, after leading for most of the three-mile race, a pattern that would continue for two more years. The IRA wasn't much better, with California coming in sixth behind Stanford at fifth. Cornell won, starting four years of domination by the Big Red.

California should have been a contender in 1956, another Olympic year. Instead the Bears lost again to Stanford by three-and-one half lengths, to Washington by four-and-three-quarters on the estuary, and by three lengths to Wisconsin on Lake Mendota. The IRA marked the very worst Cal performance since the Bears first had entered the regatta in 1921. They were tenth of twelve crews, beating only Boston University and Columbia, and even then not by very much. For the first time since he had been coaching Cal, Ky did not enter the Olympic trials.

The whole squad vowed to improve over the previous few years at the start of the 1957 season. A strong freshmen crew promised added muscle in the future. The record does show improvement—but that's all. Stanford again won the dual race by two-and-one-half lengths, after a near disaster for both crews, the "Fireboat Race."

As the regatta started there was a fire at the edge of the estuary just west of the Park Street Bridge, about 600 meters from the finish line. The Oakland fireboat berthed at Jack London Square well west of the race course had

responded and, in short order, had the fire under control. Both the freshmen and junior varsity races were held without incident. The varsity race started with the Cal crew gradually pulling out to a lead of about a half a length. About that time the Coast Guard boat that had been patrolling the race course decided it should respond to the nearly-extinguished fire. Ignoring the racing shells, and the cries of the officials, the Coast Guard boat flew by, creating a large wake. California took the worst of it and helped flatten it somewhat before it hit the Stanford shell. Ky and the officials attempted to warn the crews in vain. Both crews shipped water from the large waves, but the Bears took by far the most. Not stopping, they staggered badly. By now the Bears had lost their lead, but they began to fight back despite the excess water and again pulled ahead. The fireboat, which was built along the lines of a large sea-going tugboat, had decided the fire was out, and it was returning to its home berth at Jack London Square at full speed, leaving a very large wake. Ky, riding in the official boat, warned both crews through his ever-present megaphone, using a voice that crewmen claimed could peel paint. He urged them to ease up as the huge waves hit them, to try to ride it out before continuing. Stanford crewmen wisely heeded their rival coach and got through without shipping too much water. Cal, on the other hand, convinced it was passing Stanford, refused to ease off and plowed full tilt right into the now cresting waves. Although neither boat was damaged, which in itself was a miracle, Cal almost went under and had to finish the race with about six inches of water as extra baggage. Stanford, relatively unscathed, just picked up where it had left off and sailed on down the course in front. The Bears struggled on behind, swearing at all fireboats and firemen, convinced they were the better crew but unable to prove it owing to bad luck.

The Wisconsin race gave the Bears the opportunity to work out their frustrations and to improve the record. After five years of Badger wins, Cal oarsmen won on the estuary by two-and-one-half lengths, to their great satisfaction. The Washington race showed that the Bears still had a way to go as the Husky varsity won by six-and-one-half lengths on Lake Washington. After a frank discussion with the squad and with the athletic department, a mutual decision was made not to send a representative crew East, so the season ended. That disastrous finish back in tenth place the year before still rankled.

Although few have made note of it, Ky's performance as a premier coach of young men in his last two years of coaching, 1958 and 1959, was absolutely nothing short of outstanding. Following the 1956 plunge to the depths of his career, he had been deeply disappointed and hurt, although he never referred to it. Both Ky and the squad resolved to bounce back in 1958, and though they might

Dead Heat Finish between Cal and Wisconsin Varsities, Oakland Estuary, 1959. (Courtesy of Martin J. Cooney.)

1959 California Junior Varsity, IRA Three-Mile Champions, Lake Onondaga, Syracuse, New York. *Left to right:* #8 Don Martin, #7 Gary Anderson, #5 Gary Yancey, #6 Dave Flinn, coxswain Arlen Lackey, #1 Dick McKinnon, #3 John Christensen, #2 Tim Scofield, #4 Chris Barnes.

not have made it all the way back to the top, they certainly made it back to respectability. The Washington dual race was a hard-fought two-and-three-quarter-length win by the Huskies on the estuary. Stanford was beaten by two-and-three-quarter boat lengths, and Wisconsin was nosed out by half a second after a wild race over the one-and-three-quarter-mile course—the first Blue and Gold victory on Lake Mendota since 1950. The IRA was better, but still not what the Bears had in mind. The junior varsity came in an excellent third, and the varsity finished a hard-fought fifth to Cornell in first, Navy second, Syracuse third, and Princeton fourth. It was not up the ladder near far enough, but it was twice as good as the last time.

All who were connected with Ky's last season felt mixed emotions: honored to be a small part of such an outstanding coach's history and sad to see such a unique and remarkable career come to a close. It was not Ky's decision to put down his megaphone—in the ASUC retirement was then mandatory at age sixty-five. Everyone in 1959 resolved to ensure that Ky's last season would be one which he could look back on with pride. It may not have been all that the squad wanted for him, but the Bears were once again at a reputable competitive level.

The Wisconsin race was one for the books. For the length of the two-mile course the Bears and Badgers slugged it out without either crew gaining much. As they hit the finish line at the Fruitvale Bridge, the judges did not indicate the winner. The crews were so close, the spectators could not tell who had won. The referee, Winslow Hall, bow on the 1932 Olympic crew, asked the judges, only to be told that someone had pulled down the judging platform at the bridge, and they had no place to adequately view the finish. Hall thereupon declared a tie race, which satisfied no one, but, in retrospect, was very likely the truth. The Washington race on always tough Lake Washington was a typical tight battle with the Huskies' depth finally prevailing by two-and-

three-quarters lengths, but Cal was in it all the way. Stanford was destroyed by a resounding eight lengths.

The IRA was the wrap-up of Ky's thirty-five-year reign over the fortunes of rowing at California. The squad was determined to do him honor and, according to Ky, they did. The junior varsity rowed as gutty a race as one could imagine. They stayed right with the leaders, Washington, Pennsylvania, Cornell, and Navy, but until the last three-quarters of a mile it did not seem possible they could pull it off. As they came flying down on the finish line, they fought their way into the lead by rowing right through a faltering Washington crew which had the lead. It was a heart-stopping, come-from-behind win that Ky claimed was one of his most satisfying victories. It also represented the fourth win by one of Ky's JV crews, to go along with his six national varsity crowns and three Olympic gold medals. The 1959 junior varsity champions were:

8–Don Martin	*4–Chris Barnes*
7–Gary Anderson	*3–John Christensen*
6–Dave Flinn	*2–Tim Scofield*
5–Gary Yancey	*1–Dick McKinnon*
Cox–Arlen Lackey	

The varsity did its very best to pull off a double after the JV's thrilling win, but did not succeed. Wisconsin won it all. Cal was right there in the heat of battle, but finally had to settle for a respectable fourth, behind Syracuse and Navy. Although they couldn't win the varsity race, they took some comfort by coming in ahead of Washington, which was fifth.

Thus ended the Ebright story with the establishment of California rowing at a national and international level by a coach respected by all who row. No one man has ever had such an impact upon the sport and no man ever will. Not the least of his accomplishments was the effect he had on the hundreds of young men who were so fortunate to have him as a coach.

THE CHRONOLOGY
POST EBRIGHT 1960–1972

//

KY RECEIVED HIS FINAL HONORS as a coach at a jam-packed reception and banquet at the Claremont Hotel in Oakland attended by crewmen, past and present, faculty, administrators, and friends, and headed by University President Clark Kerr. Ky and his wife, Kathryn, received tickets for a trip around the world, including accommodations at the 1960 Olympic Games in Rome. It was a memorable night and a most fitting salute to Ky.

Ky's announcement of his successor, his freshmen coach for the past six years, was almost lost in the festivities. That skinny little kid who stood by the gate at the Marine Stadium in Long Beach during the 1932 Olympics had achieved a dream—to become varsity coach for the Cal crew. I had rowed in high school, under Pete Archer, who patterned his style after Ebright. Then, as a crew member at Cal in 1940, I was #7 on the Bears' freshmen squad, the first yearling crew to win at Seattle, and rowed #7 on the varsity in 1941 and 1942. I left the University at the start of my senior year to join the Army Air Force, flying B-17s in Europe and B-29s in the Pacific for a total of fifty-two combat missions. Returning to the University in the fall of 1945 to finish my senior year, I was one of the veterans who helped reestablish crew. I then rowed during the shortened 1946 spring season—and was one of the three seniors who graduated from Berkeley in the frigid waters of Lake Washington.

Following graduation, I was hired as a part-time assistant coach under both Ky and Russ Nagler, the frosh coach. I worked until 1951, when my Air National Guard unit was called up during the Korean War. When I returned in fall 1953, Ky needed a freshmen coach so I resigned from my job as a juvenile probation officer and took the plunge into full-time coaching. I have never regretted it.

It was both intimidating and challenging to follow in Ky Ebright's footsteps. I had rowed and coached under the man for nineteen years. If there was an Ebright

"system," I had been raised on it. Greeting the squad in the fall of 1959, I bluntly told them they no longer could depend upon Ky pulling something out of his famous hat. Now they had to depend upon themselves and upon hard work to get the job done.

The 1960 season was quite successful—unexpectedly so by most outsiders. The crews worked hard right up to the dual race with Washington. Then disaster struck in the final workout before the race. The varsity #6 man, Tim Lyman, pulled a muscle in his back and was out of the competition. After agonizing, I took a real chance and dipped into the third varsity crew to fill the vacant slot, leaving the junior varsity intact. It was a risk that showed I had been overlooking a talented man. Bruce Hansen remained in the varsity seat the rest of the season, while poor Tim, after his back had healed, had to wait until the next year; he did row in the junior varsity, however, later in the season.

The junior varsity race on the estuary was wild. Cal led from the start, but at the finish Washington was closing fast. Shortly before California went across the line, the bowman blacked out. Rather than hit the rudder to compensate for the resulting loss of power on that side, Cal's coxswain, Ralph Udick, let the boat run free, unencumbered by the drag of the rudder to cross the line ahead of the hard-charging Husky crew. The fact that the boat was going severely off course and smashed all four starboard oars on the Fruitvale Avenue Bridge pier was beside the point. The coxswain, with his quick thinking, had saved my first win over Washington ever. The varsity race was tight, but Washington won by three-quarters length over the Bears' revamped boating.

The following weekend the Bears went to Long Beach for the new Pacific Coast Sprint Championships. The regatta was at the Marine Stadium, my home course in high school. Following his experience in the race of the previous week, the JV bowman had quit rowing. Nevertheless, the junior varsity won their race by a much more comfortable margin. The varsity race was a battle. Berkeley jumped out to an early lead in the 2,000-meter sprint, rowing high and hard, but Washington began to overtake the Bears in the last 500 meters. The two crews flashed across the finish line with Cal only inches in front but a clear winner.

Feeling confident, the Bears stopped off at Madison for the Wisconsin race, which, due to high winds on Lake Mendota, was held on smaller Lake Minona. Navy, with a reputation as the strongest crew in the East, joined the race. It was another classic slugfest between Cal and Navy, with the Badgers finishing three-and-one-half lengths in the rear. The Bears held off Navy to win by six feet in what had been a real street fight.

The IRA at Syracuse still was held at the three-mile distance even though 1960 was an Olympic year. The junior varsity entered undefeated, as did a very powerful Cornell second boat. Cal put up a dogged fight, rowing the final mile as though it was a 2,000 sprint, but the Bears had to settle for second place. The varsity race was not one for faint hearts. Washington, Cornell, and Navy all started fast with the Bears hanging on just behind. As it entered the final mile, Cal began to move up, with Brown right on its stern. Finally, though Navy had slipped past a faltering Washington crew, the Bears surged in front as the winner—Cal's first varsity win in the IRA since 1949. Coupled with the junior varsity's second place, it was the best overall performance by California's crews since 1932. Happily, Cal's athletic director, Pete Newell, was accompanying me in the coaching launch to view his first crew races. Needless to say, he was an advocate for rowing at Berkeley from there on out.

Jim Lemmon, Assistant Coach 1947–1951, Freshmen Coach 1954–1959, and Varsity Coach 1960–1966.

1960 IRA Regatta, Lake Onondaga, Syracuse, New York. Cal's varsity defeats Navy in three-mile race.

Cornell's coach, Stork Stanford, graciously invited us to Ithaca to train for the 1960 Olympic trials to be held three weeks later in Syracuse. The change was delightful. The varsity, with two alternates selected from the JV, spent hours of early morning workouts on beautiful, fabled Lake Cayuga. At the trials, I felt sure the Bears were ready to take on all comers to try for an unprecedented fourth Olympic victory. It almost came off. Our crew swept through the preliminaries, defeating Cornell, Brown, and the Union Boat Club. In the semi-finals, we downed the Navy plebes, Cornell's second crew, and Penn without incident—except that I had to convince our coxswain, Lackey, that you do not protest a start after you have won the race. By the finals, Cal was clearly the favorite over the others: Navy's varsity and plebes and the Syracuse alumni. We had defeated all of the other crews except dark horse Syracuse alumni. The finals started with the Bears quickly taking the lead. Syracuse challenged at the halfway point, but they were beaten back. Then, with about 400 meters to go, Navy took over the lead. To make matters worse, they won by a full length. Some felt it was racing their own freshmen crew, rather than the fact that we had beaten them twice, that spurred them to victory, since losing to a first-year crew would not augur well for their later Naval careers.

It was a bitter disappointment for both the crew and for me, however. Still, I had been most fortunate, and 1960 was a fantastic season. We had won the IRA, and Cal's record of reaching the finals of all six Olympic trials it entered was still intact. In retrospect, it might have been a blessing that Cal was not at Rome. Rowing in Europe, especially in East Germany, was taking quantum leaps in both training methods and in equipment. The Navy crew was badly beaten, not even qualifying for a medal, so American rowing suffered a severe setback. Of course there were some of us who felt that if Cal had been at Rome the results might have been a bit different. Be that as it may, at least the Eastern domination of the IRA had been broken. It had been ten years since the West (Washington) had won, and eleven since the Bears had triumphed. Now we had to prove it wasn't a fluke.

The 1960 IRA championship crew was:

8–Don Martin	4–Marty McNair
7–Elmore Chilton	3–Bob Berry
6–Chris Barnes	2–Bruce Hansen
5–Jack Matkin	1–Gary Yancey
	Cox–Arlen Lackey

Nineteen sixty-one proved to be another banner year. A solid nucleus was back with experience in all but one position, and that was filled by Steve Brandt, a sophomore who the previous year had received the Nagler Award as most promising freshman. We won all of our dual races up to the Washington regatta by comfortable margins. In the race with the Huskies on Lake Washington, the Bears not only won their first varsity dual race since 1952, they set a regatta and course record that still stands. The varsity win was preceded by a very close freshmen race in which the Cubs finally succumbed a quarter of a length down. The JV led from start to finish, winning by just short of a boatlength. Overall results were most gratifying and the closest yet to a California clean sweep on the lake.

Two weeks later, again on Lake Washington, California suffered its first loss of the season by coming in second in the varsity event in the second Pacific Coast Sprint Championships. Washington won by just a few feet at the finish. The junior varsity won by a good boatlength; there was no freshmen race. Perhaps the varsity loss was a blessing in disguise, because after Seattle I worked the crews as they had never been worked before in preparation for the IRA. They were constantly reminded how they had let it get away up north. By the time both crews hit Syracuse they were ready to go all out.

California and Cornell fought it out in both 1961 IRA varsity events. The junior varsity entered undefeated as was the Cornell JV. Our crew did their very best, pushing to the limit a Cornell junior varsity that I felt could demolish most other varsity crews. Their fine effort was not enough, and we settled for another second place in a field of eleven. The varsity event was a classic two-boat race in a field of thirteen. Cornell and California were co-favorites and were assigned adjoining lanes in the middle of the pack. Cornell's varsity coach and dean of the IRA, Stork Sanford, shared a coaching launch with me, the most junior of IRA coaches. In fact, Stork had been Cornell's coach when I first rowed in the IRA as a sophomore in 1941. In addition to being one of the top coaches of his day, Stork was and is a gentleman in every sense.

Our two crews broke from the stakeboats dead even and began to pull away from the pack. Then California pulled into a slight lead, and during the rest of the three-mile race was never headed. At the same time Cornell was never more than three-quarters of a length down and often was just one-quarter length off the pace. It was a headwind race all the way, demanding the most of both crews. Each was suited to such a contest, with the size and strength to bull their way through the chop. I felt the Bears were one of the more imposing crews we had ever boated, averaging around six feet four-and-one-half inches and 190-plus pounds (I was reluctant to find out how much plus they were). Cornell was a mirror image. By the time the two shells entered the final mile, Cal's stroke and Cornell's coxswain were screaming to one another as to who was doing what to whom. With

1960 California Varsity, IRA Three-Mile Champions, Lake Onondaga, Syracuse, New York. *Left to right:* #8 Don Martin, #7 Elmore Chilton, #6 Chris Barnes, coxswain Arlen Lackey, #5 Jack Matkin, #4 Marty McNair, #3 Bob Berry, #2 Bruce Hansen, #1 Gary Yancey.

1961 California Varsity, IRA Three-Mile Champions, Lake Onondaga, Syracuse, New York. Cal defeats Cornell on June 17, 1961.

1961 California Varsity, IRA Three-Mile Champions, Lake Onondaga, Syracuse, New York. *Left to right:* #1 Jack Matkin, #2 Tim Lyman, #3 Bob Berry, #4 Rich Costello, #5 Steve Brandt, #6 Chris Barnes, #7 Kent Fleming, #8 Marty McNair. *Kneeling:* coxswain Chuck Orman.

2,000 meters to go both crews took off as though they had just started a sprint race. Both roared across the finish line at about forty strokes a minute, with MIT in third by considerable open water. Cal won by slightly more than one-quarter length. Both Stork and I could hardly believe the show as it unfolded. It was one of the truly great championship races in eight-oared rowing. Neither crew should have been considered a loser.

Thus the 1961 season ended with the Bear varsity and junior varsity undefeated in dual racing. The last time the varsity had defended its IRA championship was in 1934–35. This varsity win, together with JV's second place, equaled that standard set by Ky's crews in 1932 for the second successive year. Rowing at Berkeley was really back where it belonged, and it was no fluke. The 1961 IRA championship crew was:

8–*Marty McNair*	4–*Rich Costello*
7–*Kent Fleming*	3–*Bob Berry*
6–*Chris Barnes*	2–*Tim Lyman*
5–*Steve Brandt*	1–*Jack Matkin*
Cox–Chuck Orman	

There had been considerable improvements in the rail travel from the soot-laden cars without air conditioning of the twenties to the fast-moving luxury of the City of San Francisco and other legendary trains. But it was apparent that flying was here to stay, and the railroads were losing interest in hauling passengers. So, starting with the 1961 IRA, the Bears flew rather than taking the long train ride. Flying offered several advantages. No longer did the crewmen have to take their final exams as they rode across the country. Shorter travel time also turned out to be cheaper. Enough was saved to purchase shells to be stored at the Syracuse boathouse and rowed once a year at the IRA. The only real disadvantage was that the home and home arrangement with Wisconsin had to be discontinued. Today the Bears fly to all but local races and use a special trailer to haul their shells to the race site. (See chapter on transportation.)

In 1962 the veterans of 1960 and 1961, who had done so well for the Blue and Gold, graduated, and so it was another rebuilding year. The crews won their races up to the Washington dual. Cal had the lead on the estuary at the start and for most of two miles, but in the final mile Washington pulled ahead to win by one-half length of open water. The JV lost by a considerable distance. In the Pacific Coast Sprints, Washington again was the winner and British Columbia was second to California's third in both the varsity and junior varsity. The Bears, who had improved, made a good effort in the IRA, placing third among thirteen crews. Cornell won by a length of open water over Washington in second. We could not duplicate the three consecutive wins by Ky's crews in the mid-thirties, but it was a respectable finish.

The 1963 season was a very strange one, although it set up a fine following year. The crew won all of their races up to the Washington event in Seattle, where the frosh, as usual, were soundly beaten. Then the JV put on a real show, leading to just before the finish, only to have Washington go flying by for a win. The varsity race was one for the books. The Bears went out to a good lead during the first half of the race, and then Washington started to overhaul Cal. At the finish it seemed to be anyone's race, and there was no word from the judges' barge for what seemed like forever after two-and-three-quarter miles of furious rowing. Finally it was announced that the race was a tie. There had been no official camera at the finish line as was later required. A friend of mine, who had been on the barge, reported that Washington

had movies of the finish, but he doubted that I would ever be able to see them.

At the Pacific Coast Sprints the Huskies came in front of the Bears by a quarter length in both varsity and junior varsity races. The IRA, however, was another story. Cornell again won by one-half length over Navy. The Middies beat MIT by a length, and Cal was in fourth behind MIT. Washington, to everyone's surprise, was back in the middle of the fifteen-boat field at seventh.

Another Olympic year rolled around in 1964, and the rowing establishment decided that all races during that year would be at the Olympic distance of 2,000 meters to make sure that all would train for the sprint distance. We went to work and, without really meaning to, gradually developed a slightly shortened high-stroke style, even during workouts. The crews swept through their races up until meeting Washington on the estuary. It was Dean Witter's last race as chief official. Despite the fact we all knew he could still keep up with the best of them, he told me that he felt it would be better to step aside for a younger man—after all he had been officiating since 1913.

Although Washington won the frosh and JV races by about a length, our varsity set out to change this pattern. Blasting off the start they quickly forged in front and led

1963 California Varsity, finish line of Three-Mile Race, Lake Washington, Seattle. The race ended in a dead heat with the Huskies. *Left to right:* #1 Gus Schilling, #2 Gary Rogers, #3 John Sellers, #4 Don Wiesner, #5 Steve Brandt, #6 Eric Van de Water, #7 Kent Fleming, #8 Steve Johnson, coxswain Bob Shimasaki.

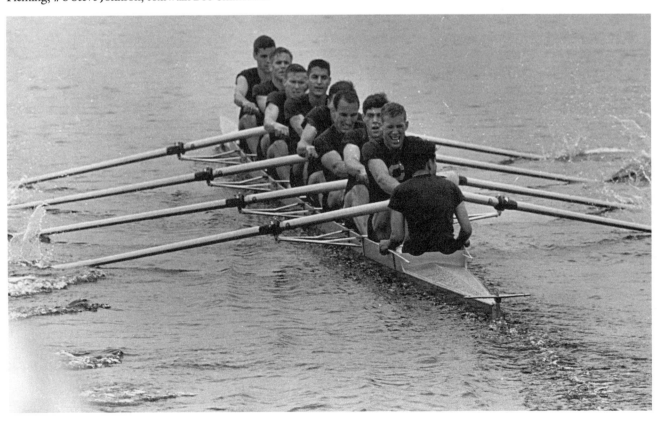

all the way to the finish at the Fruitvale Bridge. Cal looked good, rowing high and hard, coming down to thirty-eight strokes per minute only once during the whole race. Even so, they seemed relaxed and comfortable. The tough work all spring was paying off.

The 1964 Pacific Coast Sprint Championships were held on Mission Bay in San Diego. Del Beekley, a cox from the Old San Diego Rowing Club days, had started a rowing program at San Diego State College and had pushed hard for the sprints to be held there. The regatta was the forerunner of Del's dream, the now popular San Diego Crew Classic, which features top crews across the country. Weather was blustery, but the races went off anyway, not without problems. The morning heats went okay, but the wind really picked up in the afternoon. Washington won the JV by about one-half length over the Bears—even after running into a buoy. Our varsity was in the outside lane in rather heavy water. Although Washington seemed to get a slight lead at the start, Cal took over at 500 meters, and was never headed after that. There was some confusion about the margin of the victory. The timers said it was 0.3 seconds, the finish flag indicated 2.7 seconds, and those on the finish line, including Ky, said it was three-quarters of a length. But California had won, and the exact margin really didn't matter.

The 1964 IRA was interesting. By then the Bears were set in their high-stroking style, seldom rowing below thirty-nine strokes a minute. Shortly before the crew left for the East, a crewman and classmate of mine, George Blair, offered to pay for some of the new "shovel" oars popularized by the Germans and used by Harvard in the recent Eastern Sprint Championships. These oars were slightly longer, and the blades were shorter and wider. We would be using them for the first time in the IRA race. So we took the new oars as well as our conventional Pocock oars, and alternated them at Syracuse. But it wasn't until the day before the race that the crews decided they were comfortable with the wider blades. Both crews qualified easily for the finals. Our JV rowed a good race, nipping a tough Cornell crew in the last ten strokes to take second to a powerful Washington JV which had led all the way. With a strong headwind and heavy water, conditions were not the best for a high-stroking crew with wide blades, according to rival coaches and critics. Our varsity ignored these dire predictions and stormed off the start, cruising down the course at a steady thirty-nine strokes per minute. They won handily by one-and-one-half lengths over Washington, with Cornell, the favorite, two-and-one-half lengths behind.

The 1964 Olympic trials were held three weeks later at Orchard Beach, New York, so we decided to stay in the East. Cornell had planned to enter the trials and had

1964 2,000-Meter IRA Championship, Lake Onondaga, Syracuse, New York. Cal varsity wins going away with Washington in second place.

1964 IRA Regatta, Lake Onondaga, Syracuse, New York. IRA official presents Varsity Challenge Cup to Cal crew. *Left to right:* #1 Ed Bradbury, IRA official, #8 Steve Johnson, coxswain Jim Libien, IRA board of stewards member John L. Collier, coach Jim Lemmon.

invited us to train with them at Lake Cayuga again. After the IRA results, they thought there was little to gain by entering the trials and turned over to us their boathouse and facilities, as well as their motel reservations near the trials—a truly sportsman-like gesture by Stork Sanford, Cornell's coach, and his crew.

The Bears worked hard on Lake Cayuga, and again we really enjoyed that beautiful setting. We were undefeated, and certainly went to Orchard Beach as one of the favorites. The crew came through the preliminary heat without difficulty. In the semi-finals we beat Yale, with the Detroit Boat Club and Washington following. California, Harvard, Yale, and Vesper, a crew of older, experienced men, fought it out in the finals for the right to represent the United States in Tokyo later that summer. Once the race had started, it was just about over for our Bears. We had not been beaten on the racing start all year but in our most important moment of the season, our luck turned. No one really knows what or how it happened, but the crew said it felt like they hit a brick wall after just a few strokes. One entire side became hung up (crabbed), and the boat was dead in the water as the other crews sped on down the course. Cal recovered quickly and started in hot pursuit. Rowing as high and even higher than they ever had in practice, they made up ground on all the other crews. We beat Yale by one-and-one-half lengths and came within three-quarter lengths of catching Harvard. Vesper, however, was another length in the lead and had complete control of the race. Disappointment doesn't come close to how we felt. We all realized that at that level of racing you cannot so much as stumble or you're out of it. Vesper proved to be a fine representative of the U.S. when they won the gold medal in a very dramatic race rowed in the dark at Tokyo.

Shortly after the trials, I received a letter that took a little of the sting out of such a crushing defeat. The letter, sent by Allen Rosenberg, coach of the Vesper crew, read:

> Dear Jim,
>
> All too often when a competition is over, only the victor is overwhelmed with attention and good wishes. May I take this moment to tell you and your fine crew that we are, and will always be, impressed and reminded of a great, determined group of sportsmen.
>
> There were many competitors at New York. We think of California as the only sportsmen.
>
> Respectfully,
> Allen Rosenberg

I made sure each crew member had a copy of the letter. All in all it had been a wondrous season. The varsity was defeated only in the finals of the Olympic trials and had won the Pacific Coast dual race, the Pacific Coast Sprints, and the IRA championship, with the junior varsity runners-up in each of those races. The champion 1964 varsity crew was:

8–Steve Johnson	4–Mike Page
7–Gus Schilling	3–John Sellers
6–Scott Gregg	2–Alan Mooers
5–Malcolm Thornley	1–Ed Bradbury
Cox–Jim Libien	

The 1965 season was hard to classify. It ranged from the very heights to the start of a descent into the depths. The year started strong. Many had graduated from the 1964 squad, but there were some veterans returning and some strong newcomers. The crews powered through the races before meeting Washington and seemed ready to go north. The frosh led off with a two-and-one-quarter-length win over their rivals. The JV rowed a powerful race and won by three-and-one-half lengths. The varsity, under this kind of pressure, came through with a tough one-and-one-half-length win to nail down the first-ever clean sweep for Cal on Lake Washington since the series had started in 1903—a high moment in California rowing. Two weeks later the crews returned to Lake Washington for the Pacific Coast Championships. All did not go as planned, for the JV was second to Washington by one-and-one-half lengths and just feet in front of a closing Oregon State crew. Things didn't improve when the varsity came in third, three-quarter lengths behind the winner, Washington, and one-half length behind second place, British Columbia. The Bears were bewildered. Some of the problem was explained when it was discovered that the varsity #6 man, John McConnell, had an old eye injury, detached retinas, which was aggravated by the strain of the final sprint. This ended John's rowing career, although he was appointed freshmen coach in 1966 and 1967. He was one of the real power men in the boat, and there seemed to be no equal replacement. At the IRA the varsity came in a very disappointing seventh, and the JV was sixth. What a comedown after the earlier clean sweep!

The sixties had seemed so bright until the tumble in 1965. No one was prepared for the cataclysmic 1966 season. The Bears never recovered from the dive in standing after the Washington sweep. In the UCLA race prior to Washington, I tried the same tactic Ky had employed in 1940, switching the varsity and JV completely—the JV had been kicking the varsity in every run for the two days prior to the trip south. What they may have lacked in experience and strength, they made up for in drive. The result of my experiment was that UCLA posted its first-ever win against a Berkeley varsity. UCLA was on the rise at long last, and it was hard for the Bears to take. Next, it was a Washington sweep on the estuary. Our varsity lost by three-and-one-half lengths in the

1964 California Varsity, IRA Champions. *Left to right:* #4 Mike Page, #1 Ed Bradbury, #5 Malcolm Thornley, #3 John Sellers, #2 Alan Mooers, #6 Scott Gregg, coxswain Jim Libien, #7 Gus Schilling, #8 Steve Johnson.

three-mile, and the JV went down by four-and-one-half lengths, as did the freshmen. The Stanford race was even worse. Rowing on the Stanford course, the Bears were completely swept, although the frosh race was close, with California losing by only a half a second. Even the third varsity lost, as did the second freshmen. It just was not a banner day for the Bears.

The Pacific Coast, or Western Sprint Championships as the regatta was now called, was unforgettable. Several dual races had been held at a new site in front of the shipyard in Vallejo. The admiral in command of the Naval shipyards there knew and liked the sport of rowing, so he was most cooperative. All went well until race day, and then the weather took over. The wind was almost too much as the regatta progressed. The freshmen rowed a fine race, losing to Orange Coast College by half a second; Washington did not bring its freshmen. The JV just didn't have it in very rough water, and they placed last of six. The varsity race will long be remembered by those who rowed it.

First of all the stakeboats were blown away, and a floating start was necessary. In a most remarkable display

of sportsmanship, all of the coxswains worked together with the starter and, despite the now howling wind, got off even. The Bears seemed to come out of their year-long hibernation and battled the leaders, Washington and Stanford, right down the course. Somewhere in the last 500 meters the Bears' luck turned, and they ran into a wall of water that almost stopped them in their tracks. They recovered, but were now behind. At the finish it was Washington by three-quarter lengths over Stanford, who beat Cal by a quarter length.

It was a fine showing considering the season up to that point, so we decided the crew had earned a trip to the IRA. The JV, which wasn't up to snuff, stayed home. It might have been best to leave the varsity home as well, because they proved not to be representative of a good Cal crew either. In a fifteen-crew field, they came in eighth, the next to worst finish ever for California. Washington fared even more poorly, coming in eleventh. They had done quite well up to that point, and no one seemed to know what went wrong. At any rate, the Eastern crews were once again dominant.

As the crew sat down for their post-race dinner, a

shocker was in store for them. I announced that I had been offered the Dean of Men position, succeeding Arleigh Williams, who had moved up to be Dean of Students. I would leave the athletic department as of July to join the administration. Not inexperienced in the work of the Dean's office, I had served with Brutus Hamilton, the revered track coach, as special assistant to the Dean of Men for several years. I had accepted the offer just after the spring season began, but I did so with the stipulation that I would not start until the rowing season was completed, and that it would not be announced until I could tell the crew after the season ended—and, I hoped, after the IRA.

To step down from coaching, especially as the varsity crew coach at Cal, one of the top jobs in the sport in the country, was a very difficult decision. I had been remarkably successful in seven short years, with three national champions, three of seven dual race wins over Washington plus a tie, as well as finalist and favorite in two consecutive Olympic trials. I did have a disastrous final season, although this latter record had nothing to do with my choice. If anything, I considered staying to bring the crew back to a respectable level. On the other hand, how could anyone turn down the challenge of becoming Dean of Men at Berkeley? Ed Voorhees, Dean of Men during the forties, had been my mentor. I had to attempt to sit at his desk and try my best to fill his shoes. As it turned out, the pressures and confrontations of the "six-year war" of the mid-sixties on the Berkeley campus were far beyond anything I had withstood in the heat of rowing competition. To stand shoulder to shoulder with Arleigh Williams, Dean of Students, during this period was as rewarding and demanding an experience as I have had in my entire career. My status as the former varsity crew coach at Berkeley, coupled with my position as Dean of Men emeritus, makes me very humble and most grateful.

Meanwhile, I had selected Martin McNair as my successor. Marty was the #4 man in the 1960 IRA champions, and stroke of the 1961 IRA champions. Although he had no previous experience in coaching, he had rowed under both Ky and me and was well-versed in our fundamentals of style and training. He had just finished a tour of duty, which included some hazardous missions in Vietnam, in a SEAL unit, one of the most demanding outfits in the Navy. He remained in the Naval Reserve of the SEALS and has attained the rank of captain.

In the spring of 1966 he was in an MBA program at the University of Chicago. He later finished his degree at Berkeley. After accepting my offer, Marty joined me and the crew at Syracuse. The crew was told he was there to assist me as a favor and was accepted by the crew on that basis. In this way he could observe the varsity first and

Martin McNair, Varsity Coach 1967–1972. (Courtesy of Ed Kirwan.)

then, after my announcement, meet them as their new coach. Thus I stepped out of the crew picture at Cal and went on to help deal with the ever-increasing crisis on campus.

Without question the Free Speech Movement and the resultant turmoil on the campus affected the sports program. Because of its location away from campus, crew was probably less touched at first than some of the more visible sports. But at the start of fall semester in 1964 the crew was being honored for its IRA victory at the year's first University meeting in Lower Sproul Plaza when a group of dissidents marched through the gathering during Chancellor Strong's speech. This was just prior to the all out Free Speech Movement disruptions. All the teams suffered from these disturbances, and the status of individual athletes also suffered. There were times when athletes were reluctant to identify themselves as out for a sport because of peer pressure. It even got to the point where the governor of the state asked in a press interview if the football team at Berkeley wore sandals. While not an excuse for the crew program's difficulties during this era, it clearly was a factor. They were troublesome times for all involved.

Marty took over the 1967 season and established a strong program of physical conditioning based on his

SEAL training, one of the most rigorous systems ever devised. His squads were awed that the coach himself could and would lead them through drills. He introduced much, if not all, of the off-water training used by the crews at Berkeley today, including the ergometer, weight lifting, and running the stadium stairs. Rowing had been the primary conditioner, so this was a new twist for Cal crewmen, although programs elsewhere were adopting the same approach. In fact, I had recently introduced some circuit training at Harmon Gym during the off-season. Marty's requirement of a thoroughly conditioned squad all year round is still met today and with excellent results.

The first major race of 1967 was with UCLA, and the Bruins were beginning to show their teeth, as had been discovered the previous year. Although the Cal freshmen won by half a length, the JV lost by two-and-one-quarter lengths, and the varsity went down by one-and-one-quarter lengths. This continued for several seasons— UCLA had come of age in rowing. The Washington races at Seattle were a mixed bag. The frosh were destroyed by ten lengths, but the JV won by one-and-one-half lengths, never an easy task on Lake Washington.

The varsity race was a strange one. Although they lost by about five lengths, both the crew and the coaches felt it had been possible to win. Because of a disagreement or possible confusion among the crew, the race strategy seemed in conflict and the boat never got together. All thought a return match would prove different. Unfortunately, the following week two of the top oarsmen were seriously injured in a motorcycle accident on the way to the boathouse. Neither could row again that year, and it was several years before one man could resume a normal life. This was quite a blow for such a promising squad. Stanford swept its regatta with the Bears. Both varsity crews put up a good battle, however, with the JV going down by three-quarter lengths and the varsity by six feet. Still they were losses instead of the wins predicted earlier.

The 1967 Western Sprints were held in Long Beach. UCLA took the varsity race by a length over Washington, which had three-quarter lengths over Stanford. Cal, San Diego State, and Loyola trailed in that order. The JV race was incredible, with Stanford over Cal in a photo finish that could have gone either way. Washington was a distant sixth. At Syracuse the IRA was again cursed with foul weather. The storm hit when the JV race had but a mile to go. Up to that point the Bears were among the leaders rowing second or third; they were unable to handle the heavy water and fell back to seventh. Navy was the winner. The varsity race was delayed for a full two hours. When it was finally over, Penn won ahead of Wisconsin and Cornell. Cal was a distant eleventh, the worst ever for the Bears. They had been in good shape until the last mile; then they just ran out of gas. It was a

disappointing ending to a season that had started so encouragingly.

In 1968, another Olympic year, all races again were set at the Olympic distance of 2,000 meters. After winning some minor skirmishes, Cal took on UCLA on Ballona Creek in Los Angeles. The Bruin varsity won again by three lengths, with the Bears taking the JV by half a length and the frosh by three-quarter lengths. Washington swept the estuary in three good races. They won by two lengths in the varsity, by only three-quarter lengths in the JV, and in the freshmen race, they won by two-and-one-half lengths. The freshmen loss was due to a twist of fate. Cal had led until just before the Park Street Bridge, 500 meters from the finish, a tugboat pulling a sand barge got into the act. In fact, it was in the Bears' lane, despite the presence of the Coast Guard. After twisting and turning to avoid disaster, the Cal shell lost considerable ground that it could not make up.

The Stanford race started out well for Berkeley as the Blue and Gold crews won the JV by a quarter length and the frosh by one-third length. At the start of the varsity race, the water was extremeley rough. Cal led the first few strokes, but the crews were called back for a false start. In turning around, Cal shipped four to five inches of water, but started a second time. Again in the lead, after forty strokes the Cal shell swamped. Stanford also had shipped water but managed to stay afloat with four rowing and four bailing. After twenty minutes, Stanford crossed the line and claimed victory. The result was contested, but the decision stood, much to the dismay of the Blue and Gold.

The 1968 Sprints were held at Seattle. In the varsity race Washington won by a length over UCLA and Stanford tied for second. California was fourth. Orange Coast College won the JV, defeating the favored Huskies. Cal was third, Stanford fourth, and UCLA with University of British Columbia brought up the rear. There was no freshmen event. After a review of the season record it was decided not to enter the 1968 IRA or to go to the Olympic trials.

There was no improvement in 1969. Conditions on campus continued to be poor and even worsened. The Bears opened with UCLA on the estuary. The Bruins won the varsity race over the 2,000-meter course by two lengths and the JV race by one-and-one-quarter lengths. Cal's freshmen saved the day by winning a squeaker by a tenth of a second. The Bears then went to southern California to race at Long Beach. Although the junior varsity beat Long Beach State and San Diego State, and the freshmen won too, Cal did not fare well in the featured varsity race. Long Beach State won, followed by San Diego State and USC, with the Bears coming in last. The next regatta was with Washington, and both schools agreed to return to the three-mile distance for the varsities and two miles for freshmen. The Huskies swept the lake. Their varsity was in front by eight lengths, their JV by seven lengths, and their freshmen by one-and-three-quarter lengths.

The Stanford races were better. Cal's JV and freshmen won their races, but the Bear varsity lost again, by one-and-one-quarter lengths. The Western Sprint Championships were held at San Diego on the Mission Bay course. The best California could do was to come in third in the freshmen event. Washington won and Stanford was second. Cal's JV did not qualify for the finals. The Bear varsity finished last. Washington was an easy winner in this race, followed by UCLA, Stanford, UC Irvine, and Long Beach State. Again, California was not up to sending a crew to the IRA.

By the start of the 1970 season the Berkeley campus had gone through the turbulence and trauma of People's Park and the Third World Strike, and was heading for the Cambodia incident. Although the majority of the student body was not directly involved, the distractions were great. To run a disciplined sports program was a monumental job for anyone, and the strain was showing in most sports at Berkeley by then. Rowing was no exception.

The season did not get off to a good start as the varsity lost to UC Irvine by two-and-three-quarter lengths and to Long Beach State by two lengths on the estuary. The good news was that both the JV and the freshmen won. At Ballona Creek UCLA registered an historic first by rowing to a clean sweep over the three Berkeley crews, including the first-ever win by the UCLA freshmen. The next week Loyola won the varsity race on the estuary over Cal and St. Mary's. Again the JV and freshmen won. The Washington race was at 2,000 meters on the estuary. The Huskies swept again, with the varsity winning by two-and-one-quarter lengths, the JV by a close half a length, and the frosh by four-and-one-half. At Redwood City, Stanford prevailed in the varsity by three full lengths. The Blue and Gold JV won a thriller by 0.1 seconds, and the Cal frosh led across the finish line by one-and-three-quarter lengths.

The Western Sprints were held at Long Beach, with results that reflected what had been happening all season. The varsity failed to make the six-boat final but managed to win the consolation race. The JV came in sixth in a race in which Orange Coast College tied Washington for first, with UCLA third. British Columbia and UC Irvine were fourth and fifth. The frosh race was won by Washington and the Cal yearlings were fifth. Despite the record, Cal decided to return to the IRA with only a varsity four (a recently added event) and the freshmen eight. It was hoped the experience would be helpful for the first-year men. That year the housing was moved from the state fairgrounds to dormitories on the Syracuse

University campus, a much more comfortable arrangement. But the results at the IRA were a real disappointment. The freshmen were unable to qualify for the six-crew final. The varsity four lost a man to what appeared to be heat stroke in the extremely hot and humid weather. It proved too much. With a replacement in the boat, they rowed in the repechage (second chance) race but didn't qualify for the finals.

The 1971 and 1972 seasons were at much the same level as the previous few years. In 1971 UCLA again swept the Bears, only this time on the estuary. Cal did win the varsity race at San Diego over USC, San Diego State, and UC Santa Barbara in 1971, but both Washington and Stanford swept their regattas—in the Stanford varsity's case for the sixth galling year in a row. Finally in 1972 the Blue and Gold crews beat Stanford at Redwood City. On the other hand, Washington continued its mastery of California by easily sweeping the estuary.

Neither the 1971 or 1972 Western Sprints saw the Bears improve their lot by much. At Seattle in 1971 the varsity, junior varsity, and freshmen all failed to make the championship finals. At Long Beach in 1972 the Cal varsity did not make the six-boat final and was third in the consolation final to Oregon State and UC Irvine. The junior varsity was fourth in their finals, and the frosh placed second two lengths behind Washington.

For the 1971 IRA Cal sent a varsity four with cox and a pair without cox along with a varsity eight. These small-boat events that were being added to the IRA gave an opportunity for more oarsmen to compete. The varsity eight did not row well, coming in far down in the consolation final; the small boats saved the day for the Bears, however. The varsity four placed a quite creditable third behind the winner Navy and second place MIT. The pair rowed a very strong race and won. This was the first IRA pair event, and Cal ended up winning its first IRA championship in eight long years. The pair was also the first California small-boat victors since the late 1800s, when all California's racing was in small boats. The winning pair was manned by Kelly Moore, port bow, and Paul Knight, starboard stroke.

The racing season was so disappointing in 1972 that the IRA trip was canceled. In fact, Marty McNair was so frustrated that he felt it best to resign and let someone else take over. With many problems beyond his control, he could have just given up and let the program die. Luckily, he and the team survived. But for too long he had been in the right place at the wrong time. The past few years had taken their toll. Now that campus problems were finally being solved and attitudes were changing, it seemed obvious to him that new approaches were called for. In rowing circles the word was that Steve Gladstone was ready to take over a major rowing program.

Above: Steve Gladstone, Varsity Coach 1973–1980. *Left:* 1971 California's Pair Without Coxswain IRA Champions, Lake Onondaga, Syracuse, New York. *Left to right:* port bowman Kelly Moore, coach Marty McNair, starboard stroke Paul Knight, unidentified IRA official.

Steve was a former Syracuse oarsman who had started coaching in 1966 for Princeton freshmen and then took over the Harvard lightweight program in 1969. His lightweight varsity and junior varsity won the Eastern Sprint Championships four years in a row. His lightweight varsity and four without cox won at the Henley Royal Regatta in 1971. He coached the Union Boat Club to the national title in 1969 and took a U.S. National eight to Europe in 1969. In 1973 he was the U.S. National Team coach. As the record attests, Steve Gladstone was the right man in the right place at the right time.

THE CHRONOLOGY
THE RENAISSANCE 1973–1983

THERE WAS A FAST TURNAROUND of Cal's rowing program in 1973. After winning several warm-up races the Bears were ready to entertain the UCLA Bruins on the estuary. The last win over the Bruin varsity had been in 1965 and the three years previous to the 1973 regatta had been Bruin clean sweeps. The frosh opened with a half-length victory, followed by the junior varsity's come-from-behind one-and-one-half length win. The varsity completed the sweep with a solid two-length victory, and the Bears were on their way.

In an All-California regatta on UCLA's Marina del Rey course, the Berkeley varsity beat an undefeated UC Irvine eight by two lengths, with UCLA and UCSB following. The junior varsity beat UCLA by one-and-one-half lengths, with UC Irvine trailing. Although the frosh faltered, losing to UCLA's first-year men by half a length, they came in front of UC Irvine and UCSB. The moment of truth was at Seattle against a typically powerful Washington team. Although the Bears had come a long way back toward their former status as a national rowing power, the race proved that there still was far to go. The Husky crew overpowered Cal without too much effort. Their varsity beat Berkeley by just over a half length of open water, with Oregon State trailing. The JV and frosh races were equally decisive as Washington again had a sweep.

The next regatta was with Stanford. Having swept the Cards in 1972 on their home course, the Bears' challenge was unlike that in Seattle. Again the Bears came out on top in all of their races with their ancient foes. The season began to wind up with the Western Sprint Championships, scheduled for the Lexington Reservoir in Los Gatos for the first time. Each race was hotly contested, but Washington dominated by sweeping the regatta. The Husky varsity again beat the second-place Bears by one-and-one-half lengths. In the junior varsity race, Washington won over another second-place Cal by two-and-one-

half lengths. Oregon State University was third with Long Beach State, UCLA, and UC Irvine following. The Husky freshmen won by open water over a surprising USC freshmen crew, with Cal third. Orange Coast College, UCLA, and Santa Clara trailed.

After the sprints, Cal decided not to send the varsity to the IRA, but the freshmen were tagged to go. They ran into trouble facing some more experienced crews and failed to make the finals. Even so, the 1973 season gave indications that the Bear crews were coming out of hibernation. In their first year with Gladstone at the helm, the varsity lost only to Washington's Huskies by a small margin in two attempts.

The 1974 season inspired wide swings of emotion, with stunning victory and frustrating defeat. The season opened with the UCLA regatta at Los Angeles. Cal's crews dominated in each race, with both the varsity and freshmen winning by four lengths; the junior varsity won by one-and-three-quarter lengths. The Washington crews were next for California on the estuary. It started out with the same pattern as in the past eight years. The Husky freshmen beat the Cubs by one-quarter length of open water, and their JV went across the finish line one-and-one-half lengths in front of Cal. The varsity race was another matter. California broke hard and fast at the start, and Washington was unable to keep up the pace. The Bears roared across the finish just over a length in front of a surprised Washington crew. For eight straight years the Huskies' dominance had not been shaken. Now, in only his second year, Gladstone had proven to the California squad that Washington could be beaten, if the crew would pay the price. Needless to say the Cal alumni and supporters were ecstatic.

Following the Washington races, the Bears went south and swept the Newport Regatta against the southern California schools. The next weekend it was Stanford at Redwood Shores, and again Cal had a clean sweep.

1974 California Varsity. They defeat the Washington varsity on the 2,000-meter course on the Oakland Estuary.

The stage was then set for the Western Sprints and the Bears were confident. For the first time the sprint regatta was held out of the country, in conjunction with the month-long British Columbia Festival of Sports—310 sports events to be exact. The University of British Columbia hosted the races on Burnaby Lake. Again Washington showed its depth and power. The Huskies won the freshmen event by two-and-one-quarter lengths over Cal in second. Their JV took the final by two-and-one-half lengths over the Bears. Washington had revamped its varsity following the Cal race, and apparently the new combination clicked. Their varsity won the

championship heat by half a length over a surprising UC Irvine crew. A disappointing Cal crew was three-quarter lengths behind them in third. The season ended on this low note, and the decision not to go to the IRA. This choice was not only because of the poor showing in the sprints: the varsity #6 man had injured his back and could not be adequately replaced. Washington decided not to go East either, due to finals conflicts.

At the start of 1975 the crew began to discuss the possibility of a trip to the Royal Henley Regatta on the Thames in England. Racing that year actually started with a new national event, Del Beekley's dream come true, the San Diego Crew Classic on Mission Bay. Hosting the Pac-8 Sprints in 1960 convinced San Diego backers that a national event was possible. Among those invited were such Eastern powers as Harvard, Wisconsin, and Navy, which had been tops there the previous year. Also included were the Pacific Coast's strongest crews, Cal, Washington, etc. The regatta was quite successful, with a large crowd in attendance. To keep down expenses, only freshmen from Pacific Coast schools raced. Washington won the finals by two lengths over Cal's first-year men. The Bears did not fare too well in the JV race, taking fourth behind winner Washington, which was in front of Orange Coast College and Harvard. Harvard won the varsity event by two lengths over Washington, which had just under two lengths on Cal. Wisconsin, UC Irvine, and Navy trailed. All felt it was a worthwhile event even though it was so early in the racing season. It was the first regatta since the 1800s to bring all of the national powers together.

Following San Diego, the Bears went against UCLA on the estuary. The Cal crews swept their southern brothers easily in preparation for going to Seattle to take on the Huskies the next weekend. Washington decided to hold the races against the Bears as part of the Opening Day Regatta for sailing and powerboats on Lake Washington, a custom which has continued. The race site was changed to the Montlake cut, connecting Lake Washington and Lake Union, in front of the site of the old balloon hangar that had been the Washington boathouse before World War II. More often than not, some 50,000 spectators line the banks of this canal-like cut. Although the Bears had been improving, they were not up to Washington's strength and the Seattle weather. The wind gusted up to forty-five miles per hour out on the lake, and the races were rowed in driving rain. The freshmen went down by a close three-quarter lengths, the JV was defeated by two lengths, and Washington completed its sweep by beating the Bear varsity by three lengths.

The Western Sprint Championships were held again at the Marine Stadium in Long Beach. The Cal freshmen were a pleasant surprise. At San Deigo they had lost by eight seconds to Washington and at Seattle the margin had been cut to three seconds. At Long Beach the two first-year crews went neck-and-neck down the course, and the Bear Cubs flashed across the finish line .10 seconds ahead. The Huskies won the JV by three-quarter lengths over Orange Coast College, which had one-and-one-quarter lengths on Cal. In the varsity, Washington won by one-and-one-quarter lengths over Oregon State, which in turn beat Cal by three-quarter lengths. UC Irvine and Stanford followed.

It was decided to send only freshmen to Syracuse for the IRA. They started out fine in their first heat and were leading at the halfway point when they caught a crab and ended in third place behind Wisconsin and Northeastern. Then they won their repechage race, beating Cornell and Brown. The finals were delayed three-and-one-half hours by wind and waves. When they were finally run off, the Bears had apparently left their race at the float. They came in fifth behind the winner, Penn, with Syracuse, Wisconsin, and Rutgers in that order. They did beat Princeton, which took sixth and last place.

The San Diego Crew Classic was again Berkeley's season opener in 1976. Harvard, as defending champion, Wisconsin, victors in the previous three IRAs, Navy, and Penn represented the East. Cal, Washington, UC Irvine, UCLA, University of British Columbia, and Stanford were the Pacific Coast entries. The freshmen event was again just for the Pacific Coast schools. Washington won the frosh final by one-and-one-half lengths over Cal, which beat out Stanford, Orange Coast College, UCLA, Long Beach State, and UCSB in that order. The JV final was a scorcher. Penn won it by a whisker, with Cal in third just six seats back. The finals in the varsity were even tighter. Harvard successfully defended its title by nosing out Penn. California's varsity again was third but by just a half a length—despite the fact that their #6 man hurt his back in the opening heat and was replaced from the JV.

Next the Bears won several dual races preparing for the annual showdown with Washington on the estuary. When the spray settled it turned out to be an odd regatta. The Bears actually had a shot at a clean sweep but lost both the frosh and varsity races. The Cal freshmen rowed a fine race and were nosed out by only .80 seconds. The Bear JV won by just over a length. In the varsity event the Bears led all the way down the course and had open water at the Park Street Bridge (a bit more than 1,500 meters). With about thirty strokes to go the #6 man's back went out again, just as at San Diego, and he couldn't row. Cal, struggling with only seven men, couldn't hold off the Huskies, who won by .40 seconds.

A few changes were made in the boating for the Stanford races at Redwood Shores and the result was another California sweep. The frosh won by two lengths, the JV by a whopping thirty seconds (seven-and-one-half lengths), and the varsity prevailed by four-plus lengths. This time the Western Sprints were held on the San Pablo Reservoir, a dream of Ky's and mine for years. The local water district had always opposed it, but new blood on the board and modern technology for water treatment combined to turn the tide. The reservoir is a beautiful stretch of water, but it can also be a wind tunnel from late morning throughout the rest of the day. Racing was scheduled to begin early in the morning, but the field had grown out of hand. It included a number of small boat events, women's entries, and high school crews. The main events, including heats, for which the sprints were originally intended, were pushed into the later hours and the result was rough conditions. Despite a rather endless wait, when they finally were staged, the Washington freshmen rowed to a close half-length win over a hard-charging Cal shell. In the JV race Cal beat out Orange Coast College, which nosed past the Huskies. In the varsity Washington maintained control throughout the race, beating Cal by just over a length.

Once the regatta was over the Pac-8 schools decided to split off from the Western Intercollegiate Crew Coaches Association to stage their own races. This was a hard decision, because it meant cutting off some excellent competition, such as Orange Coast College and British Columbia. However, the WICCA had become a two-tiered organization with more than half of its member schools more like clubs with limited budgets and equipment. The rest had larger budgets, travel money, and professional coaches. Even within the Pac-8 this was a problem but to a much lesser degree. The answer may well be that two separate divisions should be set up for racing on the coast, much like Divisions I and II in NCAA sports.

For the first time in a number of years, all three crews went to the IRA in 1976. The results were mixed. The freshmen failed to make the finals, but did win the consolation finals over Northeastern, Dartmouth, MIT, Columbia, and Cornell in that order. The JV rowed a strong race in their finals, but came in fourth, only seven seconds behind the winner, Penn. Northeastern was second, and Cornell third—a good race but no cigar for Cal. The varsity almost did themselves in by coming in

1976 California Varsity, IRA 2,000-Meter Champions, Syracuse, New York. *Left to right, standing:* #8 Dean Wright, #7 Ulrich Lemke, #6 Bob Guthrie, #5 Neal Hoffman, #4 Joel Turner, #3 Mark Sutro, #2 Jeff Walker, #1 Keith Jackson. *In rear:* Kent Fleming, Freshman Coach. *Left to right, kneeling:* Steve Gladstone, Varsity Coach, coxswain Marco Meniketti holding Varsity Challenge Cup.

second to three-time winner Wisconsin in the heat. They saved themselves by beating Syracuse in the repechage. Prior to the IRA, Steve Gladstone had changed the varsity around with three men from the old JV and a new stroke. The new combination came into its own in the finals. They roared past Penn to win, with the Quakers nipping defending champ Wisconsin followed by Princeton, MIT, and Syracuse. Thus did Steve chalk up an IRA championship for Cal in four short years, putting the Bear crews back among the nation's elite. That Washington had chosen not to enter in recent years took something of an edge off the victory. The 1976 IRA championship crew was as follows:

8–Dean Wright	4–Joel Turner
7–Ulrich Lemke	3–Mark Sutro
6–Bob Guthrie	2–Jeff Walker
5–Neal Hoffman	1–Keith Jackson
Cox–Marco Meniketti	

By 1977 the San Diego Crew Classic had become the standard opener for the top crews in the country. This time Mission Bay proved what many old-timers knew, that it could get rough and windy. All races were over a windblown course, but came off without a hitch. In the frosh finals Orange Coast College surprised Washington, which had to fight off Cal to take second. The JV final was a catastrophe. The Bears hit a buoy, broke an oarlock, and placed last. The varsity race began bleakly for Cal with a terrible start in rough water. This undoubtedly cost them a higher finish, and they were just nosed out by Oregon State for the third spot. Penn won it all by nipping Washington at the wire.

The Bear crews won the rest of their early races while preparing for Washington at Seattle. The hard work showed as Cal provided the Huskies stiff competition. The end result, however, was a Washington sweep. Both the frosh and the JV went down fighting, losing by just a boatlength. The varsity race was also a tight one, with the lead changing hands often, but Washington won by slightly more than three-quarter lengths. Then came an unprecedented shocker. Stanford, the Bears' next opponent, suddenly canceled out of the race, and nothing could convince the crew to reverse their decision, nor did they give an explanation.

The Pac-8 crews held their own championships at Redwood Shores that year, having decided to try rotating sites for their sprints. This time Washington did not get its sweep. They won the frosh event without difficulty; then, the Cal JV pulled an upset by rowing past them at the finish for a win. The Cal varsity was stunned in their heat by being nosed out by Oregon State, which left them third in the final standings. Washington did its usual thing and beat the Beavers in

the varsity finals. At the IRA, the Bears could not defend their varsity championship as hoped. They were nosed out in their heat by Wisconsin and only got into the finals by winning their repechage. In the finals Cornell won by one-and-three-quarter lengths over Penn, which had half a length on Cal. Yale, an entry for the first time since 1897, Oregon State, and Wisconsin trailed. (The Cal varsity rowed right through Wisconsin, which had beaten the Bears in the opening heat.) The JV took a very respectable second to Penn, beating out Navy, Yale, Boston University, and Wisconsin in that order.

After the IRA, Berkeley determined to sample the competition at the Royal Henley Regatta in England. Steve, having been there before with his Harvard Lightweights, was well-versed in the necessary arrangements. Rather than sending an eight, he decided to send two fours with cox. One would represent the University, while the other was called the California Rowing Club. The crews paid their own way, so their presence was somewhat informal. Although the stay at Henley was enjoyable and educational, the results did not measure up to the crews' expectations. The Cal four lost by two-and-one-half lengths in the first round, and the Club four was disqualified after just twenty strokes for going out of its lane. So much for California's first shot at the Henley Regatta.

The 1978 season started at San Diego for the annual Crew Classic. The usual leaders of the East, including Penn and Harvard, came out to take on the best of the West. The varsity final was very tight. When it all boiled down, Washington won the varsity final by 1.7 seconds over Penn, which had .3 seconds over Cal in third and Harvard in fourth. It was not easy for either the junior varsity Bears or Huskies. Penn won, with Harvard second, Washington third, and Cal fourth. Washington prevailed in the freshmen race, followed closely by Orange Coast College and Cal.

The Stanford races were held again at Redwood Shores, and, as a Cal sweep, were really a warm-up for the Bears' contest the following week with the Huskies. Both the varsity and JV beat Stanford by six lengths and the frosh by five. The next weekend was a different story. Under ideal conditions on the estuary, Washington again scored a clean sweep, but it was not that easy. In the varsity race the Bears had a half-length lead at the halfway point, but Washington upped the pace there and rowed right through them to win by one-and-one-half lengths. The JV race ended with the same results, and the frosh went down by just over half a length after a tough battle.

The Pac-8 conference added two Arizona schools to become the Pac-10, which held its championships at Seattle on the Montlake Cut. That year the varsity final was a real show, with Washington finally pulling it out by three feet over a hard-charging California. Oregon State,

UCLA, and Washington State were left in the wash of the two leaders. The Husky JV took their final by a bit more than a length over the Bear JV, which edged UCLA's second boat by half a length. The Husky Pups won their frosh final by only half a length over the UCLA freshmen, who pushed them all the way. Cal's freshmen were third by a length behind UCLA.

The Bear varsity had been improving steadily so it was decided to make a run at the IRA, but the JV and frosh remained at home. A pair-oar without cox also was included. In the preliminary heat, the Bear eight won, defeating Syracuse by a half a length after being behind by a full length at 1,000 meters. Penn won the other qualifying heat. In the finals the Cal shell was stopped all but dead in the water by a hard crab after only a bit more than 500 meters had been rowed. The Bears never really recovered and finished last. Syracuse, which Cal had beaten decisively in the opening heat, won its first IRA crown in 58 years, beating Brown, Northeastern, Dartmouth, and the faltering Bears. Cal's only bright spot that day was when its pair-oar came in second.

The San Diego Crew Classic marked its fifth year at Mission Bay in 1979. Harvard, Syracuse, Penn, Navy, Brown, and Wisconsin were invited. In the freshmen race, Cal came in fifth after hitting a buoy. The JV race was rather disappointing too, with Cal coming in fourth, but it did beat Washington in fifth. The varsity made a real race of it all the way down the course. They finally bowed to Harvard, losing by less than a boatlength. Syracuse, Washington, Wisconsin, Penn, Navy, and Brown trailed the Bears.

A new twist in Cal's race calendar was added in 1979 following San Diego. Cornell, always a power in the East, decided to shake the rigors of late winter and early spring by coming to sunny California. This was the first time that a Big Red crew had rowed on the estuary—it was about time, too, if one remembers that California's first eight-oared shells were purchased from Cornell back in 1907. They were good races, but the Cal crews were obviously in better condition at this early point in the season. The JV won by three seats in an excellent race. The varsity won handily by two full lengths. Cornell did not bring freshmen, so Cal's first-year men raced Humboldt State and won by two lengths. The next weekend the UCLA Bruins came to the estuary for their annual battle with the Bears. Both Berkeley's varsity crews won with ease; the JV by four lengths and the varsity by three. The frosh race was a different matter. The Cal shell was behind until the very end of the race when, in a furious finish, the Bears pulled into a dead heat with the Bruins.

The Cal crews now were ready to take on the Huskies at Seattle. The usual large opening day crowd was treated to some fine racing. The Washington freshmen, always tough at home—and usually elsewhere as well—took the

measure of the Cal frosh by one-and-three-quarter lengths. Cal's JV came home one length over Washington's junior varsity. The varsity race was a real thriller with both crews even for the first 800 meters. Then the Bears pulled steadily away, silencing the partisan crowd, and won by several feet of open water. Steve, along with the Cal coxswain, was thrown into the water in appreciation of victory.

The Pac-10 Regatta was held again at Redwood shores. The Washington freshmen won the final over Cal by a length. Oregon State, Washington State, UCLA, and USC followed in the final standings. The Husky JV came out on top too but only after a tough battle with the Bears, who finally came in half a length back. UCLA, USC, Washington State, and Stanford completed the field in that order. The varsity race was California all the way—in record time. The Bears won by a boatlength over Washington. Oregon State, Washington State, UCLA, Stanford, and USC trailed behind the Huskies.

After deciding to forgo the IRA, Berkeley opted to go for broke by sending an eight-oared crew for the first time to the Royal Henley Regatta on the Thames in England. The only other time the Bears had rowed at Henley, other than the two fours entered informally in 1977, had been back in 1948 when they won their third Olympic gold medal. Henley is a superbly run regatta that has many different races in a number of classifications, and it has grown considerably in size and prestige since it began more than 130 years ago. Until the recent World Championships were organized, Henley often was the scene for the best in international competition during non-Olympic years, and it still ranks right up there. Because of its size the regatta covers about four days. All races are rowed head-to-head or two crews at a time. The precision of organization is such that three races may be going on at the same time, with one race starting, one at the halfway point, and one finishing. The first day there may be as many as eighty or more separate races with an hour off at noon for lunch and an hour off at 4 p.m. for tea. The crowd is huge and for many it is a social event where one should be seen.

For the first time, the Bears' varsity coxswain was a woman, Valerie McClain, who had considerable experience handling the tiller lines in women's crew. She had decided to see if she could handle the men. Coach Steve Gladstone soon discovered that she was quite good and used her as coxswain in his varsity boat all year. At first Henley officials refused to allow a woman to enter their historic regatta. But when Coach Gladstone threatened to pull his crew out of the race and to explain to the press why, they relented. No further problems occurred, and in recent years a number of crews have included women coxswains.

The Bear JV entered the race known as The Ladies

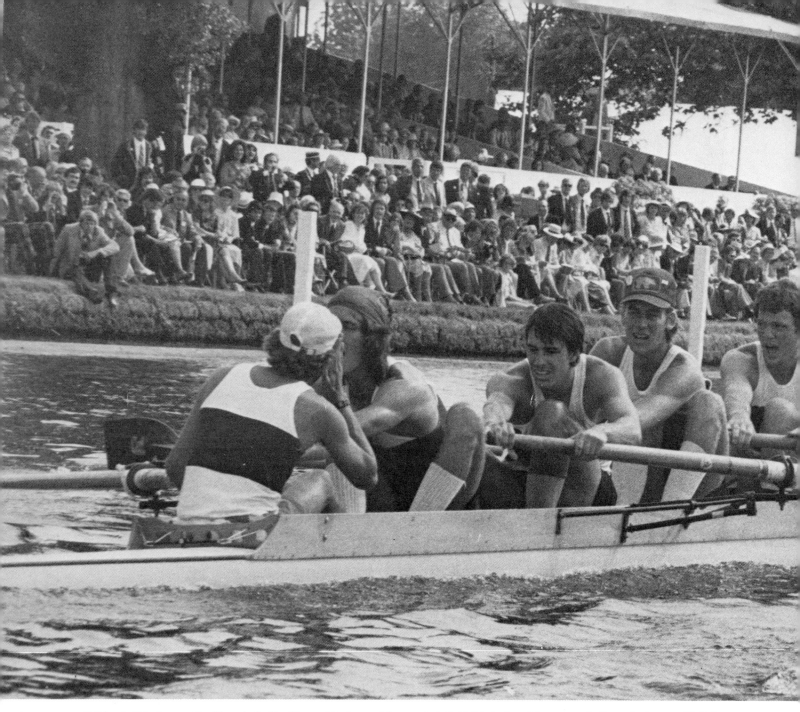

California JV wins semifinal heat in Ladies Plate at Henley-on-Thames, July 5, 1979. *Left to right:* coxswain Peter Anderson, #8 Bob

Plate, the name of its trophy. They defeated a crew from Orange Coast College by three-quarter lengths but were eliminated in the next round by a crew from the Lady Margaret Boat Club by three-quarter lengths. The varsity had the misfortune to draw the powerful British National team in their heat for the Grand Challenge Cup and lost to them in a headwind race by four-and-one-half lengths. It was terrific international eight-oared racing, the first for the Bears since they had raced down under in 1951.

In 1980 the racing season opened on a rather unusual note. After five years, the San Diego Crew Classic was canceled because spring floods had polluted the Mission Bay course. To replace the classic some excellent competition was arranged on the estuary as a season opener. Cornell's Big Red crew was invited once more to come away from the snow to enjoy good workouts and racing. Cornell's coach, Findley Meislahn, had coached with

Steve at Princeton from 1966 to 1969, so the meeting was a natural. The varsity race was much closer this time, with the Bears blowing off the start to gain a good lead. They crossed the finish in front of their Eastern rivals by a full length. The JV race was a real thriller. Cal finally won by just a foot over Cornell. The Orange Coast College crew came in third. Cornell did not bring its freshmen, so the Bear Cubs raced the Orange Coast College frosh in a very close race. At the start Cal's #5 jumped his seat, losing a full length, and that was still the margin at the end. Orange Coast College freshmen went on to win the IRA crown. The UCLA regatta was the next weekend, and all three Bear crews won by open water in a clean sweep.

The following weekend was another story. Bear fans had been waiting for Washington to come to the estuary. Washington started it off in the freshmen event by

Waggener, #7 Eric Bailey, #6 Dave Goerss, #5 Peter Mattiessen, #4 Charles Perry, #3 John Caton, #2 Greg Aplet, #1 Dale Emery.

winning by a length in a really hard fight with the Cubs. That was the end of it for the Huskies, as the JV race was neck-and-neck right down the course, and Cal won by two feet. The Cal varsity roared off the starting line and took charge. They led all the way down the course and won by one-and-one-half lengths to mark Cal's first back-to-back varsity dual wins since 1964–1965.

The Pac-10 Championships at Redwood Shores were not quite as bright for the Bears. In the freshmen final the Husky Pups increased their margin by winning by one-and-one-half lengths over the second-place Cal first-year crew. The Bear JV really got it together, however, and won their final by one-and-one-quarter lengths ahead of Washington. The varsity race was another matter. Washington refused this time to let the Cal varsity blow out on the start and stayed right with them all down the course. In a fine surge at the finish the Huskies pulled out

to win by one-third length, avenging their earlier defeat.

Cal was invited to row in the World Student Games at Milan, Italy, but the Bears chose instead to enter both varsity crews in the IRA at Syracuse. One wonders if the trip to Italy might have been the better choice, for all did not go well at the IRA. The junior varsity did do themselves proud, placing second in their final to the Cornell JV by .3 seconds. This was the crew they had defeated by one foot earlier in the year. The varsity races were different. The Bears did not even qualify for the varsity finals. In their opening heat they lost to Navy by two lengths. In the repechage they were leading at the 1,000-meter mark, but Brown and Penn went past to push them back to third and out of contention, thus ending the 1980 season.

In 1980 California had a unique freshmen coach. His predecessor, Kent Fleming '63, who had coached the

Cubs for twelve years, moved on at the end of the 1979 season, and Steve appointed an old jogging buddy, Roy Eisenhardt, Dartmouth '60, as his replacement. In addition to a solid rowing background, Roy had a law practice and taught two courses at Boalt Hall—certainly a good man to have if a problem arose in the rules of racing. Roy became distinguished among crew coaches when, later in the year, he was selected by the new owner of the Oakland Athletics, a major baseball team, to become its president. Needless to say, that ended his short career as Cal's freshmen crew coach. He had done an excellent job as his freshmen proved during their varsity years.

Not only did Cal lose Roy Eisenhardt, Steve Gladstone stunned everyone by announcing he was getting out of coaching to look for a new career. As it turned out, Steve found he could not resist the allure of coaching young men in the sport of rowing. A year after quitting at Berkeley, he took on the rebuilding of the rowing program at Brown University. There he continued the success story he had started with the Harvard Lightweights and continued at Cal by returning the Golden Bear crews to national rating. In just one year his Brown crew won the IRA Championship, and by 1986 and 1987 they had scored back-to-back wins. Steve joins Rusty Callow of Washington and Navy as the only coaches who have had IRA winners at two different schools.

Meanwhile, Berkeley's new varsity coach was once again an Easterner, Mike Livingston, Harvard '70. He became the second Harvard man to coach at Cal, following E. M. Garnett, Harvard 1887, who was the Bears'

first listed coach from 1893 to 1896 and who returned from 1904 through 1908.

Although Mike had no previous coaching experience, he had a solid background of competitive rowing. As an undergraduate, he was a member of the national championship crews of Harvard in the sixties, and he was on both the 1968 Olympic crew and the 1969 National Rowing Team. Following his graduation he continued to compete both nationally and internationally, and in 1972 he was a member of the silver medal U.S. Olympic eight. A true renaissance man, Mike has many abilities and interests. A graduate of Harvard Law School, he has practiced law; he also is an accomplished violinist and has performed in concert. At Berkeley, he continued the success cycle started by Steve Gladstone. Tim Hodges '75, Mike's selection for freshmen coach, would in time rewrite the record books.

The 1981 season started off with respected but not winning times at the San Diego Crew Classic. The final events were rowed under very rough conditions with a twenty-knot quartering tailwind. The frosh were third behind Orange Coast and Washington. The JV was second, a half a length behind Washington, and the varsity was third behind Washington and Yale. The UCLA regatta saw impressive wins in both the JV and freshmen races, but the varsity was a bitter disappointment. Clearly the favored crew, the Bears apparently rowed themselves out in the first 1,500 meters over the estuary course and ended up losing by a full length in the last 500 meters. UCLA had been well behind the Bears at San Diego, so this was quite a jolt.

Fortunately, the Washington regatta at Seattle fore-

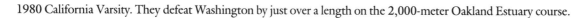

1980 California Varsity. They defeat Washington by just over a length on the 2,000-meter Oakland Estuary course.

Mike Livingston, Varsity Coach 1981–1983.

shadowed future successes when a four with cox made up of the spare oarsmen defeated its Husky counterpart, and then the frosh eight stormed to a four-length victory to end a sixteen-year losing streak on Lake Washington. The Cal JV won by just under a boatlength. Washington's varsity prevented a clean sweep with a five-second win that set a course record. Although the Huskies rated possibly the fastest crew in the country, California proved it was up to such competition. Stanford discovered this at Redwood Shores, when Cal registered another sweep. Even in the closest race, between the freshmen, the Cub crews won by four-and-one-quarter lengths.

The Pac-10s were held again at Redwood Shores, now designated as a permanent site for the Pac-10 Championships. The course, run on the two-boat head-to-head Henley format, provides interesting racing. The Cal contingent made itself known in a hurry. Both the freshmen and the JV boats sailed through the two days of racing with ease, winning the finals in record-setting time. The frosh beat UCLA, earlier winners over Washington, by three full lengths, while the Bear JV beat Washington coming from behind by three seconds. The earlier dual race defeat by UCLA meant the Bears were seeded third, and they met Washington's varsity in the semi-finals. Rowing into a stiff headwind the heavier Husky crew prevailed for the third time over the Bears by an even boatlength. Washington went on to win the

finals easily against UCLA, while Cal placed third, beating Oregon State.

Both the varsity and the JV decided against going to the IRA since final exams would be immediately afterward. The undefeated freshmen decided to take on the best the country could offer. Seeded second to Penn, winners of the Eastern Sprints, the Cal youngsters qualified for the finals despite rough water conditions. They were in third place in the finals, half a length behind Brown and a seat behind Princeton. Their season was still quite successful and a portent for the future of California rowing.

Mike and Tim added a new feature to the training cycle as the 1981–82 season got underway. Right after Christmas the varsity squad of about thirty men went down to Newport Beach, Tim's home waters, to row two-a-days using local equipment. These workouts extended over seven to eight days, and the men stayed at friends' houses and covered their own expenses. Considerable progress was made in technique as well as getting the spring season off to a fast start. The increase in squad morale was also most evident. This practice continued each year with the exception of 1986, when Tim tried keeping the squad in Berkeley with workouts on the estuary. In the end they all went on three days of cross-country skiing in the Sierras for a change of scenery, another satisfying trip.

The 1982 racing season will go down in history as one of the best non-Olympic years in California rowing, even though there were two post-season defeats. It all started with a renewal of an old rivalry with the Badgers of Wisconsin. They had been invited to take a week's break from the snow and ice to work out of Cal's Ebright Boathouse on the estuary. After enjoying their two-a-day workouts, the Badger JV and varsity were brought back to reality by losing to both of the Cal crews.

The next competition was the prominent San Diego Crew Classic, and it was one that will long be remembered by Cal crew supporters. The surging Golden Bear crews blew everyone off Mission Bay by sweeping the whole event. Both the freshmen and the JV rowed thrilling come-from-behind victories. In fact the JV won by only .44 of a second. The varsity won their final by staying comfortably in front all the way, holding off a late surge by Yale without difficulty. This placed the Bear varsity in front of Harvard, Yale, Washington, UCLA, Cornell, Boston University, Rutgers, and the rest of the Pac-10 crews. Hopes had been high, but a sweep was almost too much to expect.

Coming down from such an emotional peak was hard for the Bears when they met UCLA two weeks later on Ballona Creek. The UCLA course is very fast so there is little time for errors to be made up. The frosh had beaten the Bruin Cubs by twenty-six seconds at San Diego, but

1982 California Freshmen, IRA 2,000-Meter Champions, Syracuse, New York. *Left to right, standing:* #1 Matt Anacker, #2 Davis Bales, #3 Tony Matan, #4 Brian Cuneo, #5 Pat Graffis, #6 Matt Pribyl, #7 Sean Seward, #8 Eric Cohn, freshmen coach Tim Hodges. Coxswain Mike Shinn is in front holding trophy. An IRA official is kneeling in front.

they had to come from behind to win by six-and-one-half seconds this time. The JV fell behind early and struggled to win at last by a scant three-quarters of a length. The varsity decided not to wait and led all the way to win by three lengths in course record time.

The Washington races on the estuary were all tight and one of the most hotly contested of the long series. The freshmen, in a switch from the usual script, had the easiest time when the Cal shell took an early lead and won by better than a length. This marked the first back-to-back wins over the Washington frosh since Nagler's Cubs in 1940–41. The real war began with the Cal JV giving up a three-seat deficit to Washington's second boat and then hanging on to that margin until the very end when the Huskies added another seat to their win. It was the first defeat of any Cal crew that season. The varsity race was a scorcher, with neither crew leading the first 500 meters. Finally California began to edge ahead until at the 1,500-meter mark the margin was almost a length. At that point the Huskies started their drive to the wire and forty strokes from the finish had cut it to two or three seats. The Bears turned it on and blew across the line by one-third length in course record time. Both crews knew they had rowed a memorable boat race.

The Stanford dual race at Redwood Shores proved to be just a tuneup for the Pac-10s a week later. Despite an unbelievable collision between the Bear's varsity and JV during warm-ups, which sunk the JV shell and damaged the varsity, both crews reboated and went on to sweep the regatta following a freshmen win.

This set them up for the Pac-10 Championships the following week. The freshmen started off by finishing the regular racing season undefeated. Again the Huskies were there to push them, but that was all the northern crew could do, so Cal won by a full length and set a new course record for the first-year men. The JV race was a classic 2,000 championship. Washington gained a half-length margin in the first 500 meters, then Cal cut that down to a boatdeck difference at 1,000 meters. The Bears in the second half of the race began to pour it on and at 1,500 meters had forged ahead by just about half a length. In the final 500 meters they pulled out to a hard-fought three-quarter length win. They also set a new course record, rowing no lower than thirty-eight strokes a minute the whole length of the course. When the Cal varsity hooked up with the stakeboats at the starting line, they could smell the first-ever California Pac-10 Championship sweep. Flying off the start, the

Bears were never headed. Although the Washington varsity went down to their third straight season defeat to Cal, they didn't give up easily. Despite the fact that Cal pulled away from them all the way down the course, they gave up every foot reluctantly and drove the Bears to another course record. The margin was only a length, and every seat of it was a tough battle.

By now the national rowing format had shifted, and there was a national championship for varsity crews held at Cincinnati, Ohio. Winners of the Pac-10, the IRA, the Eastern Sprints, the Harvard-Yale race, and several other top national crews were subsidized for their travel expenses, and the victor was sent to the Royal Henley Regatta in England. Because the decision had already been made to send both the varsity and JV to Henley, sending them to the IRA didn't make sense. On the other hand, the freshmen had certainly earned a shot at the National Freshmen Championship at the IRA. The Navy plebe crew had won the freshmen event at the Eastern Sprints and was the crew the Cubs were aiming for. Indeed, the Cal freshmen won the championship finals by one second over Navy, which was followed by Syracuse, one-and-one-half seconds back, Princeton, Wisconsin, and Cornell. This was only the second Cal freshmen win in the IRA. The first was back in 1938. Thus the frosh crew and their young coach, Tim Hodges, finished an undefeated season. Members of the 1982 freshmen championship crew were:

8–Eric Cohn	*4–Brian Cuneo*
7–Sean Seward	*3–Tony Matan*
6–Matt Pribyl	*2–Davis Bales*
5–Pat Graffis	*1–Matt Anacker*
Cox–Mike Shinn	

Although the season had been outstanding, marked by clean sweeps of two major regattas, the post season was less successful. In the words of varsity coach Mike Livingston: "The Cincinnati Regatta was a gamble from the onset . . . it turned out to be a disaster." This was likely due to two factors. One, the regatta conflicted with the crews' final examinations, so the oarsmen had to arrange with their professors to reschedule their finals, which at Berkeley isn't easy. Two, there was almost a month between the crews' last races at the Pac-10 and Cincinnati. After reaching such a peak at the Pac-10s, to have a long interval in racing worked against the Bears. In addition, nothing seemed to go right. Numerous minor inconveniences, ranging from food to equipment to housing and regatta administration, did little to help the Bears regain their competitive edge. Whatever the cause, the results were hardly what California had reason to expect. Yale, winners of both the Eastern Sprints and the Harvard-Yale race, was in full command all the way,

and the Bears were passed by both Cornell, the IRA champions, and Syracuse, an added entry. A most disappointing effort for Cal.

Despite the outcome at Cincinnati, the crews carried out their plan to race at Henley-on-Thames. A contingent of Cal supporters, including Ky's widow, Kathryn, and myself, were there to root the Bears home. I had just retired from the University and a group of friends and alumni had presented me and my wife, Jean, with our first trip to Henley. Unfortunately, our support was not enough to bring the Bears victory, but it was an unforgettable event nonetheless.

1982 IRA Regatta, Lake Onondaga, Syracuse, New York. *Left to right:* varsity coach Mike Livingston and freshmen coach Tim Hodges holding the Steward's Cup which the Cal freshmen won. (Courtesy of The Bancroft Library.)

The JV had preceded the varsity and were settled in at what would be their home for the next ten days at the Bellehatch Estate, located about three miles from the race course. Both crews trained hard, knowing they would be up against some top competition.

The varsity entered the Grand Challenge Cup race, the premier event at Henley. There was a limited field in this event, down to four rather than the usual nine, due to the speed the British National Team had been displaying of late. It was the Bears' luck to draw this crew as their opening opponent. The race was settled early as the powerful British gained open water by 1,000 meters. From there they maintained race control with an awesome display of power, and they drove across the finish line with a decisive one-and-one-half length margin. They went on to defeat another British crew, thus gaining the Challenge Cup. A mature crew, averaging twenty-seven years old, the British had more than eighteen world championship medals among them. The following week they won the Pre-World Championships at Amsterdam by over a length.

The JV entered the Ladies Plate event and won their first round race by three-and-one-half lengths against an obviously weaker Christ Church crew. The following day, they came home in front of Belmont and Hereford Catholic School by one-and-one-half lengths. In the semi-finals the Cal JV came up against their Yale counterparts. At first it appeared the Bears would be in the finals without too much trouble as they opened up almost a length lead by halfway; the Yale Blues, however, made up the length and one more. In the finals Yale rowed to a dead heat with the University of London, only to lose in a re-row forty-five minutes later. And so the Bears' 1982 season came to an end. Although the season ended on losses, both varsity crews proved they were competitive with world class crews, and the freshmen went all the way without a loss.

The 1983 season could best be described as peaks and valleys caused in part by foul weather and key injuries. The winter and spring were the wettest on record with frequent high winds. As Mike Livingston put it, with typical coach-like humor, "At times it seemed our most formidable opponent for 1983 would be mildew." This, together with several injuries, resulted in considerable delay in selecting the boatings for the San Diego Crew Classic. Unlike the optimistic outlook before the last year's regatta sweep, the picture did not look promising. In the freshmen final the Cubs were well back at 500 meters behind Orange Coast and a powerful UCLA crew. In the final half they drove by Orange Coast to gain open water, but they fell to the strong Bruin Yearlings by .5 seconds. Cal's JV was up against Orange Coast, Washington, and their nemesis of last year, Yale. In the finals they rowed the pattern set by the freshmen, down

open water at 500 meters to both Washington and Yale. After that poor start they did go to work blowing by Orange Coast and Washington, gaining open water on them, but they fell short of Yale by a quarter length. The varsity race was different, with Cal only two seats down to Washington at the 1,000-meter buoy. From there on it was a horror story, and Washington won by half a length over University of Victoria followed by Yale and UCLA, leaving the Bears in fifth. The regatta results were disappointing, to say the least, after the euphoria of the 1982 sweep and hard work and changes in the weeks ahead were in order.

The UCLA dual was next and the Bears knew they would have their hands full. The freshmen race proved that UCLA had a solid boat of first-year oarsmen, as they defeated an aggressive Cal frosh boat by just under a length. In the JV race a Cal crew which had lost of one of its veterans, won by over two lengths—considerably less than the thirty-second winning difference at San Diego. The varsity race had an unbelievable finish. The Bears led all the way down the estuary and, with about 600 meters to go, were ahead by a length. The Bruins started their move at this point and cut the margin to about two seats with thirty strokes to go. Cal responded by sprinting and flew under the Fruitvale Avenue Bridge, marking the finish with a boatdeck lead—a classic finish after a hard-fought 2,000 meters.

Not content with the crews' progress, both coaches shifted their boatings halfway through the season, with the Stanford dual races but a week away. The changes worked, and the races at Redwood Shores were all California. The frosh did have a tight one, winning by half a length, but the JV and varsity were blowouts of five-plus lengths and three-plus lengths respectively.

The Newport Regatta was next. Usually it was a low-pressure event except for strong competition from Orange Coast College. That year, in addition to Orange Coast, the UCLA Bruins had been flexing their muscles and their frosh, in particular, were tough. Too tough, it turned out, as the Baby Bruins defeated Cal, which was second by a length. In the JV event the Bears downed their Bruin rivals, but fell short of the Orange Coast crew by a boatlength. In the varsity race it was all Cal and UCLA among the six other weaker and inexperienced crews. The Bears took command at the 1,000-meter mark and drove on to a two-length win.

This set up the annual shootout with the Huskies on the Montlake Cut in Seattle. It was again scheduled for the yacht season opening day. To fully appreciate how water-oriented the Seattle area is, one must attend this event. The weather proved vile, which is not unknown there at that time of year. High winds and cold fine rain made things generally miserable. The Husky yearlings, touted by their press to be the best ever, were the usual big, strong, and hard-driving freshmen who seem to crop up year after year. No matter, the Bear freshmen made a real race of it, under the unfavorable conditions, before going across the line only a boatdeck down. An added entry, the Orange Coast College freshmen came in ten seconds behind the Cubs.

Cal's JV knew they were in for a real race, because Washington had beefed up its boating following its San Diego loss and the Orange Coast crew that had defeated the Bears was the third entry. Rowing in a new shell they had picked up on arrival at Seattle, the Cal JV worked hard all down the course. They were still in third place at halfway, a full length behind Washington. In the second 1,000 meters they drove by Orange Coast and pulled up on Washington. They ran out of room, flying across the finish line a quarter length ahead of Orange Coast but down half a length to the Huskies. By now the wind was rising and the rain was driving, but the varsity race went on anyway. It was not surprising that the Huskies seemed to relish the weather and the warmer-blooded Californians were wretched. The varsity race was no contest, with Washington taking an early lead and finishing with a two-length victory.

Better weather was assured at the Pac-10 Championships at Redwood Shores. The freshmen races illustrated what can happen in Henley-style head-to-head racing. Cal easily defeated Washington State in the opening heat while Washington beat the Stanford frosh and UCLA took a bye. The next day the Cal youngsters rowed a rather spiritless race, going down by a length to Washington. Then it happened. UCLA had refused, for unknown reasons, to race Stanford, and they were matched against what seemed to be a much less competitive opponent, Washington State. Fate reached out and bit the Bruins when, at about the 500-meter mark, one of their crewmen snapped his oar. This happened well past the breakage provision for starting over, so the crew had to struggle on with just seven oarsmen. Although not a really strong crew, Washington State, with a full complement of oarsmen, had no difficulty winning. Washington wound up in the finals against a badly overmatched Washington State crew, which had only recently been organized on a club basis. Needless to say, the Huskies won in what was almost a rowover. This left Cal, Stanford, and UCLA to race it out for third through fifth place. UCLA beat Stanford to face-off with Cal. The race for third between the Bear and Bruin freshmen was without question the best race of the day. They both roared down the course with never more than a second difference between them as the lead changed hands a number of times. The young Bears prevailed at the finish but only by .2 seconds.

The JV race also proved to be a good one. Washington took an initial lead, but the Bears caught them by the 1,000-meter mark and nosed ahead. In the next 200 meters they poured it on and built a full length over the fading Huskies. After losing to Washington at Seattle, the Cal JV had vowed to not let it happen twice. With that in mind they held a full boatlength advantage across the finish and won their fourth straight Pac-10 championship. The varsity race was close and hard-fought all the way down the course, but Washington gradually crept ahead. At 500 meters it was a seat in their favor, at 1,000 it was a quarter length, and at the finish it was three-quarter lengths. Cal had been in it all the way but couldn't quite stay with the Huskies. This ended the varsity racing season.

The IRA again conflicted with spring quarter finals, with several critical examinations for some of the varsity, and it was felt best to skip it. Both the JV and frosh were able to adjust their exam schedules and were charged up to go to Lake Onondaga, confident that they could do well there. Both crews had favorable draws in the initial heats, but the weather seemed to do the freshmen in. Rowing in whitecaps the first 1,000 meters, they couldn't get going and lost to Navy by three-quarter lengths. In the repechage it was even worse. They lost to Northeastern by one-and-one-half lengths and by one to Stanford, a crew they had beaten three times during the season. UCLA, which they had defeated in the Pac-10s, finished fourth in the finals. The JV did a little better by winning their heat despite poor conditions, finishing better than a length ahead of Cornell. In the finals, however, after a strong 1,000 meters, they faded badly to finish in fourth place. Brown, coached by former Cal coach Steve Gladstone, won the varsity race.

So the season ended. Although the Bears didn't win them all, they did quite well overall. The varsity lost by only three seconds to Washington at the Pac-10s, and the Huskies missed out on the nationals at Cincinnati by only .2 seconds. The JV was loser only to Yale at San Diego and won the Pac-10 event decisively. The frosh came on strong during the season, defeating an excellent UCLA crew at the Pac-10s and showing promise for future varsity years.

The crew was stunned, therefore, when Mike Livingston announced that he was going to retire from coaching for personal reasons and move to Hawaii. Mike had done much during his brief tenure to solidify the rowing program at Berkeley, which had been revitalized by his predecessor, Gladstone. His approach to the sport of crew is eloquently stated in his remarks to the 1983 Awards Banquet at the campus Faculty Club (see Appendix H). Mike is a very remarkable individual. He will long be remembered by Cal crewmen as standing for the very best in rowing.

THE CHRONOLOGY
THE HODGES PERIOD 1984–1987

WHEN IT CAME TO REPLACING THE Bears' head coach, there was no need to look further than Mike's freshmen coach, Tim Hodges. Tim had become the most successful frosh coach Cal has ever had. His crews beat Washington two out of three times, and two of those years, 1981 and 1982, were back-to-back. In addition, his 1982 freshmen were undefeated and wound up their season by winning the IRA. Tim had his start in rowing at Orange Coast College, and he stroked Cal's varsity in 1974 and 1975 under Steve Gladstone. His 1974 crew beat Washington's varsity for the first time in eleven years. He graduated from Berkeley in 1975 with a degree in English, coached at Orange Coast as an assistant for a year, and then spent three years in business. Clearly he was well qualified to continue the Gladstone-Livingston winning tradition.

The 1984 season opened at the San Diego Crew Clasic. Mission Bay was characteristically smooth in the morning and somewhat rough by afternoon—nothing like the estuary the previous week, when all five crews swamped in a line squall during the interclass race held for Alumni Day. The freshmen lost a squeaker in the opening heat to Orange Coast and in the finals ran out of gas to place third. Orange Coast won the race with Stanford in second. The JV races were disappointing, with a third place in the heat, and a fifth in the finals, which Washington won with ease. The varsity races were better. Qualifying easily in the morning, the Bears got into a really tough one in the finals. It was between Washington, Navy, and California right from the start, with the others falling open water to the rear. With 500 meters to go, Washington had a length, and Navy was even with California. The Bears took command over Navy as the crews drove for the finish and made up half a length on the Huskies, as Washington won by two seconds. A good race, but no cigar.

The Stanford dual was more to the Bears' liking. A well-rested frosh crew won their race by two full lengths, avenging their loss to Stanford at San Diego. Both the varsity and the JV had no contest, winning by at least three lengths. The UCLA races were closer, but still a sweep for California. This set the stage for the Washington dual on the estuary. It opened with a decisive freshmen victory, thus racking up an unprecedented three out of four frosh wins in the past four years. Unfortunately, the rest of the regatta went against the Bears. The JV lost by over ten seconds, still two lengths better than they had done at San Diego. The varsity race was not much better, with a fast Husky crew dominating a crippled Cal crew: the stroke suffered from a chronic shoulder injury.

In 1984 the Pac-10 Championships moved to Lake Natoma, near Sacramento, to join with those non-Pac-10 schools that were rowing on the Pacific Coast. The idea was to have the two divisions, Pac-10 and Western Intercollegiate Crew Coaches Association, determine their champions on Saturday, and then on Sunday race the top three finishers in each division for the respective Pacific Coast Championships. The Cal freshmen again defeated Washington and all the rest to win the Pac-10 Championship. Both the Bear JV and the varsity improved but still lost to Washington. The races Sunday were a rerun of the Cal-Washington rivalry in the varsity and JV events, but the freshmen race had the added spice of a strong Orange Coast College crew. Each had a win against the other, with the last one Cal's by one second. The race was a real barn-burner, as Cal, Washington, and Orange Coast broke out of the pack at the start. At 1,500 meters the three crews were bunched within four seats. The Huskies gave under the pressure, leaving Orange Coast and Cal to slug it out. Cal held a slight advantage going across the line and won by .5 seconds to become the freshmen Pacific Coast Champions. Unfortunately, the freshmen win was all Cal got. The JV cut one more second off of Washington's winning margin, and the varsity hung on for the first 1,000 meters but could not hold off the Huskies' strong finish. Both varsity crews did win second place in these championships with relative ease, but they had been aiming for more.

The varsity and freshmen crews went back to the IRA, leaving the JV home. A highlight of the trip was stopping off at Ithaca, New York as guests of the Cornell crew and coach Findley Meislahn to work out for four days on Lake Cayuga. Training there went well, with some good hard runs on the lake. The crews had seemed fit and ready during the last part of training, but upon arrival at Syracuse a serious, albeit temporary, illness had hit one of the freshmen. They were able to row in their initial heat but had to go easy there and then try to qualify for the final through the repechage the next day, when it was hoped they would be well. As fate would have it, they drew Princeton for their second race and lost by less than what the Tiger first-year crew had in winning the finals the next day. The Cubs were out of the championship, and although they won the petite finals with ease, it didn't seem to mean that much. It should be noted that the freshmen crew included the second woman, Amy DeFiebre, to be a Cal coxswain.

The varsity qualified for the finals easily, but their race was tough. Navy and Penn were the leaders, with an advantage of better water. Cal came in a respectable third, leading Syracuse, Cornell, and Brown across the line. The Bear varsity took some solace in their hard-fought battles with Washington when the Huskies won the National Championship at Cincinnati a week later.

The 1985 opener at the San Diego Crew Classic was not at all like past years in that the weather was miserable, with a strong cold wind. The races, therefore, were shortened. The freshmen handled the poor conditions and won going away, followed by Orange Coast, UCLA, Stanford, British Columbia, and UC San Diego. The JV race was a good one, as Washington beat out Cal at the wire. The varsity race was tight all the way. Washington went out fast and won by a length, but the Huskies were hotly pursued by Cal and Navy going at each other neck-and-neck all down the course. At the finish the Bears nipped the Middies by a seat for second, with the other crews spread out well behind.

The next regatta was a dual race first. Cal hosted UCLA on Briones Reservoir, a delightful site, nestled in a sylvan setting in the hills above San Pablo. As was true of the larger San Pablo Reservoir, the East Bay Municipal Water District had only recently allowed racing there. Several years earlier the crews, under Marty McNair, staged an Alumni Day and interclass race on Briones in a great experiment. Now several crews work out there, including the Cal women and nearby St. Mary's College men. Usually Briones is well sheltered from most winds, but at times it can get rough and 1985 was one of those

Tim Hodges, Freshmen Coach 1981–1983 and Varsity Coach 1984–1987.

times. Cal won the freshmen race, and the junior varsity won by a comfortable margin. The varsity race was a real brawl. UCLA broke into the lead off the start, but the Bears hung tight on its stern right down the course. Shortly before the finish Cal caught the Bruins and nosed in front by .4 seconds to win a tough one. No longer can the UCLA Bruins be considered an easy touch as might have been the case when they were just getting underway.

The Washington races were again at Seattle; the Montlake Cut has become the main race course for 2,000-meter events. It can be tricky to race in, but it offers the best vantage points for spectators. The Cal freshmen arrived with high hopes, but ended up half a length behind their rivals. The JV race was a heart-stopper, as Cal took an early lead only to lose it at the 1,200-meter mark because of a bad crab. Recovering fast, the Bears dug in and came back to win by a quarter length. The varsity race was Cal all the way, despite a Washington charge at the finish. Two varsity wins at Seattle isn't all that bad. The Stanford regatta was a warm-up for the Bears, and all three crews won handily.

The Pacific Coast Championships results at Lake Natoma were not what the Bears had hoped for after Seattle. The freshmen race came out exactly the same as before: Washington won by half a length. Stanford was third, five seconds behind Cal; Orange Coast was one-and-one-half lengths back, and UCLA and UC Irvine followed. The JV race did not go at all well, with Cal third behind the winning Husky crew and Orange Coast in second. In the varsity race Washington proved it had learned its lesson well and would not let the Bears blow by at the start. Both crews stayed right together until the last 500 meters, when Washington pulled out to a full-length win. UCLA was third, with Stanford, UC Irvine, and Long Beach State following.

It was decided to send only the varsity to the IRA and to regroup the Bears with the possibility of getting another crack at Washington in the nationals at Cincinnati. Although there had been good workouts prior to the races at Syracuse, Cal just didn't have it, placing sixth and last in the final. This loss was all the more frustrating after the way the crew had rowed at Seattle. A reprieve appeared when California was invited to fill in the six-boat field at Cincinnati. But the result was no different, with a sixth-place finish. Harvard won, defeating Princeton in second place and the defending champs, Washington, which took third. Both Cornell in fourth and Wisconsin in fifth were also in front of the Bears. What had seemed such a promising season, with two solid varsity wins over the Huskies on their home water, ended on a low note.

The very first day of the 1986 season started with the goal of building on strengths of the previous season and putting aside its frustrations. The San Diego Crew Classic showed there were brighter days ahead. The freshmen had a wild bout with Orange Coast College, and it finally had to be rerowed following a protest by Cal over the winning Orange Coast crew's lane violation. The Cubs won this one by a quarter length. The JV race was really between the winner, Washington, and Orange Coast in second, with Cal two lengths behind the leaders. The varsity race was the usual thriller one has come to expect on Mission Bay. Penn, the early favorite and later winner of the Eastern Sprint Championship, took charge and won from wire to wire. Cal, on the other hand, had a slow start, but then rowed right through the pack closing on Penn. They fell short by half a length but were six seconds in front of third-place Navy and eight seconds ahead of Washington—satisfying even though the gold was not theirs. After all, it was a really inexperienced crew with only three veterans, and Washington had returned 100 percent of its fine 1985 crew.

The UCLA regatta was next on the Ballona Creek course. The Oxford crew came over from England for the first time to make it a triangular event, which generated considerably more press hype than the annual dual races. The freshmen race went to Cal without too much trouble. The JV race was much closer. The junior Bear boat

had suffered some injuries but still managed to win by a quarter length. In the varsity event, Cal went out to a quick lead and won by a length of open water. The really interesting portion of the race was the hot contest UCLA and Oxford waged all the way to the finish line. At the end UCLA just managed to nose its English rivals for second place.

The Redwood Shores Crew Classic was a new regatta, which started in 1986. Although not as all-encompassing as San Diego, several top crews are invited from the East to meet their counterparts on the West Coast. The difference is that all racing is Henley-style, head-to-head or two crews per race, with East Coast versus West Coast races scheduled as often as possible. In 1986 Wisconsin and Brown were invited to race UCLA, Stanford, Washington, and California. The frosh entrants were all from within the state, and the Cubs won their event by better than a length over Orange Coast. The Cal JV had won their heat and in the finals ran up against a fast Brown JV. It was a good race at first, but a loose outrigger foiled the Bears' hopes, and they lost by open water. The final heat for the varsity promised to be fascinating as pupil, Tim Hodges, faced teacher, Steve Gladstone, Brown's coach. Brown had beaten Stanford and Washington with real speed, especially against the latter. Cal had defeated both UCLA and Wisconsin without too much trouble. The final faceoff was a real scorcher. The Cal boat inched ahead of its rival starting at the 1,000-meter mark and flew across the finish line with a length lead, setting a new course record.

The Washington regatta was rowed on Cal's home waters on the estuary. Conditions were poor, especially in the first 1,000 meters. In the frosh race Washington won by a comfortable margin. In the JV race Cal made up four seconds of the eight it had been behind at San Diego, but it still meant the Bears were a length behind the Huskies. The varsity race started out as if Washington would have little trouble gaining a clean sweep. Cal started poorly in the rough water and caught a crab, ending up six to seven seats behind. By 1,000 meters the Huskies had a full boatlength lead. The second 1,000 meters was a different story. Cal started moving and proceeded to overtake a faltering Washington boat. In the last 200 meters the Bears rowed right through the Huskies and by the last forty strokes had a full length lead. All three of the Cal crews had easy wins in the following regatta with Stanford and seemed ready for the Pacific Coast Championships.

The races at Lake Natoma were a mixed bag. The freshmen rowed a disappointing race, coming in a distant fourth. Washington won, with Stanford a surprising second, and Orange Coast was third. UCLA and UC Irvine came in behind Cal. California's fortunes began to improve in the JV race. Cal came in second to Washington by .5 seconds after a tight race the whole way. Orange Coast was six seconds back with UCLA, Stanford, and UC San Diego trailing. The varsity race was Berkeley all the way. Blasting off the start, the Bears wasted litle time pulling out in front of the pack. They continued to add to their lead all down the course and stormed across the finish with open water over Washington and the rest of the crews. Stanford was third, with UCLA, Long Beach State, and UC Santa Barbara following in that order.

Tim Hodges decided to forgo the IRA and to point for the nationals at Cincinnati. A delightful change of pace in training occurred when Gus Schilling '64 offered use of his family's spectacular home at Lake Tahoe. It is doubtful whether the crew ever had such a magnificent setting for training following final exams. The fact that the conditioning would be at high altitude was an added advantage. Certainly it was a far cry from the estuary.

Arriving at Cincinnati with high hopes after such a successful season, Cal was unprepared for what happened. Conditions were excellent, the crew seemed ready, and the borrowed equipment was fine. The race, however, was a nightmare. The Bears came in fifth behind the winner, Wisconsin, and Brown in second. Both of these crews had fallen to the Bears earlier in the season. The crew and coaches were at a loss to explain the Bears' downfall. More than likely, it was hard to achieve another peak after the long five-week interval between the Pacific Coast and National championships. What a way to end such a fine overall season!

As training began, the 1987 season appeared as promising as any in recent times for Berkeley. Only the bowman had graduated from the varsity, and there were a number of eager candidates waiting to fill that slot. An added incentive was the opportunity to make up for the loss at Cincinnati the previous year. But during preseason training sessions, Coach Hodges had to put *five* port oarsmen, all top crew members, on the injured list—surely unprecedented in Cal's rowing history. At first it did not seem he had enough men to man a JV for the San Diego Crew Classic. Finally, after picking up some candidates who had dropped out earlier, Cal was able to enter a full complement at San Diego, but it was a makeshift, patched-together squad. The freshmen rowed a good race but still lost by half a length to Orange Coast College. UC Irvine, Stanford, UC Santa Barbara, and University of San Diego followed in that order. A truly substitute JV qualified for the finals but that was about all, as they came in sixth and last. Harvard beat out Washington to win this race, with Penn, UCLA, and Orange Coast leading Cal. The varsity also took last in the finals, only this time it was seventh. The Harvard Crimson won, adding to their earlier JV victory. Washington was second, followed by Navy, Wisconsin, UCLA, and Stanford. This was the worst that Cal had rowed since the San Diego Crew Classic had begun twelve years before.

The next races were with UCLA in a dual regatta on the estuary. By this time some of the wounded were recovering, and the crews were obviously stronger. The frosh won their race by a bit more than a length. The JV, still undermanned but better, rowed a vastly improved race but lost by open water. The varsity perked up a bit and won their race by a good boatlength. The Redwood Shores Crew Classic was the next event on the race calendar, with Brown, Wisconsin, and Dartmouth providing the Eastern opposition. The freshmen lost to Stanford's yearlings by three-quarter lengths, after beating them at San Diego. The JV was still outclassed, losing first to Brown and then to Wisconsin. In the opening heat, the varsity lost to a very fast Brown crew by a length of open water, but in the next heat they beat Wisconsin, the defending national champions. In a somewhat anticlimatic final heat, the Bears easily defeated an outmanned Dartmouth crew to take second in the overall standings. Washington had lost to both Brown, the overall winner, and to Wisconsin.

The next opponent was Stanford. The Stanford freshmen again proved they were tough by downing the Cubs by a length and a half. The junior varsity was finally getting some reinforcements and were able to down the Cardinal second boat by a good two lengths. The varsity race was close all the way, but the Bears prevailed by two lengths. The next regatta normally would have been the Washington races, but the Huskies had scheduled the Russian eight for a first-time appearance in Seattle. Washington may have had second thoughts afterward, for the Russians proved to be much too strong and won handily.

The Pacific Coast Championships at Lake Natoma had by now become a fixture in view of its excellent facilities. The freshmen did not row at all well for some reason and came in sixth and last in their finals. This hotly contested race was won by Orange Coast by .7 seconds over Stanford. UC Irvine nosed out Washington for third, followed by UC Santa Barbara with Cal trailing. The Cal JV rowed its best of the season, losing a good tough race to Orange Coast. The Husky JV faded badly in this contest. By the time the varsity race rolled around the Bears seemed ready. For about the first time that season all of the men were healthy. Cal started strong from the start. By 1,500 meters the crew had open water. At this point UCLA made up some ground on the Bears, while Stanford took over third ahead of Washington. It still seemed a Cal victory from wire to wire when disaster

Bruce Beall was appointed Varsity Coach in Fall 1987.

struck, fifteen or twenty strokes from the finish line. The Cal stroke caught a full crab over his head and before he could recover, UCLA slipped by for the win. Even though Cal was second, the Bears were bitterly disappointed.

Some consolation was gained at the Washington regatta the following weekend with two varsity wins and a close frosh loss. The freshmen rowed what was probably their best race of the season despite losing their regular coxswain who severely injured his neck in a freak accident right before leaving for Seattle. The race was tight, and Cal's yearlings led twice, but at the end they were unable to hold off Washington, which won by a bit of open water. The JV really put it all together and won the race right off the start, finishing open water over their rivals. The varsity race went about the same, as the Bears stormed off the start and crossed the finish a good length and a half ahead.

Despite the good showing of the frosh and JV in their final races, only the varsity was sent to the IRA. If they did a good job at Syracuse, then they would make another try at the National Championships. The crew, dogged by injury most of the season, seemed fit and ready to go. In their opening heat the Bears made a strong showing, beating Princeton and Northeastern with ease. The finals were another matter. The Cal boat

could not seem to get untracked and was sluggish. The Brown shell clearly dominated the entire race, and the Bears, after hanging on in the initial stages, faded badly to sixth and last. So the season that had been anticipated as one of the more promising in recent years ended.

Before the season had come to an end, word was out that surprised the alumni and undergraduates alike. Varsity coach Tim Hodges, one of the most successful Cal coaches in history, announced he was stepping down. Tim felt that he had done what he could and did not look forward to a lifetime career in the coaching ranks. His early business experience had challenged him, and he wished to return to it.

Cal's athletic director Dave Maggard searched long and hard for Tim's replacement. He discussed possible prospects with several of the leading coaches in the country, drawing on their knowledge of current possibilities. It wasn't until the end of the summer of 1987 that his selection was announced: Bruce Beall (pronounced "bell"), Washington '73, was Maggard's choice. Bruce came with excellent credentials, having been an assistant freshmen coach at Washington after his own rowing career there. He then was appointed freshmen coach at Boston University, and from there put in a five-year hitch as the lightweight coach at Harvard. He was at MIT as the varsity coach for two years prior to coming to Berkeley.

In addition to his years of coaching, Bruce has had extensive experience on U.S. national crews competing here and overseas. In 1971 he was #5 in our eight in the Pan-American Games and won a silver medal. In 1973 he was in the pair with cox in the European Championships at Moscow. At the 1974 World Championships he was in the pair-without. In the Pan-Am Games of 1979 he was a member of the quadruple scull that won a bronze medal. In 1983 he was an alternate for the World Championships, and in the 1984 Olympics he again was a member of the quadruple scull. It is obvious that Bruce not only has a solid coaching background and strong undergraduate oarsman experience, he has had considerable international competition. The Cal rowing program cannot but benefit from his expertise.

The results of Bruce's tenure will have to wait for another to record. It does seem clear that the program at Berkeley is in good hands, and it seems certain that the Bears will continue to be a force in rowing. In view of the heavy graduation losses of 1987, Bruce's start as coach will entail at least one rebuilding year. But he is not the first man to come here from Washington, and his predecessor from the north started a career in 1924 that was unparalleled. May Bruce be so lucky.

THE CHRONOLOGY
EPILOGUE

///

So this chronology ends with the 1987 season after a shadowy start in the late 1800s. It has been most enjoyable compiling this history of rowing at Berkeley. Soon it will be for another to update it as the crews continue to make their mark through the years to come—which they surely will, for our friends and alumni have made this a certainty. There have been some long hard struggles, especially in those early years. There have been some glorious victories, including the first three in 1899, 1904, and 1905, along with the remarkable three Olympic championships and the ten national IRA championships. There have been some bad times, such as the burning of the boathouse and all equipment in 1895 and the sinking of the old *Amador* in 1913. Even Ky saw some seasons when nothing went right.

At first the crewmen numbered in tens, and then it was hundreds who had labored endless miles up and down the estuary. By now several thousand have shared this singular experience. Through it all, this remarkable sport has been the means of teaching young men their true measure. Mike Livingston phrased it eloquently in his final statement to the crew in 1983 when he referred to "the discipline of the body . . . the discipline of the mind . . . and the discipline of fellowship."

California's proud record has not been written by one crew or by one coach. It has been the history of all who have been so fortunate as to be involved: lettermen and non-lettermen, champion and also-ran, coxswain and manager, coach and trainer. That is what this history of rowing at California has been all about. Long may it continue.

EQUIPMENT CHANGES: THE HIGH-TECH REVOLUTION

///

ALTHOUGH THERE WERE A NUMBER of men who designed and built racing shells and work boats for the various clubs and schools that were rowing in the early 1900s, by the 1920s in the U.S. one man began to dominate: George Pocock, who had learned his craft from his father in England. Pocock, with the encouragement of Hiram Conibear, the University of Washington coach, set up his shop at the Husky boathouse before World War I and began turning out racing shells. (His brother started doing the same at Yale a few years later.) Before long a George Pocock shell was a must for a school to enter topflight competition. His work force soon became a close-knit group, almost a family of craftsmen proud of its product. Aware that money was a problem in rowing programs, Pocock did his best to keep costs down, particularly during the Depression. Pocock oars and racing shells were used from the thirties through the sixties by virtually every school that rowed. The U.S. Olympic rowing teams of that period also used Pocock equipment.

A Pocock eight-oared racing shell was sixty feet long and twenty-five to twenty-six inches wide at its widest point. It had spruce frames and ash shoulders. A three-sixteenth-inch close-grained cedar skin was applied, and the bow and stern sections had a varnished silk deck. (Canvas was used in some of the later shells.) Clog-type footboards were used with copper heelcups and a broad laced leather band to hold the feet down. The shell weighed from 300 to 320 pounds. The outriggers holding the oarlocks out and away from the side of the shell have not changed much since 1911, except in the early thirties Ky introduced the single-bar outrigger (as oppposed to the double-bar outrigger that caused trouble in rough water), and stainless steel, when available, replaced the galvanized iron previously used.

A Pocock oar was spruce with an iron bark backing and had poplar wood blades with copper tips. The blades were seven inches wide and thirty-three inches long. The oars were between twelve-feet-one-inch and twelve-feet-three-inches and weighed nine-and-one-half to ten pounds. For many years the rudder was attached to the sternpost and was about seven to eight inches long and about six inches deep. A metal fin was attached to the keel of the shell behind the coxswain to provide a pivot for steering and was about six inches long and four inches deep—a rather small but vital item as any coxswain who has lost one while his shell was underway will tell you.

By the 1960s equipment and oar design and material changes began to appear, originating in Europe. The first innovation was the shovel oar used by the East Germans, with wider and shorter blades than the conventional Pocock. Some said they were not new at all and had been used by several crews at Henley in the early-1900s. Both Harvard and California, among others, used them starting in 1964.

Currently there are four shell manufacturers competing quite successfully with Pocock. They include Empacher in Germany; Vespoli in Connecticut; Schoenbrod in Maine; and Kaschper in Ontario, Canada. Of the five types of shells, Vespoli is probably gaining the most favor and Pocock the least. Pocock, however, is coming out with a new shell, which should be competitive. George Pocock died several years ago, and his son, Stan, took over for him until going into semi-retirement recently. Bill Titus now runs the Pocock shop and is pushing its new trend in design and materials.

The new shells are pretty much the same overall, but with significant modifications. They are fifty-seven feet long as opposed to the old Pococks' sixty feet. Their weight varies from 215 to 270 pounds versus the old Pococks' 320 pounds. The main difference is in the construction material. The skin is a fiberglass-like Kevlar impregnated by an epoxy, a polymerized resin. Both Schoenbrod and Kaschper use a one-eighth-inch skin with spruce frames and ash shoulders. Empacher, Vespoli, and the new Pocock use a thicker one-quarter-inch skin with a honeycomb core which eliminates a lot of the framework. Nylon, rather than brass, wheels are now used for the sliding seats, and the tracks they run on are adjustable fore and aft. The tracks also are much longer than the old Pococks, thirty-one or thirty-two inches as opposed to twenty-seven inches. Shoes are used in place of the old clogs for footboards. Some boats have footboards with adjustable height and angle.

Fabric boatdecks are no longer used; instead a honeycomb or foam with a deck of Kevlar is applied. This eliminates all framing at both bow and stern. The rudder is much smaller—and also less efficient—and usually located right behind the fin or skeg. In many of the four-oared shells and some of the eights the coxswain has been relocated and now is in a prone position in front of the bow man with only his head showing—a strange sight indeed for the traditional crew fan.

Another high-tech addition is the cox box, which is located in front of the coxswain between his legs. It consists of an amplifier system so every man in the boat can hear via several small speakers, a stroke-rate meter with constant readout that has a sensor on the stroke's seat, and a digital stopwatch for elapsed time. The outriggers are much more complicated. The oarlock pin is adjustable fore and aft and also adjusts in or out (shims are no longer needed). The Schoebrod has an outrigger that is adjustable to fit any position in the boat, whereas the others only fit a particular position.

The oars have undergone much the same change as the shells. Now the only wood in the commonly used oar is the handle. The loom, or shaft, is now carbon fiber, and the blade is carbon fiber on a foam core. The oar is five

inches longer at twelve-feet-six-inches to twelve-feet-eight-inches. The blade is shorter and wider at eight-and-one-quarter inches wide and twenty-three inches long. Although longer the new oars are lighter at seven pounds as opposed to nine-and-one-half to ten pounds. (Equipment specifications were furnished by Mike Fennelly, UC Berkeley boatman/rigger.)

These changes are quite radical when one considers that the basic design of racing shells and the material used (wood) did not change very much in 100 years. Suddenly, within the last twenty years, completely new materials and drastically modified design have swept through rowing worldwide. The result is lighter and much more durable equipment, needing much less maintenance, leading to faster times, particularly when improvement in equipment is coupled with the more intensive training techniques currently employed by coaches. It is a fact that top crews are posting times under no-wind, no-current conditions that were unheard of not too long ago.

Oar blades. *Left:* currently used style. *Right:* Pocock blade.

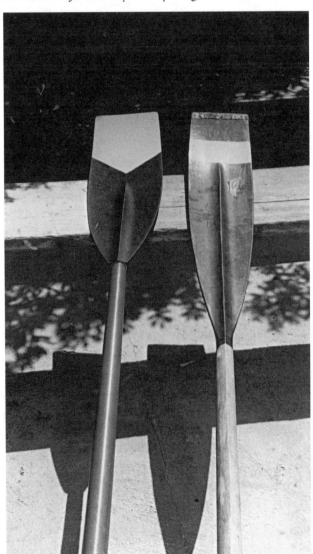

TRANSPORTATION OF EQUIPMENT

///

ONE OF THE THORNIEST LOGISTICAL PROBLEMS in the sport of rowing is the transportation of the necessary equipment from the home boathouse to another race site, most especially when moving eight-oared shells which are sixty feet long and exceedingly delicate. In the very early days, the teams and their shells traveled via ship between the Bay Area and Seattle. Soon the mode changed to trains with a baggage car for the shells and oars, and also was the way the crew traveled East for the IRA.

An arrangement was usually made with the railroad to purchase sufficient tickets to take up an entire passenger car, which would cover the cost of a baggage car. Two or three shells would be carefully loaded into the car on specially built racks and then secured to withstand the severe jostling inherent in a long rail trip. The oars, including spares, would be boxed and loaded. Then the varsity coaching launch would be put in on blocks to complete the shipment. Unbeknownst to the rail authorities, more often than not additional baggage was included: several junior managers or reserve oarsmen taking a free ride to the regatta in somewhat rough and often soot-and-smoke-filled quarters. They would provide extra hands to help the boatman/rigger and the senior manager, so the coaching staff conveniently overlooked their presence.

With train travel, there was always the possibility of leaving a squad member at one of the way stations following a brief stop. In fact this happened several times. However, most crewmen have never heard of one case which happened late one night when Ky Ebright stepped off the train at a stop to get some toothpaste. As he came out of the nearby all-night drugstore, Ky watched the train pull out of the station. After a moment of panic, he found a taxi stand and caught a cab, offering a handsome reward if the driver could beat the train to the

Loading shells on top of old Crew Bus at Lake Merritt, Oakland. (Courtesy of Albert Kayo Harris.)

Early shell transportation. "You turn to starboard, and I'll turn to port." (Courtesy of The Bancroft Library.)

View of inside of baggage car as shells are being loaded.

next station. Ky was able to swing back on board as the train paused there briefly. Only after the train started up again did Ky remember that this was the last stop before it crossed the desert. It is doubtful he could have ever caught up later on. The senior manager was beside himself until he saw Ky back on board. Needless to say, Ky swore him to secrecy. Only years later did Ky tell this story and explain how hard it would have been to face the squad if he had missed that last stop.

Another time one of the oarsmen discovered he had accidentally kept the keys to his girlfriend's car after driving with her to the station. As the train pulled out of Berkeley, the oarsman asked me what he could do. I arranged for a train representative to pick up and return the keys when the train stopped in Sacramento, but I also gave the forgetful oarsman a bad time about the keys. Then the squad checked into the hotel in Madison, Wisconsin for their race with the Badgers. As I reached into my coat pocket I froze—inside were my wife's car and house keys. My wife and two young daughters had seen me off in Berkeley, and I had left them a carefully locked car. Fortunately, Kathryn Ebright had also seen Ky off and was able to drive my family back to our house to get a spare set of keys. I had to pay for the kitchen window they broke getting into the house.

Train travel was at times monotonous but could be educational. In those days few of the squad had even been out of the state, let alone back East, so Ky developed a system of using different routes for their return trip from New York. They would go back East as directly as possible, taking five days and four nights to Chicago, where there was always a four-hour layover, and another day and night to Poughkeepsie or Syracuse. On the return, Ky would route them home one year by way of New Orleans, another by way of Canada. The tickets home were good for sixty days, so there was ample opportunity for stops along the way.

In the post-World War II period the train trips back East were rather singular, due to the semester system inherited from the wartime trimester plan. It meant the crews left before final examinations. A proctor accompanied the squad to administer the finals as close as possible to the time they were being given back in Berkeley. Professor Jerry Marsh of the speech department invariably chose this honor. When he was not busy overseeing the exams, Professor Marsh was an excellent instructor in the card games of hearts and bridge, which helped while away the long hours on the train. It was not uncommon to see a crewman sitting in a train station, or in the passenger car, or even under a tree beside Lake Onondaga, taking a final exam. When the crews started flying, this was thankfully no longer necessary.

The use of trains with baggage cars continued up to the 1960s, but after that the crew started flying to the regattas, taking only their oars and personal luggage. This was much more convenient and much less time-consuming, and made possible in the dual races because almost every eight-oared racing shell used in the country was a Pocock. Most crews kept two sets of racing boats, one for their own team, and the other set for the

Loading shells in baggage car in front of Ebright Boathouse.

Coach Ben Wallis (with hand on megaphone) and friends in launch *Oski I*. (Courtesy of The Bancroft Library.)

opposing crews. There were some problems in the Pacific Coast Sprint races because the local schools were not able to furnish a large enough pool of comparable boats, but compromises were worked out.

For awhile it worked to everyone's advantage to fly and use the host crew's shells, which assured that the rival boat was the same age and shape as the host's. Such an easy solution did not last, however, because of the advanced technology of imported European-designed boats. East and West Germany in particular had made a number of changes in design and materials, an advantage that could not be overlooked. Quickly there were a number of different designs available, and different teams were using different boats. The unfortunate result is that each school now must depend upon using its own boat to remain competitive. Every shell requires time to get used to and often a change in technique is required, so borrowing is usually not a good idea. Today almost every school has its own specially built trailer and hauls its shells and equipment to the various race sites, even back to the IRA at Syracuse. (With the savings gained through flying to the IRA, Cal purchased two shells to store permanently at Syracuse.) It does make one wonder at the idea of "progress." When Ky Ebright saw this problem looming on the horizon, he would say, "Best that you are racing men against men, not competing to see who has the best equipment." At times one feels the latter is more the case.

Transportation of Coaches

Coaches, in order to properly coach, must be able to keep up with the boats as they progress down the work course. They cannot follow during a race and certainly cannot coach then. Cal coaches over the years have used a variety of craft ranging from single sculls or pair-oars to tired old outboard motorboats to specially designed inboard-craft. Ky even used a bicycle at the 1948 Olympics, when the crew worked out the last few days on the Olympic course at Henley. They had been staying at Marlow, down river, where Ky could use a coaching launch; however, at Henley coaching launches were not allowed. Ky's solution was to obtain a tandem bicycle and use Jim Yost, the senior manager, as its primary manpower. There is no record as to what shape Yost was in when this began, but it is certain he was much fitter by the time Olympic racing got underway.

The best-known launches at Berkeley were the Oski series. There was an *Oski I*, but little is know about it. Apparently it was an inadequate inboard of dubious lineage, which Ky inherited from Ben Wallis and used only until *Oski II* was available. There were times that Ben Wallis used a pair-oared shell as a coaching boat, drafting an extra oarsman to row the opposite side. This was not eagerly sought duty; Ben, an accomplished oarsman, expected his partner to keep the shell on course so he could coach properly.

Coach Ky Ebright in bow of *Oski III*. (Courtesy of The Bancroft Library.)

One of Ky's stipulations when he accepted the post of coach at Berkeley was that proper equipment be provided, including a new boathouse, new shells, and new coaching launches. Ky wanted launches that would provide a certain amount of protection for the coach in bad weather; privacy, via a front cockpit, from others in the launch; and enough room in the back to carry a few spectators or a swamped crew. Hull design was also important in order to keep the following wake of the boat as small as possible so it would not interfere with other boats on the estuary. *Oski II* was the first attempt, commissioned shortly after Ky started, and built by the Stephens Shipyard in Stockton. *Oski III* followed and was a bit larger with an improved design. A well-traveled launch before its demise in the late sixties, *Oski III* made innumerable trips to Seattle, Poughkeepsie, and Syracuse via baggage car. It went by ship to the Sloten Canal for the 1928 Olympics, and it was at Long Beach for the 1932 Olympics. In addition it went hundreds of miles up and down the Oakland Estuary, as did *Oski II*.

After having its ribs and planks replaced as many times as possible, and an unknown number of engine replacements, and all but sinking after an encounter with an oil barge, *Oski III* was sold for junk, as was *Oski II* (which was in even worse shape), in 1969. What was left of the hull of *Oski III* lay weathered and bleached, rotting in a vacant lot until a few years ago. Alan Furth '43, who collects and rebuilds old wooden boats, obtained blueprints from the shipyard that built the boat and reincarnated the old launch. Today *Oski III* glides across Lake Tahoe, sparkling in its fresh coat of blue and gold paint and its new brass fittings, looking every bit as fit as when Ky first launched her on the estuary. The two outboard runabouts that replaced the Oskis do their job but lack the class of the older, more dignified launches.

Transportation of Men

The most vexing problem of rowing at California is getting from the Berkeley campus to the boathouse on the Oakland Estuary and back again after a workout. In the early days it was the crewmen's responsibility to make it down and back. This meant a ride in the horse-drawn trolley down Telegraph Avenue to the estuary, and then a walk of some blocks, usually through mud and debris, to the bleak boathouse.

When Ky had the boathouse relocated, it was even more difficult to get there on one's own, so Ky obtained a bus to transport the crewmen between the boathouse and campus. The old "Blue Goose" was already of doubtful vintage, with benches running down each side of its

Above: Crewmen depart from Sather Gate enroute to Boathouse in 1920s. (Courtesy of John C. Rogers.) *Left:* The Telegraph Avenue Trolley. The trolley was an alternative form of transportation to the boathouse in the 1920s. (Courtesy of John C. Rogers.)

interior rather than conventional seats across. Most remember it as a faded blue-grey vehicle that was tired before its time, but at least it was transportation. The "Blue Goose" lasted into the late thirties, and then was retired to the junkyard. Its replacement was a new blue and gold bus with a suggested capacity of around forty. Seldom were there that few. Once normal capacity was reached using the jumpseats in the aisle, the gap between the jumpseat and the adjoining seat would be used. When the gaps were all used, passengers would be handed back hand over hand and stretched across the laps of those already seated. It made quite a load.

A tradition which started on the "Blue Goose" and continued with its replacement was singing to while away the time. The crewmen may not have been the University Glee Club, but the freshmen quickly learned their Cal songs. In fact they learned a lot more than the traditional fight songs and University hymns. Some were traditional all right, but you wouldn't include them, say,

in letters home. There were times when Ernie Madson, the longtime bus driver, and Matt Franich, his successor, would pull the bus over and refuse to continue until things quieted down.

Following Ky's retirement the replacement bus finally wore out and had to be junked. It was impractical to buy another bus at then-inflated prices, so the crew entered into a charter arrangement with Oakland's AC Transit Company. This deal was not too satisfactory, and for awhile various of the crew were subsidized to drive their own cars carrying passengers. At one time a refurbished Checkers taxi limousine was pressed into service.

The current system, three large vans, seems a far cry from the days of raucous singing coming from a tired old blue and gold bus as it made its way up Telegraph Avenue. Be that as it may, although transportation to and from the boathouse has always been a problem, it has never prevented the crews from getting their job done, even if it did mean a late dinner back on campus.

RECRUITMENT OF CREWMEN

THERE ARE NO ATHLETIC SCHOLARSHIPS or grants-in-aid in crew to attract prospects, and most of the prospects know little about the sport, so recruitment of men for rowing is entirely different than for other sports. Until the mid-thirties there were no high school or prep school programs in the West to furnish experienced recruits. This was also true in the East to a certain extent; however, there were a number of prep schools in that area which did row. For most of Cal's history, rowing has been the one varsity sport composed of athletes who had no previous experience in the sport before coming to college. There may have been an occasional isolated case of someone having rowed with a club, but this was so rare it didnt' have much effect.

Lack of previous experience might seem a disadvantage. Actually it can be an advantage when almost all of the freshmen squad are inexperienced. First, it provides an opportunity for an athletically inclined youngster to start a major competitive sport on an equal footing with just about everyone else on the squad. His status does not depend on what he did in high school and the number of awards he's received. Second, rowing is a repetitive sport insofar as stroking an oar is concerned. Just as with a golf swing, bad habits become quickly ingrained and are difficult to change. If a prospect from a prep school, for instance, was taught a different style or had picked up bad habits because of an inattentive coach, he would soon find himself at a disadvantage. In working with a prospect who had no previous experience the coach at the college level can shape his stroke in the desired style and keep a watchful eye on him as he establishes his basic habits. Today, even though there are more experienced freshmen prospects due to real growth at the high school level, a check of the top varsity crews across the nation will disclose that most, and often all, of them have no previous rowing experience.

On the other hand, most crewmen have previous athletic experience in high school and competitive interest is at a high level. Swimming, cross country track, and basketball are always well represented. Football players who may not be quite big or heavy enough or are one step too slow, are often eager to continue in a competitive sport. Those with knee injuries are other likely candidates. Then, too, a number of our top crewmen were bluechip prospects in a sport that was more individually oriented, and they are attracted by the intense teamwork aspect of rowing. An additional attraction stressed by the coaches in their recruiting is the now almost yearly opportunity for good crewmen to qualify for international competition with trips to Europe, South America, etc. Since the mid-seventies a number of Cal crewmen have taken advantage of this. (See section on national crew.)

Rowing also provides an opportunity, which is limited at the college level, for the really small youngster to qualify for a major competitive sport. Coaches are always on the lookout for small men, average five-feet-six-inches and 125 pounds, who seem quite confident and extroverted. Such a small individual makes an excellent coxswain, steering the shell and giving the orders. The available positions are admittedly limited in that there is just one per crew. It is an exceptional learning experience as the coxswain must take charge of a situation, give orders and have them followed, and make quick decisions under considerable pressure. It is something to see when one of the little guys is in complete charge of eight large, strong men—and makes them like it. It is a longtime tradition that the only recourse an oarsman has to get back at the coxswain, who often resorts to verbal abuse under trying conditions, is to throw him in the drink, and that is allowed only when the crew wins their race. (The coach can suffer a similar fate following a championship race, possibly for the same reasons.)

From the early twenties through the early sixties all

underclassmen were subject to compulsory ROTC and as a group were the main source of candidates for the crew. One of the coaches and several of the varsity oarsmen would stand by the string-draped poles or the tape on the wall just beyond the ROTC area, watching for anyone who had to duck under the string set at six feet or who would top the tape set six feet off the floor. Any man who seemed to qualify was stopped and told about the rowing program. If he had committed to another sport he was passed on. If not, he was given the hard sell about rowing for Berkeley. His name, address, and phone number were recorded, and he was advised of the day and time of the crew orientation and sign-up meeting.

Shortly after I took over from Ky the registration line was eliminated due to registration by mail. Fortunately at this time an even better method of screening prospects was developed. All new students still had to take a full physical exam at Cowell Hospital on campus at the start of the semester. Arrangements were made with the director of Cowell to have two volunteers to work at the mens' height-weight station during the examinations. The fact that they happened to be varsity crewmen allowed them to screen every freshman and sophomore man for the crew: six feet or more and 170 pounds or more. If they met the standards, their exam forms were marked so they could not leave Cowell without talking with the freshmen crew coach stationed near the exit. During this period a number of fine prospects were directed to the boathouse. It had been determined years ago that if you could just get a candidate to the boathouse to see the slick shells and the pictures and records on the clubroom walls, he usually would give the sport a try.

Finally, in the late sixties, the compulsory physical was discontinued, and this made finding crew prospects much more difficult. Tables with crew information and sports interest cards now are set up and manned by one of the coaches during each of the summer orientation programs for new students (CALSO). Various forms of advertising the sport, such as posters, throwaways, and ads in the *Daily Cal* were and still are used. In addition, all the coaches starting with Ky have had various systems of writing to high schools throughout California, pushing rowing as the sport to start in college. Word of mouth utilizing the current crewmen, both in their living groups and their home communities, has also been employed, often with considerable success. Several of the coaches, starting with Ky, developed training films, including actual races, to show to high schools, alumni groups, and at the crew orientation meeting at the start of the semester. These have been well received.

Today the program is many-faceted. For the experienced oarsman or coxswain, who now make up twenty to twenty-five percent of a first-year squad, contacts and inquiries are continually made to various preparatory schools on a local, national, and even international basis. These range from letters to personal visits when appropriate, and will intensify in the future according to the current coaches. For the inexperienced and uninformed prospects, there are a number of ongoing approaches. A crew brochure is sent yearly to every high school in California. The work in the summer orientation program for new students has continued as in the past, and every student participant receives an athletic interest card. A crew brochure with orientation meeting time and place is furnished each entering male student. Ads are placed in the campus newspaper. Coaches and varsity volunteers make a point of roaming the campus during pre-registration and the early days of the semester looking for likely prospects. In short, everything possible has and is being done to get the word out to young men who might be interested in becoming a part of that tradition known as California crew.

CONDITIONING: ON AND OFF THE WATER

ALONG WITH THE CHANGES IN ROWING equipment, there have been revolutionary changes in conditioning of oarsmen. Until well into the sixties, most, if not all, of the crewman's conditioning was done on the water during squad workouts. Occasionally some running was prescribed, and there were some who pumped iron when weight-lifting became popular. Most coaches, however, felt that miles under the keel made for fast crews. When the races were over longer distances of three and four miles, this was true. Today's emphasis on year-round training didn't exist. Very few of the oarsmen rowed in the summer with the clubs, and fall training was limited to about eight weeks. In fact at Cal, both Ky and I excused our senior oarsmen in the fall to concentrate on less experienced candidates. Any of the old-timers will tell you that the spring workouts, which were hard and demanding, meant that the crewmen were in top condition come race day.

Crewmen today train for a different goal, which affects the type of conditioning required. Earlier they aimed at achieving sustained effort for fifteen to eighteen minutes at a lower stroke, while currently the crew races for a shorter period of six minutes or less at a much higher stroke. The contrast is analogous to the difference between a two-mile and 440 race in track. Vastly different techniques are involved both in competition and training. Today's college crewman competes almost the year round if he is a truly top-caliber athlete. January through June is devoted to college rowing and racing with the spring regattas in mind. During the summer there is a scramble for places on the national team and then international competition. The fall and early winter months allow some letup, but there are more and more fall regattas albeit of an informal nature.

Off-water training has become an important part of rowing programs. The rowing tanks of the East and Midwest were developed to allow indoor training during the harsh winter months, thus neutralizing the weather advantage on the milder Pacific Coast. Some tanks are mechanical miracles with regulated water flow. The latest mechanical aid used by almost every team and the bane of the oarsman's existence is the ergometer. An ergometer is basically a rowing machine for off-water conditioning which measures the oarsman's output. The oarsman uses the same rowing style as in a boat—leg drive on a sliding seat, arm pull, and body swing—but instead of going anywhere he propels a flywheel that registers each revolution. The number of revolutions achieved in a given period of time with the same resistance setting of the flywheel determines the score. If one goes all out, "erg" workouts can be the ultimate in punishment, but they do measure the ability of an individual to sustain a certain amount of physical exertion over time.

Another standard off-water workout at most colleges and universities, especially those with large football stadiums, is the almost diabolical practice of running the stadium stairs. Any long flight of stairs will do to develop the leg drive, but an unbroken flight of sixty-five or seventy rows is the most demanding. Weights are used a great deal these days, but the emphasis is on repetitions rather than maximum lifted weight. Also there is more stress on aerobic-type exercise to build up an individual's oxygen intake capacity.

Oarsmen training on ergometers.

THE OTHER PACIFIC COAST CREWS

//

BERKELEY WAS THE FIRST TO START organized rowing at the university level on the Pacific Coast in the late 1800s. Stanford and Washington joined Cal in the 1900s, and these three crews had the only college-level crews on the Pacific Coast. Other schools eventually followed suit, but none were on the same competitive level until after World War II. Oregon State University and the University of British Columbia boated crews on a club level prior to the war. UCLA started rowing in 1933, following the 1932 Olympics, and slowly grew in strength.

Ky always encouraged the spread of the sport. He felt to have other teams, as well as the Big Three, racing would be to everyone's advantage. With his encouragement, Sacramento Junior College started rowing in the 1930s and provided good competition for the Bear freshmen up to World War II. It also trained several oarsmen for Cal, including Ed Salisbury, stroke of the 1932 Olympic champions and Jack "Pappy" Stack, bow on the 1948 Olympic champions. Bob Hillen, USC coach, also was a Sacramento Junior College coxswain.

Ky helped start rowing at the high school level as well. Teams from Long Beach Poly High, Long Beach Wilson High, and Compton High raced in the Marine Stadium in Long Beach from 1934 until the war. A number of these crewmen continued rowing at Berkeley. Alameda High rowed during this period and for a while was working out of the Cal boathouse. Alameda was the runner-up in the National Schoolboy Championship in 1936, and several crewmen from Alameda found their way to Berkeley. Although there was no rowing in racing shells in the San Francisco schools, there was a very successful whaleboat program. Rowing these large heavy craft was quite different, but it was rowing nonetheless. These high school programs were discontinued during World War II and never reactivated. Today there is rowing at Berkeley High, at some of Oakland's high schools, and at Redwood High in Marin County. Washington has long had a high school program at Green Lake.

In Long Beach both Poly High and Wilson High had the same coach, Pete Archer. He consulted with Ky constantly so that his graduates could fit into Ky's program if they so chose. There were always men from Long

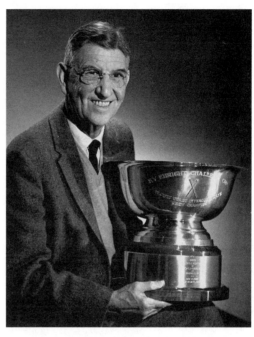

Ky Ebright with the Ky Ebright Challenge Cup he established as a symbol of the Pacific Coast Intercollegiate Crew Championship.

Beach on Ky's crews from 1936 through 1946. Pete Archer contributed much to high school rowing on the Pacific Coast. Following his retirement from teaching, he continued his interest in rowing as a volunteer boatman/rigger for Long Beach State and the Marine Stadium. In 1987 he was still at it.

Prior to World War II there were six college crews rowing on the Pacific Coast. Growth following the war was phenomenal. One factor in the sport's sudden upsurge in the West was the post-war emphasis on 2,000-meter races as opposed to the traditional three-mile races. Few schools could find enough water for a three-mile race, but almost any nearby reservoir could handle 2,000 meters (one-and-a-quarter miles less one yard). There now are thirty-three schools boating crews on the Pacific Coast. By 1987 the original six had expanded to the following:

California Maritime Academy
California Polytechnic University, San Luis Obispo

Gonzaga University
Humboldt State University
Long Beach State University
Loyola University
Orange Coast College
Oregon Institute of Technology
Oregon State University
Pacific Lutheran University
Sacramento State University
San Diego State University
Santa Barbara City College
Santa Clara University
Seattle Pacific University
Stanford University
St. Mary's College
University of British Columbia
UC Berkeley
UC Davis
UC Irvine
UC Los Angeles
UC San Diego
UC Santa Barbara
University of Oregon
University of San Diego
University of San Francisco
University of Southern California
University of the Pacific
University of Puget Sound
University of Washington
Washington State University
Western Washington University

As rowing on the Pacific Coast expanded, scheduling became quite complicated and organization was clearly indicated. The nine schools most involved met in Berkeley on September 6, 1957 and the Western Crew Coaches Association (WCCA) was formed. The following were present: Paul Baptiste, varsity coach, Orange Coast College; Karl Drlica, varsity coach, Oregon State University; Bill Lockyer, varsity coach, Long Beach State University; Lou Lindsey, varsity coach, Stanford University; R. J. "Bus" Phillips, athletic director, and Frank Read, varsity coach, University of British Columbia; Ky Ebright, varsity coach, and Jim Lemmon, freshmen coach, University of California, Berkeley; Bob Schaeffer, varsity coach, and Cliff Fagin, freshmen coach, University of California, Los Angeles; Bob Hillen, varsity coach, University of Southern California; and Al Ulbrickson, varsity coach, University of Washington.

Ky Ebright was elected the first president of the fledgling organization, and the president' term was set at one year. A constitution was written and adopted. Annual fall meetings rotated among the member campuses. The group had two main purposes: to work out the race schedules for the coming season and to establish a championship regatta. In fact, it wasn't until 1960 that the first regatta actually was held.

For a time the WCCA worked quite well. Scheduling became systemized, and the regattas were planned out fairly well in advance. As more schools joined the association, the need for such an organization became ever more apparent. During the early seventies a slight but significant name change was made: the Western Intercollegiate Crew Coaches Association (WICCA). Although this name had been discussed at the initial meeting, it was assumed that the group was limited to coaches who were working with either college or university crews. As the organization grew, club and high school coaches wanted to be included. Because the problems of these crews were quite different, it was felt best to limit the WICCA to the college-level coaches.

The success of rowing on the Pacific Coast proved to be the downfall of the WICCA. The continued growth of the sport put strains on the organization in both scheduling and in the format of the championship regatta. With a much larger number of schools competing, the level of the competition differed drastically. The older schools were competing on a national level with large squads and sizeable budgets, whereas some of the schools were lucky to have one shell and a single crew. Finally matters came to a head at the 1976 championship regatta on San Pablo Reservoir. It was too large and the competitive level too varied. Although it started quite early in the morning, it went on so long the winds had come up and the featured races were rowed under very poor conditions. The result was that at the WICCA fall meeting in 1976, the Pac-8 schools decided to withdraw. This was unfortunate and destroyed the unity that the founding members thought so imporant. But it was inevitable under existing conditions.

The Pac-8 crews formed their own group (and later became Pac-10). In 1977 they raced at Redwood Shores on San Francisco Bay, and in 1978 they went to Seattle. In 1979 they decided to return to Redwood Shores and to remain there, which they did through 1983. The other schools continued as the Western Intercollegiate Rowing Association and held their own regattas. In 1984 the two groups cooperated in a joint regatta at Lake Natoma near Sacramento. This proved to be an ideal site for all. The first day the two groups raced separately to determine their own champions, and the following day the best crews from each raced for the Pacific Coast Championship. By 1985 the two factions rejoined insofar as racing was concerned and scheduled one big two-day regatta, which has continued.

Scheduling on the West Coast remains a big problem. It may well be that the various schools with crew should be separated into divisions, as in the several NCAA sports. This could be done on the basis of having a division I class, requiring that the sport be considered part of the intercollegiate program with an appropriate budget, and a division II class for those crews who have a club status and depend on their own funding.

THE TRAINING TABLE

//

FOR MANY YEARS, one of rowing's main drawbacks was getting back to the campus after normal dinner hours. The crew bus left from campus at 4 p.m. for weekday workouts, and the crews usually got on the water just before 5 p.m. They were off by about 6 p.m., and then it was a mad dash back to campus. Dinnertime on campus was normally 5:30 or 6 p.m. at the latest, which meant the crewmen ate late—and usually cold—dinners. Ben Wallis had started a short-lived training table in 1916 in the Sigma Chi house, and from the beginning Ky had fought for a training table for at least the varsity boat. By the twenties football and basketball already had training tables.

After his 1932 success, Ky finally was successful in gaining a budget item for a training table, which consisted of dinner for the varsity and JV served in the coffee shop of the old Stephens Union. It started a month before the Washington race and was for only the first two varsity crews. Changes in the boatings caused changes in those eligible for training table, usually on a weekly basis. This was additional incentive to make a position in one of the top boats. Needless to say, the food was plentiful and gratefully accepted. In the depression days of the late thirties it was the only decent meal for more than a few. The freshmen first boat was included for the week before the Washington race in the late thirties and early forties, and to be so honored was one of the high points in a first-year crewman's life.

An obvious benefit of a training table is that the coach, with advice from his trainer, can make certain that his men are eating the right food. Crewmen, among all athletes, are acknowledged to be tops in putting away the groceries. As knowledge of the effect of appopriate diet has increased over the years, training table fare has changed accordingly. An excellent example is the drastic change in the typical pre-race meal. For many years athletes were served a large thick rare steak, even if the

contest was in the morning. Even if their nerves would allow them to eat the steak—and many couldn't—crewmen say that it would sit like a hard lump in their stomachs for hours. Nutritionists now push a high-carbohydrate meal such as pasta, spaghetti, or pancakes to provide quick energy. This type of meal is prescribed for a day or two before the contest, and the race-day meal is quite light, perhaps toast with honey and a little tea. The present day athlete is much better off with this more sensible approach.

But, for those lucky enough to qualify, the training table was more than just a hot meal. It provided a real boost in crew morale, a moment of relaxation when the men could really get to know one another. There was a definite bonding effect that did wonders for crew unity. When the freshmen were included it signified an initial phase of bringing them into the total program. Unfortunately, the athletic department's budget cutbacks, which started in the late sixties, meant the end of a regular training table for crew by 1975. (Training tables have continued, however, for gate sports.) Since the crews now work out before classes, due to increased boat traffic on the estuary in the afternoon, the problem of cold dinners no longer plagues them, and it may no longer be an issue.

A variation of training table was introduced during the days before World War II, when the spring semester ended several weeks before the crews headed east to Poughkeepsie and the IRA. Because all the living groups and boarding houses closed at semester's end, Ky developed a program that continued until rowing shut down for the duration. For several weeks after final exams, the crew took over the old Delt house and the entire team was housed and fed there while they rowed two-a-days. The squad by then consisted of just the first three crews, plus the freshmen if they were going East, and they really got together in spirit as well as in body.

Ky claimed the squad often accomplished as much during these two weeks as they did for most of the prior season. The record backs this up—in 1934, 1935, and 1938 Washington won the dual race, only to be defeated by Cal in the IRA. The same underlying purpose of promoting team unity was used in the early sixties, when the Varsity Rowing Club took over the Zete fraternity house for the spring break. And in the eighties, coaches Mike Livingston and Tim Hodges also have tried similar "training tables."

Those crewmen fortunate enough to have spent such times together will never forget those days of complete immersion in the rowing program with the resultant camaraderie and mutual respect. It may be that, with the University back on the pre-war semester system after years of the fragmented trimester or quarter system, this means of uniting the crews can be reinstituted. Living together for awhile when classes are out, or simply having a meal together on a regular basis, is a true morale booster and creates closer bonds among the team.

Small-Boat Annex to Ky Ebright Boathouse.

SMALL-BOAT ROWING
AT CALIFORNIA

THE USE OF BOATS SMALLER than the eights is a luxury that the Cal rowing program has enjoyed only during recent years. Once the program graduated to the more prestigious eights in 1907, the use of fours, pairs, and singles fell off rapidly, primarily due to space and financial limitations, plus the fact that for many years collegiate events were generally restricted to eights. For a number of the Olympics, some colleges would break up their varsity and/or JV crews to man the small-boat events. Most of the rowing clubs concentrated on small-boat events, leaving the eights to the colleges. There were, of course, some notable exceptions such as the great Penn Athletic Club eight of 1932 and the Olympic championship Vesper Rowing Club eight of 1900, 1904 and 1964. The coaches knew all along that smaller boats would enhance a program, both in teaching better "watermanship" and in providing flexibility in dealing with numbers of men rowing.

The smaller the boat the more an oarsman's skills come into play. One individual's effect in moving the boat and setting it up is much more apparent, both to the oarsman and to the coach, in a four than in an eight—and even more so in a pair. After a period of small-boat rowing, shifting back into the more stable eight is a revelation to an oarsman. The experienced club oarsman has known this all along, whereas many college crewmen do not enjoy such an opportunity due to program limitations.

When Ky Ebright came to Berkeley the new boathouse was constructed on its present site. Despite his efforts to obtain an additional boat bay, only two were provided, and, as the program quickly grew, there was just enough space for the necessary number of eights. For most of the Ebright era there was only one four with cox of questionable origin that was used by the reserve crews when they were short of men for an eight.

Shortly after I took over from Ky, the picture began to change somewhat. Having done some club rowing in small boats at Long Beach before coming to Cal, I knew of the advantages of small-boat rowing and wanted to somehow incorporate it into the Cal program. Through the generosity of the newly formed Lake Merritt Rowing Club in Oakland, I was able to achieve this to a limited extent. The only times boats could be borrowed was during the one-week University spring vacation, when the crews rowed twice a day. I borrowed some fours from the club and in the mornings I could race the bow fours of my crews against the stern fours as an example. This proved quite helpful to the program. Also, in 1961, we obtained from Washington a secondhand four, in excellent shape, to replace the old and rapidly failing four that had been in the Cal fleet for so long.

Steve Gladstone laid the groundwork for collecting the fleet of small boats Cal now owns. Through the help of the Alumni Rowing Club, later known as Friends of California Crew, Steve first obtained a straight pair (pair without cox) and, as time went by, added a few more. Both Mike Livingston and Tim Hodges expanded the small-boat fleet which now consists of four fours with cox, one four without cox, six straight pairs, and seven single sculls.

As these boats were acquired, it swiftly became evident that the old boathouse was going to overflow with boats of every description. A small-boat addition was constructed adjacent to the Ebright Boathouse to store some of this overflow, thanks to several alumni, including Willis Andersen Jr. '54, who bankrolled the project; John Bacon '77, who donated the lumber; and Craig Huntington '76, who donated his architectural expertise. Already the annex is overflowing.

THE SCOW AND THE SHELL BARGES

///

TWO ROWING AIDS FROM THE OLD DAYS of Ky's and my reign, which alumni oarsmen remember with mixed emotions, are the old scow and the shell barges. The old scow was patterned after Pocock's model but was much more solidly built for the often choppy estuary. A very heavy, quite ungainly, large flat-bottomed craft, about forty feet long and about six feet wide, it had eight rowing positions on each side with full slides and footboards. Cast-iron outriggers were used as well. A walkway down the center of the scow allowed the coach to work personally with each toiling new prospect. Balance, so critical in a shell, was not a problem, given the scow's broad beam, and prospective oarsmen could concentrate on how to coordinate arm pull with leg drive, the basic feature of rowing in a racing shell. The scow weighed a ton or more, and with the added weight of sixteen oarsmen, several coxswains, and a coach or two, it was not the fastest of craft. Old oars, with cutdown blades to keep breakage to a minimum, afforded the budding oarsman a chance to learn the secrets of the sliding seat coordinated with the rather long and often unwieldy oar. The typical crewman spent several weeks in the scow before the coach dared to put him in a thin-skinned shell.

After the scow, the next stage was the shell barge. Although they were built roughly along the lines of a racing shell, these two large clumsy craft were wider and had heavy double skins able to withstand hard treatment. They held up quite well under treatment rough enough to really damage a more fragile racing shell. It took two crews to carry them out of the boathouse and put them in or take them out of the water. Intended to be a transition craft for new oarsmen, the shell barges carried a crew of eight and a coxswain seated in the same manner as in a regular shell. Easier to balance than the regular shell, the shell barge still offered more of a challenge than the scow and the oarsmen had to master balancing or "keel" before they could graduate to old racing shells, which took a

beating. The new shells were held back for racing season.

The main problem caused by the shell barges was the amount of time they took out of a very limited workout period because of the difficulty of launching and returning them to the boathouse. When Pocock designed a double-skinned racing shell, the problem was solved. Although a little heavier than a regular racing shell, one crew could handle it about as easily. It had a flatter bottom too and was easier to set up or balance. Early in my career I decided to use these double-skinned shells instead of the shell barges, much to the relief of both the oarsmen and the rigger. The new shells today, with their fiberglass-type Kevlar skin in place of the old fragile cedar, can handle very hard wear. Thus the newest oarsmen can be put into a regular shell right out of the scow. The balance problem is handled by rowing only four or six of the eight oarsmen and having the others hold the shell on keel with their oars as extended outriggers.

The scow also was time-consuming— always an issue at the boathouse because time is available in such limited amounts. During rowing season when tied up to its float the scow usually had to be pumped out before workouts. Taking it out for the winter overhaul and returning it in spring took hours on end and was even a bit dangerous because of its enormous weight. Moreover, by McNair's era in the late sixties, it was becoming increasingly difficult to repair after a hard fall season. Marty solved this dilemma by making a deal with Berkeley High School, which recently had begun rowing at Berkeley Aquatic Park at the foot of University Avenue. Berkeley High accepted the old scow and used it for its new oarsmen. Cal could use it briefly for new oarsmen at the start of its fall season. This arrangement worked fairly well for several years, but the scow was deteriorating badly. Finally it broke its back while being pulled out for repairs. It still resides in the Aquatic Park parking lot as a barrier to prevent cars from entering.

The old training barge or scow.

The old scow has been replaced by a newer, better-built model that is used sparingly the first week or so of a new season. The term "newer" is used advisedly in that it is an old Pocock model which UCLA had traded to Steve Gladstone in exchange for the shell *Mariposa*. The new scow has been moved to smoother water up on Briones Reservoir in the hills behind Berkeley.

But most alumni still can recall their early days on the estuary making like galley slaves in the old cumbersome scow and then graduating to the shell barge, always looking forward to that great day when one could actual-ly get into a sleek racing shell. The scow and shell barges did give flexibility to the freshmen program, in that it was possible by using student coaches to have three different types of workouts going at the same time. A coach could encourage the quick learners and those with previous experience, yet bring others along more patient-ly. Today the scow is used only for about the first week, and it does cause transportation problems getting men to and from Briones Reservoir. Still, it is possible to get the new men into actual shells, giving them a better sense of what rowing in a racing shell is all about.

THE VARSITY ROWING CLUB

IN 1933 KY EBRIGHT AND THE CREW established the Varsity Rowing Club as an auxiliary support group. All crewmen and managers who have been part of the rowing program for one full school year become members of the club. Its officers include the commodore, first mate, and bursar. Charlie Chandler, #3 in the 1932 Olympic championship boat, was the first commodore and wrote the original initiation ceremony, which is quite creative and uses rowing terms and symbols. He set in motion what was to become a very active group.

One of the club's main functions from the start was to help raise funds for the crew's trip East to the IRA. There were two main fundraisers during the late thirties and early forties. One was the Varsity Rowing Club dance at the Claremont Hotel, traditionally the first organized all-campus dance each year. Ky knew the owner of the hotel, a crew supporter, and was able to rent the ballroom for a token one dollar fee. Always very popular, the dance was well-attended and showed a good profit. The other club activity was an annual raffle with a large, usually donated prize such as a car. These efforts provided the club with a purpose and kept its members quite busy. The club helped organize the squad and taught good leadership skills.

Shortly before crew stopped for World War II, Ky finally succeeded in getting the ASUC to include travel expenses to the IRA in the crew's annual budget. Consequently, the Varsity Rowing Club lacked a reason for being and began to languish. After Ky retired and I took over, the club had a resurgence. Due to a complicated series of personnel changes among the boatman/rigger, bus driver, and mechanic positions, there were two less hands to maintain crew equipment. So I decided to put

the Varsity Rowing Club into action. The club held a workday for both varsity and freshmen on the Saturday after the end of fall rowing. Each boat was gone over carefully, and minor repairs were made where possible. Major work was duly recorded for more expert attention. After a few years' worth of these workdays, the exterior of the boathouse was painted, the concrete sidewalk was laid along the west side of the boathouse, the dock and float were repaired, and much landscaping was accomplished. The workday always ended with a big barbeque.

Another effective rowing club project which I devised was the spring vacation training period. For one week, the crew took over the Zeta Psi fraternity house and the Varsity Rowing Club, through its officers, ran the program, hiring a cook, planning menus, and assigning various jobs, while each crewman paid his own way. Most evenings alumni speakers were invited to have dinner with the squad and share rowing stories. The freshmen were made to feel they were an important part of the program, underscored by being assigned a varsity roommate. Even the Zeta Psi brothers were happy about the week—they claimed that their house was never as clean as when the crew left it. Unfortunately, when the campus shifted to the quarter system in the late sixties, the vacation period was dropped, and the program had to end.

The years have slipped by, and once again there seems to be no active role for the Varsity Rowing Club. Membership is maintained and officers are elected but that's about all. In order to survive, traditions must have a purpose; perhaps in the future a new role for the club will arise.

THE BOATMAN/RIGGER

//

THE BOATMAN/RIGGER, USUALLY KNOWN AS the rigger, is a unique individual, very often self-taught because few know the required skills. The term "rigger" stems from the rigging of the racing shell, and a rigger adjusts the outriggers that support the oarlocks which in turn provide leverage to the oarsman. The outriggers' height from the water and attitude, or slant, are critical to efficient rowing. This is the most specific task of a rigger, but there is much more to his job description. He is the man behind the scenes who keeps things going for the crews. He must understand every type of maintenance for the complicated racing machines we know as shells. The job includes a myriad of other skills and esoteric knowledge, such as sliding seat height relative to the rigging or the wetting factor of certain finishes.

In the beginning coaches tried to handle these responsibilities, but as programs grew, being a rigger became a full-time job. Boat maintenance, especially during the years they were made of wood, is a neverending task: varnish has to be renewed, simple splits have to be repaired immediately, oars have to be repaired and repainted. Coaching launches must be maintained (unless there is a separate mechanic on staff). Often the coach consults with the rigger when an oarsman is having problems in rowing up to his potential. Sometimes a minor adjustment in equipment can make a real difference in performance. Few coaches in large programs these days have the diverse skills of a rigger or have time to do his job, so they really rely on this critical position.

California has had at least seven riggers of record, and all have contributed much to the Bears' rowing program. The first we know of was Joe "Portuguese Joe" Francis, mentioned by former crew captain Harold Pischel '19 in a crew banquet speech in 1942. Joe helped move the old boathouse from the Alameda side of the estuary to the foot of Washington Street on the Oakland side. He was said to have moored his scow, in which he lived, along-side the boathouse so he could keep watch over it. Ben Wallis also mentions Joe as his boatman.

When Ky arrived and the boathouse was completed in 1925, Albert "Mac" McGregor was hired as the rigger and served through 1934. His successor was Alex Thompson who served from 1935 through 1943, when rowing was discontinued for the duration. None of these men had prior experience, but their knowledge of working with wood and their ability to adapt their skills to the position's requirements served them well. Crewmen of those days remember them with affection.

One man, who really doesn't fit the description of rigger but who was an important contributing member of the program, was Ernie Madson. Ernie was hired to drive the first crew bus to the boathouse and to maintain the coaching launches. He also helped the incumbent rigger as needed, serving in this capacity from the late twenties until 1947, when he quit to go into private business as a mechanic. Later he returned to the athletic department as equipment manager. Ernie was a tough-talking, hard-shelled individual who was fiercely protective of "his" crew bus and "his" coaching launches. He was the enforcer for the senior manager, keeping the managerial system in line, making certain all duties were properly performed. Underneath he was a pussycat and would do anything for his crewmen.

After World War II, as Ky and Ernie labored to rehabilitate the boathouse and the dock facilities, Jack Donnelly was hired as the rigger. Jack was a cabinet-maker, but he quickly picked up the necessary lore to take care of the boats. (Ky knew as much, if not more, than any rigger and could train his own people.) Jack served as rigger from 1946 until his retirement with Ky in 1959. His health in his later years was not good, and he needed more and more help from Matt Franich, who had succeeded Ernie in 1948.

Citing his health, Jack declined to go East for the IRA

in 1954. I had been hired as freshmen coach that season and was pressed into service as the rigger for the IRA trip. I had had some rigging experience, having worked during the thirties with Walt Bush, a Long Beach racing shell builder. At Syracuse, I was fortunate enough to have the Wisconsin and Navy riggers take me under their wings. They were the top two riggers in the sport at the time, so my instruction came from the very best. This, plus Ky's expertise, gave me a background that helped considerably in my later coaching years.

When Ky retired in 1959, an adjustment was made in the crew staff, which had consisted of the varsity coach, freshmen coach, a part-time assistant coach, the rigger, and a mechanic/bus driver. Because the crew bus was constantly breaking down, it was decided that it would be best to go to a charter agreement with the local bus system. No longer needed as a bus driver, Matt Franich was hired as rigger and the job of mechanic, for launch upkeep, was included in his job description. He served in this capacity from 1960 through 1980, and, in the process, he became known as one of the best riggers in the sport. From the very start he was welcomed into the circle of established riggers whose main goal was to keep their complicated equipment in top racing shape. It was not uncommon at the IRA to have a number of the riggers pitching in to help one of their fellow craftsmen when he was faced by an emergency such as a badly damaged shell. Their mutual goal was to provide equipment in the best possible shape for their crews on race day. A loss because of equipment failure was a shared nightmare they all strived to avoid. Matt was quickly recognized as an equal by this esteemed group. Even though he has retired, he still follows the various regattas closely and is quick to offer his services when they might be needed.

Matt's successor was Mike Fennelly, who started in 1981 and is the incumbent rigger. A former lightweight Cal oarsman, Mike coached the lightweight crews for a brief period. He worked with Matt for several years learning the trade. Together they made the transition from the long-established wooden shells and oars to the current high-tech array of plastic/fiberglass shells, outriggers with an infinite number of possible adjustments, and graphite/fiberglass oars with wood only in their handles. Much of this almost space-age technology is a far cry from the world of George Pocock, known to generations of crewmen. Many former crewmen find it hard to believe that in some crews the coxswain lies down in the bow of a shell with just his head showing. Thus far Berkeley has not succumbed to such heresy.

Boatman/Rigger Matt Franich. He is checking out a shell in one of the Ky Ebright Boathouse bays at the Oakland Estuary. Matt was boatman/rigger 1960–1980. (Courtesy of Howard Erker.)

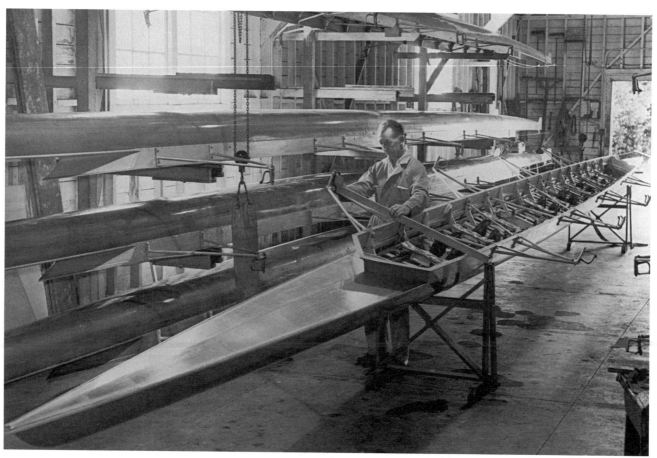

THE MANAGERIAL SYSTEM

THE MANAGERIAL SYSTEM IN Cal's athletic program was highly organized and contributed much to both sports and to the individuals involved. Almost all of the sports had managers, and nowhere did they contribute more than in crew. Organized like a pyramid, the system's top was the senior manager. His assistants were several junior managers. The main work force was a large group of sophomore managers, whose numbers depended upon the recruiting ability of those above them.

The senior manager in each major sport was awarded a Big C equal to that of the varsity letter winners. He was a letterman just as they were. From the very beginning there was competition among the managers at each class level. Usually four junior managers were selected from among six to eight sophomores, and one senior from the four juniors. In crew the varsity coach supervised the selection process with advice from the outgoing senior manager.

It was recognized early on that the senior manager could relieve the coaching staff of the myriad housekeeping tasks and many of the equipment allocation problems inherent in athletics, certainly in rowing. The crew's senior manager also enjoyed a privilege not found in other sports—driving the coaching launches. Now the coaches usually drive their own small outboards, and some glamour definitely seems lacking.

The senior manager supervised the rowing program at the boathouse, and, if he had good juniors helping him and was well-organized, all went smoothly without too much effort. He came into his own whenever the crew traveled. Particularly during train trips, the senior manager had a crucial job. The head coach would advise the athletic department's business manager of travel plans well in advance, but it was the senior manager's job to work out all the timetable details; to pick up tickets; to arrange and pay for meals; to load equipment under supervision of the rigger; to pack racing uniforms, including the appropriate race shirts; to check hotel reservations; and to schedule wake-up calls and meal times. It was a job calling for topnotch organization and the ability to improvise at a moment's notice. Being a senior manager was an education in itself and worth every bit of recognition. Senior managers took a real burden off the coaching staff and contributed much to the sport.

One incident involving a senior manager became near-legendary. One year the squad pulled into the Chicago train station for the obligatory four-hour layover before continuing on to Syracuse. The men were allowed to go where they wished, and some visited relatives, some went to baseball games, and some went sightseeing. On this occasion the senior manager had been talking about looking up an old girlfriend. The freshmen coach and trainer were watching the squad scatter throughout the station, when they noticed the senior manager dash up to a phone booth, make an extended call, and then hurry to catch a taxi. They also noticed when he left the phone booth, he did not have the large briefcase he carried everywhere with him. The briefcase held all of the squad's tickets, money orders, and cash for meals, and all of the housing arrangements and reservations. He had left it in the booth. The coach and trainer retrieved the briefcase and deposited it in a locker for safekeeping. They then stepped back and waited. Moments later one of the station's outside doors flew open, and a completely distraught young man raced to the phone booth, only to come out empty-handed and white-faced. He looked about wildly and seemed at a loss. When he appeared about to have an attack, the two men ended his panic. The trainer handed him the key to the locker without having to say a word. It all ended well, and everyone noticed the senior manager was *never* without his briefcase the rest of the trip.

A typical group of Crew Managers in 1950s. *Front:* senior manager. *Next row:* junior managers. *Back two rows:* sophomore managers.

The old managerial system was a victim of campus unrest during the sixties. Being a sports manager seemed to have lost its attraction. Some considered such a position demeaning, and it became difficult to recruit students to help the squads. There still are senior managers, but often they are seniors in name only. Coaches are lucky to find someone who will serve, although in most cases they are fine, hard-working young men. There no

longer exists the reserve of student help and the career ladder to assure the desired leadership and experience that went into molding a traditional senior manager. But for those who joined the ranks, it was a worthwhile system and provided an opportunity for a young man to participate in a sport when he was not able to meet its often rigid physical requirements. A roster of senior managers from 1924 through 1987 is in the appendix.

INTERCLASS RACES AND ALUMNI DAY

IN THE FIRST DAYS OF CALIFORNIA ROWING the only competition the crews met was among themselves. In fact, an ornate trophy for the interclass championship sits in the Hall of Fame crew case at Memorial Stadium. Early in his career Ky started a tradition that still stands today. He took a page from the early days of rowing at Cal and staged an interclass regatta, starting off the year with a rallying point to excite alumni interest in the upcoming season. Representative class crews raced each other, in front of a completely partisan crowd of alumni, to determine which class was fastest. Afterward, the bravest of the alums were encouraged to suit up and prove they could still set up a boat. Although urged to take it easy, they did not always comply. Most found rowing is like swimming—once learned, never forgotten. On Alumni Day men who have not held an oar for ten or twenty years have gone out and performed quite well.

Before World War II the squad was large enough to boat two crews in each class, so two different events were held: first boats and second boats racing one another. Occasionally the second boat of a senior class or even a junior class was augmented by lowerclassmen, but this was overlooked in the heat of battle. One reason the squad was so large was that there was not yet a separate lightweight division, and many of thsoe rowing then were in the lightweight classification. Of course, many smaller lowerclassmen grew eventually and became bona fide heavyweight varsity candidates.

The result of the interclass rivalry usually was predictable. The more experienced seniors and juniors fought it out for first, while the sophomores did their best to keep the freshmen in their place—lowest on the totem pole. Sometimes a very strong sophomore crew took over, as in 1941 and 1948, and in 1925 and 1957 a freshmen crew prevailed. These latter victories did not augur well for that year's varsity season but held promise for strong teams as the younger crews matured.

The interclass races have continued down the years, although now there is only a single race due to smaller squad size. Often classes hold their reunions on Alumni Day, and when several are being celebrated simultaneously, alumni crews stage mini-races to prove superiority. Given the questionable physical condition of the participants, the coaching staff discourages such events but to no avail. How do you convince a Dave de Varona not to go all out? After the racing and alumni row-bys everybody enjoys a picnic at the boathouse, while the kids take launch rides with Oski.

Over the years Alumni Day has been held in all kinds of weather, but the 1984 regatta was one of the most dramatic. It started out as a beautiful day. The 1964 IRA champions were holding their twentieth reunion, many of the 1932 and 1948 Olympic gold medalists were there, and everyone was having a fine time. Just as the interclass race was to start, however, the weather began to turn. It seemed as if there would be plenty of time for the five boats to race before the bad weather arrived. But as the crews lined up for their start beyond the Coast Guard station on Government Island, a furious line squall came speeding up the estuary. Before the crews could do much about it they were engulfed in sheets of driving rain and at the mercy of waves they could not handle. All five crews swamped, and the coaches and officials had a mess to untangle that was unprecedented on the estuary. After the crews were rescued and the swamped shells were towed home it was discovered that, wonder of wonders, there were no injuries or damage. It was eloquent testimony to the fine discipline and high morale of the entire squad and the coaches. What could have been a real disaster turned into a first-rate salvage operation that will long be remembered. The only losers were the small fry who missed out on the usual launch rides with Oski.

SWAMPINGS AND DUNKINGS

///

THE EIGHT-OARED SHELL USED BY OUR college crews is hardly a surf boat. Even so, it's amazing how much rough water a shell can survive when properly handled. There is a limit, however, as more than one crew has discovered. Some of the most painful incidents, albeit the most spectacular, are now historic: the first eight-oared race for Pacific Coast supremacy, when Cal, Stanford, and Washington all swamped on Richardson Bay; the 1929 varsity race and the 1940 JV race at the IRA on the Hudson River; the first racing post-World War II on Lake Washington in 1946, when all the participants swamped after the race ended, thanks to the spectator fleet of powerboats; the IRA race on the raging Ohio River, when all three of Navy's crews went under; and the protested race with Stanford in 1968.

Some swampings of note have occurred during workouts. Ky was fond of describing the time in the mid-thirties when Washington ran into one of the large nun buoys in San Leandro Bay—not once, but twice, the second time in a borrowed Cal boat. On both occasions the bow section of the shell was badly damaged. The embarrassed Husky crew took the damaged Berkeley boat back to Seattle for Pocock to repair at their expense.

Another swamping during a workout in the sixties involved a famous Cal shell, the *George Blair* of 1948 Olympic fame. I had a four crew workout getting underway, when a large tugboat wake came rolling up the estuary, building ever higher against the outgoing tide. Normally a shell can turn parallel to such a wave and then bob over it like a cork. That day there was not enough room to turn all the shells, and the *Blair* was trapped in the middle. The wave swept over the bow and down the length of the shell, hitting the oarsmen waist high. As the wave passed, the following trough left three feet of daylight beneath the #5 man before the now water-filled shell broke in half.

The boatman/rigger, Matt, to the amazement of all,

rebuilt the shell. Several years later the *Blair* again was in a bad swamping, seemingly beyond repair. Recognizing its sentimental value, Matt proceeded to convert the shattered shell to a rather diamond-shaped four with cox by joining the bow and #2 positions with the stroke and #7 positions. The middle section was unusable. The Redwood High rowing program in Marin County used the rebuilt *Blair* for a number of years. It was last seen as a relic, its bow section mounted on a wall in a Fresno bar. Cal alumni have been trying to rescue it and restore it to dignity in the University's Hall of Fame.

Not only shells get swamped; oarsmen can be catapulted right out of the boat. Rare and impressive, it also is most embarrassing for the oarsman. Dunkings happen only in certain circumstances, usually when an oarsman catches a crab. The oarsman's grip slips slightly so the oar is turned just beyond the almost flat position which it normally assumes on recovery of the stroke, or the oarsman might over-bevel the oar past the flat position. If the boat is on balance, or set up, he may get away with it. If, however, the boat drops to that side or if an errant wave covers the blade, the result can be ruinous. The over-beveled blade acts as a diving plane, forcing the blade down and the handle up. Meanwhile, the shell, carrying the weight of nine men, is speeding along at ten to twelve miles an hour, while the oar is stuck in the water trying to go straight down. There can be only one of three outcomes. In the least damaging, the oarsman is knocked flat and the oar handle flies over his head, allowing the oar to trail in the water. The next worse scenario is when the oar handle pins the oarsman in the bow end of his slide and the oar blade is buried in the water acting as a brake. Occasionally the timing is such that the oar catches the oarsman in the stomach and flips him out of the boat. This happens so fast most victims remember rowing one minute and swimming the next.

A crab can happen to anyone, even the most experienced crewmen. Very often it is not the victim's fault, having started on a previous stroke when someone on the other side of the shell gets caught in the water, usually at the finish. For example, the 1948 crew was in a very close time trial on the estuary one day. The JV had been given a head start and the varsity caught them at the Park Street Bridge. Just as they flashed under on their way to the finish line at Fruitvale Avenue, the most experienced man in the crew and undoubtedly one of the finest #7 men to row for Cal, senior Dave Turner, went flying out of the boat to end up treading water in the wake of the now disappearing shell. The stroke, his brother Ian, said he felt the boat lurch as it passed under the bridge, and then he saw his brother bobbing in the water behind the boat. Needless to say, the old veteran Dave took quite a ribbing for this exploit.

I will long remember being out on the Bay, well past the mouth of the estuary, on one of our traditional Saturday morning workouts. Claude Hutchison, then an undergraduate oarsman and subsequently president of the California Alumni Association and a Congressional candidate, took an involuntary swim. For some reason, a man in the water out in the Bay seems even more spectacular than within the confines of the estuary.

When a dunking happens in an actual race, it is a disaster. A seven-man crew cannot compete with a full complement of eight. Once at Seattle in the fifties a Washington man went out shortly after Cal passed them down near the finish. And in a hotly contested race against Long Beach State in the early sixties, the Long Beach coxswain managed to hit a floating log despite warnings by the race officials for the previous half mile. The Long Beach #7 ended up in the drink, and the race was settled right there in the Bears' favor by default—no way to row a crew race!

One of the most memorable dunkings took place during an early afternoon fall workout. I was pulling away from the float for a training spin with a scow load of new freshmen. Ky Ebright was helping to launch the scow by swinging the bow away from the float. He had not changed out of his coat and tie and was carrying two newly repaired stop watches in his pocket. Just then two freshmen, who were late, came running down the ramp onto the float with oars in hand. As they jumped for the scow they swung their oars in an arc, neatly sweeping Ky off the float into the cold estuary water, hat, coat, tie, watches, and all. Without a word, Ky pulled himself back onto the float and stomped a very wet path back into the boathouse. My freshmen charges and I watched all this in open-mouthed amazement, powerless to prevent it. The two culprits, immobilized with shock, waited for Ky's roar of rage, which never came. In fact, he never said anything about the incident. Then at the end of the fall workout, some weeks later, I presented the two perpetrators with a certificate stating that they were the only Cal oarsmen ever to put Ky in the water.

THE FRESHMEN COACH

///

FEW REALLY UNDERSTAND THE VITAL significance of the freshmen rowing coach. Unlike other sports, in rowing, most, if not all, of a first-year squad must be taught *how* to row and *how* to handle the equipment. They also must learn a whole new vocabulary. A freshmen coach must keep in mind that his primary job is developing men for the varsity boats. He must teach the style the varsity coach employs, whether or not it suits his personal preference. He must develop depth in those positions that are thin on the varsity level or which will be when strong senior men graduate. A freshmen coach, therefore, may boat a freshmen crew that is not all to his liking or have a squad that seems imbalanced.

One pleasant aspect of the job is that the freshmen coach can afford to get close to his men by the end of their first year, whereas the varsity coach must maintain complete impartiality. Often the freshmen coach acts as a buffer for the squad by presenting their problems to the varsity coach. But it can be frustrating for the first-year coach because the varsity always takes precedence, whether in allocation of equipment or workout times. It's all part of a kind of freshmen rite of passage.

The record lists fifteen Cal freshmen coaches (There may have been more, but they were not labeled as such in the early days.) Two freshmen coaches, whose crews beat Washington and assured a sweep when the varsity and JV came through, were Dave Turner on the estuary in 1952, and Tom Dunlap at Seattle in 1965. Only two coaches were able to beat the Husky frosh two years in a row:

Russ Nagler in 1940 and 1941, and Tim Hodges in 1981 and 1982. Roy Eisenhardt probably became the most famous freshmen coach—after he went on to become president of the Oakland A's. But the one most alumni recall best is the coach with the longest tenure, Russ Nagler, freshmen coach from 1923 through 1942 and from 1947 through 1951.

Russ came with Ky from the University of Washington, the first full-time paid coaches at Berkeley. He quickly recognized the role of the freshmen coach was to develop men for future varsities, and he did just that for a quarter of a century with success unmatched within the coaching ranks. Small even by coxswain standards, Russ weighed about 100 pounds. What he might have lacked in size, he made up for with a caustic, sarcastic manner of speech and as classic a knowledge of profanity as was ever displayed by a salty seafarer or earthy muleskinner. He had a way of making a verbal point that few could forget, although his wry sense of humor took any personal bite out of stinging observations on one's rowing style. Together with Ky, Russ developed some of the finest crews the world of rowing has ever seen. In the background most of the time, he was the one who taught those future champions their basic rowing technique. Ky certainly refined their style, provided motivation, and came up with strategy, but the foundation was laid at the freshmen level. It was in this that Russ excelled, and, rather than by a somewhat mediocre record against Washington, it is by this that he should be judged.

CREW FINANCES

///

IN ITS EARLIEST DAYS, ROWING WAS supported primarily by private donations and Boating Association membership dues. The ASUC took over financial sponsorhip of the rowing program in 1906 and continued until July 1959, when the entire athletic program was established as a separate department within the university administrative system. It receives no state funding. In the early days budgeting was rather simple and expenses were at a minimum. As time passed, costs in all sports mounted. The crew budget usually covered only normal season costs, and post-season trips, such as the IRA, called for separate fund-raising.

When Ky Ebright started coaching at Berkeley in 1924, he understood at once the importance of alumni in providing support to the program. He encouraged and developed alumni support beginning with a file of current alumni addresses that he kept on his desk, adding names as each class graduated. Later he started the annual Alumni Day centered around interclass races. At the suggestion of Jim Dieterich '40, he created an annual newsletter, *The Log*. In order to avoid an alumni group dictating coaching policy, Ky requested assistance only at specific times for specific reasons—a needed shell, help for the trip East, pressure on the athletic department when the sport was threatened. By the time he retired in 1959, Ky had an alumni file of about 1,000 names and addresses. Alumni Day was an annual fixture, and "The Log" provided a summary of the previous season and a preview of what was coming up for Cal.

I continued Ky's approach to the alumni, but also developed an endowment fund for the financial support of the crew at Berkeley. In 1960 I had discovered almost all of the established Eastern crews had long been fully endowed and didn't have to worry about football receipts. About that time Lou Penney '17 was considering a rather large legacy for the crew. At a meeting hosted by Dean Witter '09 at the Pacific Union Club, I met with several of the older alumni, and they agreed to support the establishment of the Crew Alumni Memorial Fund. By 1962 the fund had been approved by the University; Dean Witter started it off with $5,000. He contributed several thousand dollars in subsequent years, but he became disenchanted because of its slow growth and the problems on the Berkeley campus in the late sixties. As a result, we lost a large bequest which he had hinted at earlier. Even so the fund soon began to provide at least a set of oars each year, and by 1979 totaled about $40,000.

When Martin McNair took over as coach in 1967, athletic department support was beginning to erode. Marty decided the time had come for more personal alumni involvement, so he started the Alumni Rowing Club, or ARC. Incorporated in 1967, ARC was tax-exempt, with a board of directors and by-laws. Initial efforts were centered on increasing the Memorial Fund.

By 1973, when Steve Gladstone was coaching, the athletic department's financial picture was becoming quite grim because of spiraling costs and declining income from student fees. A recommendation to drop freshmen crew was seriously considered during the budget review. Matters came to a head when Steve was given a choice in the 1978 budget of funding the trip East for the IRA or the trip to the San Diego Crew Classic. An agreement was reached that the athletic department would fund the regular crew season, including the San Diego Crew Classic, and the alumni would raise money for all post-season travel.

A change in organization and expansion of alumni efforts was called for, so in 1978 ARC became the Friends of California Crew in order to include those who had not actually rowed such as parents or friends. The Friends committed to an annual fund drive for contributions to go directly to the rowing program. A goal of $22,000 was set to fund the IRA trip, with any additional money to go into the Memorial Fund. Don Martin

'60, a dentist in San Francisco, organized the fund-raising and established year captains and ten-year captains from among the alumni. The old address card file had already been put on computer, thanks to Jay Jacobus '66, and was constantly updated. The athletic department provided a weekly progress report on the drive. It was so successful that crews were sent to the Henley Regatta in England under both Steve and his successor, Mike Livingston. Since 1979, the Friends have raised an average of more than $40,000 per year—"the margin of excellence" over and above the basic budget provided by the athletic department, it represents about twenty-five percent of the total budget.

In 1980 the Lou Penney Fund was established through a sizeable bequest in Lou's will. Shortly thereafter the income generated by the Penney fund and the Memorial Fund was sufficient to take over the "margin of excellence" that is vital if Cal is to remain competitive on a national basis. The Friends now could concentrate on increasing the endowment, so the California Crew Permanent Fund was established in 1983 under the leadership of Claude Hutchison '59. Its goal is to fully endow the sport of rowing at Berkeley, which would take at least two-and-a-half million dollars.

By June 1985 the total of the four funds came to more than one million dollars, so in fall 1985 Gary Rogers '63 kicked off a campaign to complete the endowment. A whirlwind effort, with the rallying cry "Cal Crew Forever," began and by May 1986 two million dollars had been reached. A portion of this amount is in stock, thus its value fluctuates, and a good portion is in pledges and bequests, so the crew still is dependent on the athletic department budget. But rowing is all but assured of becoming Berkeley's first fully endowed sport.

THE NATIONAL TEAM

THE UNITED STATES, represented by several different university crews, won the gold medal in the eight-oared rowing event in every Olympics from 1920 until 1960. There had been intense debates between the college eights and the rowing clubs for many years, but with a single exception, clubs had been unsuccessful in Olympic trials.

After World War II, sports recognition became a part of international power politics, and most countries began an intensive drive to develop strong national teams, including rowing. A highly-organized support system with solid financial backing blurred the amateur status that had been such an ingrained part of rowing. The Eastern-bloc countries were the first to achieve impressive success with state-supported national teams, and they were quickly followed by West Germany and other countries. They held mass training and screenings, emphasized high-tech equipment improvements, and selected older, more mature oarsmen with years of competitive experience. Performances that heretofore had been considered impossible became the norm.

The United States was slow in accepting the need for a national rowing team to remain competitive with other countries. Gradually, the Olympic committee became convinced. In 1960 the United States, represented by Navy, lost the eight-oared race in the Olympic Games for the first time. Four years later, a carefully-recruited club crew, Vesper, won the gold medal for the United States in the finals at Tokyo, making a good case for a national crew. Then Harvard's crew lost in the 1968 Olympics, while Washington had a poor showing in the Pan-American Games. It was the final blow, and the Olympic committee agreed that an open selection process nationwide was the only way for the U.S. to again defeat the elite eight-oared crews of other countries. It seemed clear that the club crews had been unsuccessful in competing against the college teams only because the clubs depended on local part-time oarsmen who held down full-time jobs.

After 1968 U.S. rowing authorities organized broader-based selection methods to find the most qualified oarsmen throughout the nation. They established training camps all over the country. They screened coaches to seek the best in the various regions where rowing tryouts were held. The process took several years to perfect. Gradually American rowing on an international level improved considerably.

The U.S. national team in recent years has started to climb back to the top. The U.S. eight in the 1984 Olympics was an excellent example; they were the top international eight in Europe and rowed unbelievably fast times. At the Olympics in Los Angeles, they had to settle for a silver medal, due to a tactical error—they ignored a fast Canadian crew, whom they had soundly defeated previously, until it was too late, sitting on top of the defending New Zealand champions instead. Still, it was obvious from their overall performance that the U.S. had regained its top rating in eight-oared rowing.

The ultimate goal of a national team is to have the eight most qualified oarsmen in the country in one boat, one crew. Such a truly representative U.S. crew would have no trouble winning its share of gold medals. The greatest change for the oarsmen in the revised selection method is that, if properly done, it assures that each candidate will be judged upon his own ability, not rise or fall by his original crew's record. Of course, there can be no question of politics, regional bias, personal prejudice, or favoritism, all of which has been intimated as the national program has grown. Although recent years have disproved these rumors, the danger does exist and must be guarded against at all times.

California's crewmen have fared rather well on the national team, considering that for a time the Bears were suffering from a down-cycle in the win/loss column. As their fortunes have improved, so has their selection record. Since the national team began in the seventies, a number of undergraduates and an even larger number of recent graduates have been invited to the national camps for tryouts or have entered open trials for international competition. One by-product has been an increased emphasis on small boats at Berkeley: an oarsman who aspires to international competition had better have a foundation of small-boat racing if he expects to have a chance.

The number of Cal candidates has increased each year, starting in 1975 with Pat Hayes, who rowed in the four with in the Pan-American Games at Mexico City. In the pre-Olympic year 1983, no fewer than nineteen Cal crewmen, undergraduate and alumni, were invited to national camps or were in open competition. Not all of them made it, but Berkeley definitely has contributed its share of talent:

Pat Hayes '73
Four with, 1975 Pan-American Games, Mexico, gold medal
Four with, 1976 Olympics, Montreal

John Bacon '77
Lightweight eight, 1981 World Championships, Germany

Paul Prioleau '79
Four without, 1979 World Championships, Yugoslavia
Member, 1980 Olympic squad

Chris Clark '82
Pair with, 1983 Pan-American Games, Venezuela, silver medal
Pair without, 1985 World Championships, Belgium

George Livingston '82
Pair with, 1983 Pan-American Games, Venezuela, silver medal

Mark Zembsch '82
Cox, 1983 Pre-Elite eight
Cox, eight, 1985 World Championships, Belgium, bronze medal
Cox, four with, 1986 Goodwill Games, Russia, silver medal
Cox, eight, 1986 World Championships, England, bronze medal
Cox, pair with, 1987 World Championships, Denmark

Chris Huntington '83
#4, Pre-Elite Eight, 1981 Thames Cup Championships, England

Port alternate, 1984 Olympic squad
#7, eight, 1985 World Championships, Belgium, bronze medal
Four with, 1986 Goodwill Games, Russia, silver medal
Four with, 1986 World Championships, England, bronze medal
#4, eight, 1987 Pan-American Games, Indianapolis, gold medal

Dan Louis '83
Stroke, Pre-Elite Eight, 1981 Thames Cup Championships, England
Port alternate, 1983 Pan-American Games, Venezuela

Dave DeRuff '83
#7, Pre-Elite Eight, 1981 Thames Cup Championships, England
#7, eight, 1983 Pan-American Games, Venezuela, gold medal
Pair without, 1984 Olympic squad

Ted Swinford '83
Pair with, 1985 World Championships, Belgium
Four without, 1986 World Championships, England, gold medal
Four without, 1987 World Championships, Denmark, bronze medal

Eric Klug '84
Lightweight eight, 1983 World Championships, West Germany

Henry Mattiessen '84
Four with, 1985 World Championships, Belgium
Pair with, 1986 World Championships, England
Eight, 1987 Pan-American Games, Indianapolis, gold medal

Tony Matan '85
1983 Pre-Elite Eight

Brian Cuneo '85
1983 Pre-Elite Eight

Eric Cohn '85
Stroke, 1982 Pre-Elite Eight, England, gold medal
Stroke, 1982 Pre-Elite Eight, Holland

Stewart Huntington '87
Lightweight eight, 1986 World Championships, England

Chip McKibbon '87
Port alternate, 1987 Pan-American Games, Indianapolis

Tim Ryan '90
Junior National Eight, 1985 and 1986 World Junior Championships, silver medal

GLOSSARY

Note: This is not intended as a complete glossary of rowing terms. It covers some of the most common terms which may confuse the layreader or which appear in this text.

AFT: at or toward the stern end of the boat.

BEVEL: the act of turning the oar blade from the almost flat position it assumes on the recovery to the vertical position at the catch.

BLADE: the spoon-shaped end of the oar that gives purchase in the water. Depending on its design, it varies from seven to nine inches in width and twenty-three to thirty-three inches in length.

BOWMAN: the oarsman sitting in the front of the boat. Also called the bow position or the #1 position.

BUTTON: the wide leather or plastic collar attached to the shaft or loom of the oar to prevent the oar from slipping through the oarlock.

COXSWAIN OR COX: the crewman who is responsible for steering the boat and for giving commands. To save weight, he usually is much smaller than the oarsmen: about five feet six inches and 125 pounds. Usually he sits in the stern of the boat facing the stroke oarsman. In a few boats he lies on his back in front of the bowman and inside the boat with just his head showing. This arrangement provides better frontal vision and better weight distribution. Despite a popular misconception, the coxswain does *not* set the cadence. The stroke oarsman sets the rhythm and raises or lowers the stroke beat. The coxswain takes the count off of the stroke's oar blade.

COX BOX: contains an amplifier that connects with several small speakers spread along the inside of the boat so all can hear the cox's commands. (He no longer needs the traditional cox's megaphone strapped to his head.) It also connects with a sensor located underneath the stroke's seat and gives a constant readout of the stroke cadence or strokes per minute. In addition it has a stopwatch to show elapsed time. It plugs in in front of his seat in the boat.

CRAB: occurs when the oar blade, caught in the water, acts as an immediate brake on the forward progress of the boat. Usually occurs when the oar blade is turned past its normal, almost flat position on the recovery of the stroke. If the oar blade catches in the water in this position, it acts as a diving plane, forcing the blade down and the handle up. The result can pin the oarsman at the forward part of his position or even catapult him out of the boat. Until it is disentangled a crab can stop a boat completely.

DECK OR BOATDECK: the covered portion of the boat located at both ends. The bow deck starts just forward of the bowman's position and the stern deck starts just behind the coxswain's position. The covering is varnished silk or a thin plastic sheet.

DRIVE: the power part of the stroke cycle between the catch and the finish. It is accomplished primarily with the legs, with the arm pull and shoulder swing distributing the leg drive for the pulling part of the stroke. It is for this reason the seat has wheels.

EIGHT: a racing boat or shell that employs eight oarsmen with an oar apiece and a coxswain to steer.

FEATHER: the act of turning the oar from the vertical position at the end of the drive to the almost flat position for the recovery. At the same time the oar handle is somewhat depressed and pushed away from the body. The blade thus comes cleanly out of the water while describing an arc.

FIN OR SKEG: a small thin piece of metal attached in a vertical plane to the keel of the boat just behind the coxswain's position. It acts much the same as a centerboard on a sailboat and helps to hold a straight course.

FINISH: other than the end of a race, a finish is the end of the drive portion of a stroke cycle. As the finish is completed, the oarsman immediately initiates the recovery of the stroke by feathering the oar, pushing his hands away from his body, and swinging his body away from the bow. The legs have been driven completely down, the arms have pulled the oar handle almost, but not quite, into the body, and the body has swung a bit past perpendicular.

FORE: at or toward the bow end of the boat.

GUNWALE: the horizontal strip of wood running along the uppermost part of the boat. It is the point of attachment for the ribs, knees, and skin surrounding the open portion of the boat where the oarsmen and coxswain sit.

HANDLE: where the oarsman grips the oar. In today's oars, the handle is the only part of the oar that is wood; the rest is primarily carbon fiber.

HEEL CUPS: metal or plastic cups at the bottom of the footboards to help keep the feet in the footboards.

HENLEY-STYLE RACING: a regatta with heats of two boats at a time as at Henley-on-the-Thames, England.

HOLD OR HOLD WATER: a command given by the coxswain to an individual position, to one of the sides (i.e. port), or to the entire crew. It is used to turn, slow down, or stop the course of the boat by holding the blade vertically in the water.

KEEL: the structure at the very bottom of the boat that runs its full length. It marks the centerline of the boat and is the point of attachment for all the other portions (i.e. ribs). It also is used as a term of balance, as in "Get the boat on keel." A boat is "on keel" when there is no tilt to either side.

LAYBACK: the amount of body swing of the oarsman past the vertical toward the bow.

LEATHER: a piece of leather or plastic about four inches long, which surrounds that portion of the oar that is in the oarlock and protects it from excessive wear in the lock. The button is located at the handle end of the leather.

LOOM: the shaft of the oar between the handle and the blade.

OARLOCK: a U-shaped metal or plastic device that rotates around a pin attached to the outrigger. The oar is placed in the oarlock's open end and is then locked in by a bar or "gate" that winds across the open end of the U. The button on the loom of the oar keeps the oar in place by snugging up against the oarlock.

OPEN WATER: more than a boatlength.

OUTRIGGER: two or three metal tubes attached to the gunwale that converge opposite an oarsman's position at a point about thirty inches from the centerline of the boat. A very small platform at this location supports a rigid pin for the oarlock. The oarlock rotates about the pin as the oarsman rows. In normal placement or "rig," outriggers are at each oarsman's position on alternate sides of the boat. It is the force of the drive against this pin when the blade is locked in the water that propels the boat forward.

PORT: the left side of the boat when facing the bow. In conventional eights, fours, and pairs the stroke position is on the port side, although some coaches use a starboard stroke. Port oarsmen use the right hand to bevel and feather the oar, letting it turn in the grip of the left hand, whereas starboard oarsmen do the opposite.

PUDDLES: the circular disturbance made in the water with each stroke of an oar. The eight makes four puddles on each side of the boat for every stroke. The distance between each set is called "run" or "spacing."

READY ALL: the preparatory command to start rowing, followed by the command of execution such as "row" or "hike." At this first command the oarsman assumes the catch position at the stern end of his slide, ready to catch together on the command of execution. Although this command is used by many, it has been replaced in official racing by the international commands which are in French and used in the Olympics and the world championships: *"Êtes-vous prête? Parte,"* or "Are you ready? Row."

RECOVERY: that portion of the stroke following the feather release. The oar is out of the water, beveled, the body swings back past vertical as the arms re-extend from the body and push the blade back towards the bow, and the seat travels back down the slides toward the stern. It is a blended movement coordinated by the crew.

RELEASE: when the power cycle ends and the oar is feathered out of the water. It is essential that this is done cleanly, without catching in the water and slowing the boat down. Just as a crew must catch together, they must release together.

RIB: a thin strip of wood from the keel to the gunwale to hold the shape of the skin.

RIG: the arrangement of outriggers down the boat, usually on alternate sides from bow to stern. Germans rig the #4 and #5 positions on the same side and alternate others. Italians rig stroke and bow positions on alternate sides and the rest alternate in pairs.

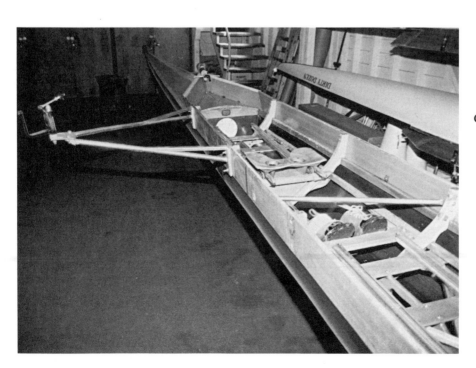

Close-up of a conventional outrigger.

ROWOVER: to win a race a crew must row the full distance and cross the finish line even when the other crew(s) have canceled or been disqualified. If there is no other opponent the remaining crew may row as slowly as it desires.

RUDDER: a vertical attachment in the stern underwater portion of the boat that can swing in a partial arc on a pin and is used to steer the boat. In older shells it was attached to the very stern end. Now it is a much smaller metal, fin-like rudder located behind the fin. It is controlled by the coxswain using pulleys and rope lines.

RUN: the distance the shell glides between strokes. It can be judged by noting the space between the sets of puddles. At a very high stroke there is little to no space between puddles, hence "a crew is catching its puddles."

SCULL OAR: one of two such oars used by one man, it is between nine and ten feet long and weighs three to four pounds. Scull oars are used by one man in a single scull, by two men each with two in a double scull, or by four men, each with two, in a quadruple scull or "quad."

SEAT: a wooden seat molded to fit the oarsman's buttocks and mounted on wheels that run back and forth on tracks. The main purpose of this sliding seat is to enable the oarsman to engage his leg power against the oar when it is "hooked" in the water. In a conventional rowboat, all the work is done by the back and arms. With a sliding seat the most powerful muscles of the body, the legs, are brought into play, while the back and arms are used mainly to distribute the leg drive evenly. After the release, when the legs are driven down, the seat is used to reposition the crewman back at the stern end of his slide, ready for the catch of the next stroke.

SINGLE SCULL: a shell with one oarsman rowing with a sculling oar in either hand.

STAKEBOATS: a series of small skiffs or rowboats anchored in a line at the start of the race course with one in each lane. Each skiff is occupied by an individual who holds onto the stern of the racing shell so the crews are lined up evenly. This can be difficult if there is a crosswind and/or a strong current. Many race courses have turned to a starting platform, a pier-like structure or large float with slots for each lane.

STARBOARD: the right side of the boat when facing the bow. In a standard rigged boat the odd numbered positions are starboard and the even numbered are port. The starboard oarsman uses his left hand to feather and bevel the oar, letting it turn in the grip of his right hand. Being right- or left-handed has nothing to do with which side an oarsman is rowing.

STRETCHER: two footrests to keep the foot down, either a footboard with a heel cup and wide laced strap or, in the newer shells, a light shoe. The stretcher is a single unit and attaches to the gunwale at the top and the keel at the bottom. The unit may be shifted fore and aft so that the oarsman can use the maximum amount of the slides as his leg length will allow. Set in position with thumb screws, it becomes the very foundation of the leg drive.

STROKE: the movement is the complete cycle from catch to catch: catch, drive, finish, recovery, and catch. It should flow together in one blended action with no noticeable change from one phase of the stroke to another. The bladework of bevel and feather also must be blended in at the appropriate time. Each oarsman must coordinate every phase of his stroke with his fellow oarsmen to keep the boat balanced or "on keel" at all times.

The individual called the stroke is the man in the #8 position who sits right in front of the coxswain. He sets the beat or cadence, and it is his sense of rhythm that sets the swing for the rest of the crew. If the coxswain counts out the cadence, he takes it off the stroke oar.

STROKES PER MINUTE: the crew's pace is measured in strokes per minute. A stroke is the full cycle from catch to the following catch. Coaches use a stopwatch calibrated for three or four strokes which show the rate per minute. The cox box gives a constant readout of strokes per minute. Different stages in a race, as well as the length of the race, determine the rate of strokes per minute. The first ten to twenty strokes in a racing start may be in the range of forty to forty-four strokes per minute as is the sprint at the finish of many races. The rate for the middle of the race differs with the distance to be rowed. The international, and now national, distance of 2,000 meters is considered a sprint race, with most conditioned crews seldom dropping as low as thirty-six strokes a minute. The previous distance races of three to four miles were rowed in the twenty-eight to thirty-two range.

SWEEP OARS: a single oar used by each man in an eight four, or pair oared boat. It's about twelve-and-a-half feet long and weighs seven pounds, with a blade about two feet long and eight inches wide.

WASHING OUT: when the oarsman lets his blade pull out of the water while still in the drive. This is usually caused by pulling the oar handle down in the lap and can pull the boat off keel and cause a wave of white water that oarsmen in front of him encounter on their recovery.

WAY ENOUGH: command by the coxswain or coach to stop rowing.

Close-up of sliding seat, tracks, and footboards.

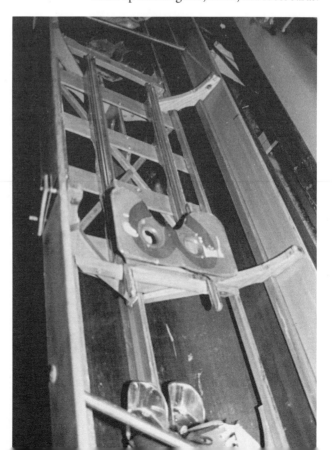

APPENDIX A
ANNUAL BOATING OF CALIFORNIA CREWS

//

THIS LIST IS BASED UPON HOW the coach listed his crews at the end of the season on the oar blades and plaques in the club room at the Ky Ebright Boathouse. In some years various combinations of men may have been used in various races; when the coach recorded oarsmen from earlier in the season, they are listed below following the coxswain. Every effort has been made to obtain both first and last names, although in some cases that was not possible.

1893
No crew listed: start of the Boating Association

1894
Honorary listing

8–Russ Avery 4–S. S. Sanborn
7–Stanley Easton 3–N. C. Trew
6–Joseph Pierce 2–E. P. Foltz
5–C. H. E. Laughlin 1–David A. Porter
Cox–Peter Browning

1895
4–N. C. Trew 2–W. E. Cole
3–C. H. B. Laughlin 1–Hutchinson
Cox–R. E. Easton

1896
4–Wilson 2–Allen
3–Wittenmeyer 1–Peck
Cox–Danforth

1897
4–Cole 2–Dean
3–McDonnell 1–English
Cox–Hammer

1898
4–Trew 2–Prendergast
3–Grinwood 1–Hopper
Cox–Clausses

1899
Astoria Regatta Junior Champions

4–Clifton H. Tracy 2–Roy Waggershouser
3–Roy Fryer 1–Jimmy Hopper
Cox–Francis A. Wilder

1900
4–Frank V. Kington 2–David Goodale
3–J. W. Barnes 1–Minot E. Scott
Cox–unknown

1901
Class Regatta Winners

4–Cerf 2–Moore
3–Smith 1–Pitchford
Cox–Smithson

1902
Senior Crew

4–Foster 2–Pickett
3–Childs 1–Duden
Cox–Baird

1903
4–Harley 2–Smith
3–Dandy 1–Grindley
Cox–unknown

1904
Pacific Coast Champions

4–Bunnell 2–Anloff
3–E. A. Bannister 1–Grindley
Cox–J. P. Loeb

1905
Pacific Coast Champions

4–E. A. Bannister 2–D. E. Evans
3–George C. Jones 1–Edgar V. Dodge
Cox–J. P. Loeb

1906
4–Schmidt 2–W. K. Tuller
3–George C. Jones 1–McFarland
Cox–E. J. Loeb

1907
Varsity

8–Dean Witter 4–F. W. Bush Jr.
7–W. K. Tuller 3–R. F. Williams
6–C. R. McKillican 2–Ivan J. Ball
5–G. F. Ashley 1–L. Evans
Cox–Paul A. Myers

Freshmen

4–Austin Sperry
3–W. R. Schroeder

2–H. H. Ashley
1–O. H. Robertson

Cox–A. F. Bray

1908
Varsity

8–Dean Witter
7–T. A. Davidson
6–O. H. Robertson
5–H. H. Ashley

4–G. F. Ashley
3–W. H. Schroeder
2–Ivan J. Ball
1–H. H. Dignan

Cox–Paul A. Myers, L. McSpaden

Freshmen

8–Langstroth
7–B. L. Cope
6–Nelson Bowen
5–D. P. Hardy

4–H. L. Jensen
3–S. E. Jackson
2–F. A. Randall
1–J. A. Dias

Cox–H. C. Kelly

1909
Varsity

8–O. H. Robertson
7–T. A. Davidson
6–Ivan J. Ball
5–H. H. Ashley
Cox–Lewis McSpaden

4–D. P. Hardy
3–H. H. Dignan
2–Harvey L. Davis
1–I. G. Markwart

Freshmen

8–A. P. Cox
7–B. R. Small
6–L. L. Doud
5–R. E. Maynard

4–A. L. Beal
3–R. C. Ingram
2–C. A. Quitzou
1–Steve Malatesta

Cox–Duff, J. S. Halbert

1910
Varsity

8–Steve Malatesta
7–T. A. Davison
6–Everett L. Ball
5–H. H. Ashley

4–D. P. Hardy
3–I. G. Markwart
2–B. B. Blake
1–S. P. Colt Jr.

Cox–Lewis McSpaden

1911
Varsity

8–Steve Malatesta
7–T. A. Davidson
6–Everett L. Ball
5–Rey Maynard

4–D. P. Hardy
3–A. L. Beal
2–B. L. Cope
1–S. P. Colt Jr.

Cox–H. C. Kelly

Freshmen

8–R. C. Miller
7–C. E. Denman
6–R. S. Fuller
5–H. D. Ulery

4–R. C. Shaw
3–F. C. Cordes
2–G. C. Ferch
1–L. P Hunt

Cox–T. C. Hutton

1912
Varsity

8–D. P. Hardy
7–C. E. Denman
6–M. A. Lee
5–Rey Maynard

4–R. C. Shaw Jr.
3–J. S. Halbert
2–Arthur Eaton
1–Steve Malatesta

Cox–T. C. Hutton

Freshmen

8–I. F. Davies
7–L. C. Morehead
6–R. N. Hellner
5–B. T. Rocca

4–Herbert Hardy
3–C. Z. Sutton
2–R. E. Merritt
1–F. D. Halbert

Cox–H. H. Hope

1913
Varsity

8–Arthur Eaton
7–L. W. Georgeson
6–R. C. Shaw Jr.
5–C. J. Williams

4–R. N. Hallner
3–R. E. Merritt
2–O. W. Young
1–C. Z. Sutton

Cox–L. T. Coombs

Freshmen

8–T. E. Gay
7–B. H. Pratt
6–J. P. Anderson
5–H. A. Norris

4–W. B. Augier
3–R. J. Still
2–J. E. Wright
1–F. D. Heastand

Cox–J. C. Howard

1914
Varsity

8–R. E. Merritt
7–M. A. Lee
6–R. C. Shaw Jr.
5–W. A. Falck

4–Herbert Hardy
3–L. W. Georgeson
2–F. C. Cordes
1–C. Z. Sutton

Cox–J. C. Howard

1915
Varsity

8–L. H. Penney
7–Fred Darnell
6–R. C. Shaw Jr.
5–B. H. Osborn

4–W. A. Falck
3–C. R. Kierulff
2–R. E. Merritt
1–John Burns

Cox–J. C. Howard

Freshmen

8–Day
7–W. B. Carter
6–A. C. McFarland
5–Frank Lamb

4–Miller
3–L. D. DeMund
2–M. Thornburg
1–McNeil

Cox–Humanson

1916
Varsity

8–W. A. Falck
7–L. H. Penney
6–E. P. Congdon
5–Frank Lamb

4–Herbert Hardy
3–H. M. Black
2–J. W. Clune
1–H. R. Hogaboom

Cox–Ernest Camper, Guy Gale
L. D. DeMund, G. L. Ebner

Junior Varsity

8–T. Wilson
7–G. L. Ebner
6–L. D. DeMund
5–E. B. Butler

4–W. B. Carter
3–H. T. Howard
2–M. Thornburg
1–A. J. Swank

Cox–G. Gale

Freshmen

8–H. Y. Stebbins
7–Merril Brown
6–J. T. Donnellan
5–L. R. Dykes

4–M. W. Jones
3–C. W. Farmer
2–R. A. Gardner
1–F. A. Reed

Cox–J. S. Ward

1917
Varsity

8–W. P. Thomas	4–H. Y. Stebbins
7–L. H. Penney	3–W. A. Falck
6–C. L. Tilden Jr.	2–M. W. Jones
5–L. R. Dykes	1–F. A. Reed

Cox–Guy H. Gale

Freshmen

8–G. S. Hinsdale	4–Jack Okell
7–W. A. Martin	3–H. R. Johnson
6–Neville Edwards	2–S. A. Anderson
5–J. J. Kemp	1–J. R. Wagy

Cox–A. J. Houston

1918
World War I (No crews)

H. Y. Stebbins elected as honorary captain of the varsity crew

1919
Varsity

8–H. D. Pischel	4–L. H. Henderson
7–H. R. Johnson	3–W. A. Martin Jr.
6–C. L. Tilden Jr.	2–G. S. Hinsdale
5–R. C. Downs	1–R. W. Griffin

Cox–A. J. Houston

Junior Varsity

8–A. E. Larsen	4–H. E. Simi
7–F. G. Meehan	3–J. M. Rogers
6–T. W. Nelson	2–W. Lyons
5–B. B. Knight	1–G. N. Nash

Cox–J. W. Winstead

Freshmen

8–C. T. Burnham	4–Henry de Roulet
7–J. H. Reinhardt	3–R. K. Wheeler
6–H. R. Blohm	2–W. R. Baillard
5–J. M. Ahlswede	1–K. E. Kunze

Cox–P. J. Goldschmidt

1920
Varsity

8–A. E. Larsen	4–Henry de Roulet
7–R. C. Downs	3–F. G. Mehan
6–J. H. Reinhart	2–G. S. Hinsdale
5–E. F. Marquardson	1–J. M. Rogers

Cox–J. S. Winstead

Junior Varsity

8–W. Lyons	4–Dan A. McMillan Jr.
7–L. A. Brown	3–B. B. Knight
6–A. F. Lawrence	2–C. E. Reynolds
5–T. J. Kemp	1–E. McAllister

Cox–K. H. Repath

Freshmen

8–M. S. Jacobus	4–J. M. Reynolds
7–A. C. Holler	3–J. E. Jardine
6–J. H. Threlkeld	2–M. L. Hoen
5–G. A. Williams	1–T. D. Huls

Cox–H. S. Gunn

1921
Varsity Pacific Coast Champions

8–A. E. Larsen	4–T. J. Kemp
7–F. G. Mehan	3–L. A. Brown
6–Dan A. McMillan Jr.	2–E. F. Marquardson
5–R. C. Downs	1–J. M. Rogers

Cox–K. H. Repath

Junior Varsity

8–M. S. Jacobus	4–C. R. Steinort
7–G. A. Williams	3–J. E. Jardine
6–H. F. Blohm	2–M. L. Hoen
5–B. H. Howell	1–W. W. Davison

Cox–F. Hellman

Freshmen

8–H. R. Peacock	4–R. J. Donahue
7–J. L. Howard	3–A. J. Donnels
6–R. W. Bolling	2–J. A. de Armond
5–V. W. Rosendahl	1–E. de R. Morton

Cox–J. B. Dixon

1922
Varsity

8–Dan A. McMillan Jr.	4–C. R. Steinert
7–G. A. Williams	3–L. A. Brown
6–Porter Sesnon	2–R. W. Belling
5–Burl Howell	1–Brooks Walker

Cox–Paul Knight

Junior Varsity

8–J. M. Rogers	4–R. Gardner
7–C. Loskamp	3–H. Bailey
6–W. Linstrum	2–J. Threlkeld
5–H. Langley	1–H. Dunn

Cox–F. Hellman

Freshmen Pacific Coast Champions

8–T. Halton	4–Livingston
7–H. Gall	3–Carson
6–Barlow	2–Rea
5–Stanton	1–Stewart

Cox–Renick

1923
Varsity

8–R. F. Gardner	4–J. W. Lindstrum
7–W. G. Donaldson	3–H. W. Bailey
6–G. S. Cranmer	2–H. A. Dunn
5–G. A. Williams	1–C. V. Laskamp

Cox–J. B. Dixon

Freshmen

8–F. M. Holland	4–K. G. Morton
7–S. W. Moncure	3–R. H. Drews
6–R. H. McCreary	2–K. M. Emery
5–G. A. Gibbons	1–M. J. Carr

Cox–O. E. Hotle

1924
Varsity

8–G. S. Cranmer	4–W. T. Beard
7–W. G. Donaldson	3–J. H. Stewart
6–F. M. Holland	2–Brooks Walker
5–E. L. Harbach	1–C. V. Laskamp

Cox–O. E. Hotle

Junior Varsity

8–K. Craycroft	4–W. Linstrum
7–S. W. Moncure	3–H. B. Bolton
6–K. G. Morton	2–W. T. Walker
5–G. A. Gibbons	1–E. Morton
	Cox–A. Armstrong

Freshmen

8–Joel Geddes	4–Neal Dixon
7–Warner Burke	3–John Sanders
6–Hardy Hutchinson	2–Neal Roberts
5–Shasta Green	1–J. Don Locke
	Cox–Don Blessing

1925
Varsity

8–G. S. Cranmer	4–H. C. Hutchinson
7–S. W. Moncure	3–E. L. Harbach
6–C. P. de Jonge	2–W. Murphy
5–E. W. Berlin	1–J. D. Locke
	Cox–O. E. Hotle

Junior Varsity Pacific Coast Champions

8–F. M. Holland	4–D. Dunwoody
7–T. O'Sullivan	3–J. Long
6–K. G. Morton	2–W. T. Beard
5–G. A. Gibbons	1–C. Morse
	Cox–Don Blessing

Freshmen Pacific Coast Champions

8–Al Moe	4–Jack McKenzie
7–Jack Valentine	3–Budge Holland
6–Charlie Dressler	2–Ed Jasper
5–Al Rydlander	1–Ward Von Tillow
	Cox–George Richardson

1926
Varsity

8–Al Moe	4–Ross H. Babcock
7–Marvin Stalder	3–C. P. de Jonge
6–E. W. Berlin	2–H. C. Hutchinson
5–Harold Hoover	1–Ward Von Tillow
	Cox–Don Blessing

Junior Varsity

8–Tom Beck	4–Charlie Dressler
7–Jack Valentine	3–Budge Holland
6–Dave Dunwoody	2–W. T. Beard
5–Al Rydlander	1–Wyman Vernon
	Cox–Owen Hotle

Freshmen

8–Pete Donlon	4–Jack Brinck
7–Willard Graham	3–Fran Frederick
6–Bill Thompson	2–Harry Fawke
5–Al Drout	1–Ed Meadows
	Cox–Vincent Mullin

1927
Varsity Pacific Coast Champions

8–Pete Donlon	4–Carrol Dressler
7–Fran Frederick	3–C. P. de Jonge
6–Bill Thompson	2–H. C. Hutchinson
5–Al Rydlander	1–Ward Von Tillow
	Cox–Don Blessing

Junior Varsity Pacific Coast Champions

8–Al Moe	4–Harry Fawke
7–Harry Miller	3–Marvin Stalder
6–Edson W. Berlin	2–Dave Dunwoody
5–Harold Hoover	1–Terry O'Sullivan
	Cox–Vincent Mullin

Freshmen

8–Jim Workman	4–Gale Powers
7–Bill Dally	3–Hays
6–Bob Beinhorn	2–Stimson
5–Bell	1–Gilmore
	Cox–Jimmy Logan

1928
Varsity Olympic, IRA, and Pacific Coast Champions

8–Pete Donlon	4–Bill Thompson
7–Hub Caldwell	3–Fran Frederick
6–Jim Workman	2–Jack Brinck
5–Bill Dally	1–Marvin Stalder
	Cox–Don Blessing
	Al Rydlander, Carrol Dressler

Junior Varsity

8–Al Moe	4–Hugh Habenicht
7–Bill Dally	3–Marvin Stalder
6–Jim Workman	2–Stimson
5–Allen Goode	1–Gilmore
	Cox–Vincent Mullin

Freshmen

8–Victor Owen	4–Ken Stowell
7–Howard Wells	3–Lee Pope, Meade
6–Phil Condit	2–Hodge Stevens, Knight
5–Harvey Granger	1–Walt Silver
	Cox–Julian Montgomery

1929
Varsity Pacific Coast Champions

8–Pete Donlon	4–Jim Workman
7–Hub Caldwell	3–Fran Frederick
6–Bill Thompson	2–Jack Brinck
5–Bill Dally	1–Ward Von Tillow
	Cox–Vincent Mullin

Junior Varsity

8–Richard Knight	4–Smith
7–Hays	3–Lee Pope
6–Phil Condit	2–Hodge Stevens
5–Bill Woodward	1–Harvey Granger
	Cox–Jimmy Logan

Freshmen Pacific Coast Champions

8–Duncan Gregg	4–Bert Jastram
7–Mike Murray	3–Davie Nelder
6–Herm Holman	2–Bill Van Voorhis
5–Dave Dunlap	1–Virgil Carlson, Bill Mason
	Cox–Norris Graham
	James Blair

1930
Varsity

8–Duncan Gregg	4–Bert Jastram
7–Hub Caldwell	3–Dave Dunlap
6–Herm Holman	2–Jack Brinck
5–Bill Dally	1–Harvey Granger
	Cox–J. E. Logan

Junior Varsity

8–Ed Salisbury	4–Ed Goldeen
7–Lee Pope	3–Andrew Davie
6–Jim Workman	2–Burnel Hyde
5–Morris Mathewson	1–Bill Woodward
	Cox–Julian Montgomery

Freshmen

8–Reg Rhein	4–Luther Everett, Moore
7–Bob Peterson	3–Joe Demeter, Fred Enmark
6–Frank Archibald	2–Howard Lackey, Roy Jacobes
5–Lewis Newman	1–Normand
	Cox–Lloyd Scouler

1931
Varsity

8–Reg Rhein Sr.	4–Spencer Duguid
7–Bill Woodward	3–Herm Holman
6–Duncan Gregg	2–Burt Jastram
5–Dave Dunlap	1–Harvey Granger
	Cox–Norris Graham

Junior Varsity

8–Ed Salisbury	4–Harold Tower
7–Lee Pope	3–Carl Pedersen
6–Bill Hudgins	2–Henry Gage
5–John Irwin	1–Glenn Rogers
	Cox–Julian Montgomery

Freshmen

8–Taylor	4–F. Dunlap
7–Van Winkle	3–Chamberlin
6–Ed Hagen	2–Dundon
5–Roger Chickering	1–Emanuels
	Cox–Blunden

1932
Varsity Olympic, IRA, and Pacific Coast Champions

8–Ed Salisbury	4–Burt Jastram
7–James Blair	3–Charlie Chandler
6–Duncan Gregg	2–Harold Tower
5–Dave Dunlap	1–Winslow Hall
	Cox–Norris Graham
	Herm Holman, Carl Pedersen

Junior Varsity

8–Jack Dennison	4–Ed Hagen
7–Herm Holman	3–Joe Demeter
6–Hayes McLellan	2–Bill Hudgins
5–Bill Van Voorhis	1–Morris Mathewson
	Cox–Phil Shipley
Louis Neuman, Glenn Rogers, Bob Dyk, John Irwin	

Freshmen

8–George Jamieson	4–Bob Walker
7–Marshall Haywood	3–Elmer Moore, John Stage
6–Tevis Thompson	2–Jim McKinney
5–Harry Jones	1–Ward Klink, Jack Martin
	Cox–Reg Watt
	Bengstrom

1933
Varsity

8–Harold Tower	4–Howard Lackey
7–Winslow Hall	3–Charlie Chandler
6–Hays McLellan	2–Reg Rhine Sr.
5–Bill Van Voorhis	1–Morris Mathewson
	Cox–Norris Graham, Reg Watt

Junior Varsity

8–Jack Dennison	4–Ed Hagen
7–Joe Demeter	3–Green
6–Nathan Rubin	2–Henry Gage
5–Harry Jones	1–Beinhorn
	Cox–Phillip Shipley

Freshmen

8–Bob Malone	4–Jack Sexson
7–Frank Dunlap	3–Charles Schuster
6–Norm Sutcliffe	2–Ken Oulie, Evald Swanson
5–Joe Pease	1–Ed Goree, John Wrenn
	Cox–Tom Kruse

1934
Varsity IRA Champions

8–Dick Burnley	4–Carroll Brigham
7–Larry Dodge	3–Evald Swanson
6–Ferd Elvin	2–Jack Yates
5–Ray Andresen	1–Frank Dunlap
	Cox–Reg Watt
Martin, Chandler, Bob Walker, Ed Goree	

Junior Varsity

8–Norm Sutcliffe	4–Ed Hagen
7–Charles Schuster	3–Joe Pease
6–Ken Oulie	2–Bob Walker
5–Harry Jones	1–Ed Goree
	Cox–Elwin Gregory

Freshmen

8–Stevens	4–Bill Franklin
7–Tymstra	3–Botman
6–Addison Bowers	2–Tickner, Bob McNamara
5–Howard Barney	1–Harvey Fremming
	Cox–Grover Clark

1935
Varsity IRA Champions

8–Gene Berkenkamp	4–Carroll Brigham
7–Larry Dodge	3–Evald Swanson
6–Tevis Thompson	2–Jack Yates
5–Ray Andresen	1–Harley Fremming
	Cox–Reg Watt
LeRoy Briggs, Elmer Moore, John Stage, Jim McKinney, Addison Bowers	

Junior Varsity

8–Dick Burnley	4–Addison Bowers
7–LeRoy Briggs	3–Elmer Moore
6–Ferd Elvin	2–Jim McKinney
5–John Stage	1–Frank Dunlap
	Cox–Tommy Maxwell

Freshmen

8–Larry Arpin	4–Al Daggett
7–Henry Steinmetz	3–Bob Knowles
6–Henry Peters	2–Wayne Gregg, Kurt Rocca
5–John Hoefer	1–Pete Porterfield

Cox–Rush Clark, Henry Kueny

1936
Varsity

8–Larry Arpin	4–Gene Berkenkamp
7–Larry Dodge	3–Evald Swanson
6–Tevis Thompson	2–Carroll Brigham
5–Al Daggett	1–Harley Fremming

Cox–Grover Clark, Tommy Maxwell
Charles Schuster, Jim Graves, Frank Dunlap,
Jim McKinney

Junior Varsity

8–Ken Oulie	4–Tevis Thomson
7–Charles Schuster	3–Elmer Moore
6–Henry Peters	2–Jim McKinney
5–Jim Graves	1–Frank Dunlap

Cox–Tommy Maxwell
Pete Porterfield, John Hoefer

Freshmen

8–Warren Moorehead	4–Emil Berg
7–Steve Frost	3–Forrest Dubois
6–Rollin Moore	2–Gwynne Sharrer
5–Dave de Varona	1–Jackson Coley

Cox–Jim Dieterich
Bob Ball, Bill Yates

1937
Varsity

8–Larry Arpin	4–Emil Beerg
7–Pete Porterfield	3–Jim Schaeffer
6–Rollin Moore	2–Gwynne Sharrer
5–Dave de Varona	1–Steve Frost

Cox–Harry Kueny
Curt Rocca

Junior Varsity

8–Gregory Peck	4–John Manross
7–Peeter Arpin	3–Benson Roe
6–Henry Trobitz	2–Jerry Roberts
5–Jack Collins	1–Roger Bell

Cox–Dan Shinoda

Freshmen

8–Dexter Webster	4–Ray Talcott
7–Chet Gibson	3–Linton Emerson
6–Stan Freeborn	2–John Hansen
5–Bernard Schulte	1–Al Gilcrest

Cox–Reed
Bert Schwartz, Harry Dubois

1938
Varsity

8–Kirk Smith	4–Linton Emerson
7–Chet Gibson	3–Emil Berg
6–Stan Freeborn	2–Jack Manross
5–Jack Hoefer	1–Benson Roe

Cox–Jim Dieterich, Harry Kueny
Kurt Rocca, Henry Peters

Junior Varsity

8–Bill Beal	4–Gwynne Sharrer
7–Ray Talcott	3–Bernard Schulte
6–Henry Trobitz	2–Stan Backlund
5–Pete Porterfield	1–Steve Frost

Cox–Harry Kueny
Gregory Peck

Freshmen IRA Champions

8–Bob Andresen	4–Dick Andrew
7–Conrad Oberg	3–Bill Blevins
6–Jack Klukkert	2–Dave Rice
5–George Talbott	1–Earl Serdahl

Cox–Art Gassaway
Ed James, Bill Lamoreaux, Harry Connolly

1939
Varsity IRA and Pacific Coast Champions

8–Kirk Smith	4–Linton Emerson
7–Chet Gibson	3–Dave de Varona
6–Stan Freeborn	2–Stan Backlund
5–Emil Berg	1–Benson Roe

Cox–Jim Dieterich

Junior Varsity Pacific Coast Champions

8–Les Still	4–John Hansen
7–Bob Olson	3–Jim Schaeffer
6–Jack Klukkert	2–Ray Andresen
5–Bill Blevins	1–Gwynne Sharrer

Cox–Norm Soderstrand

Freshmen

8–Walt Casey	4–Harcourt Hervey, Watters
7–George Nikkel, Ed Garvey	3–Schaer
6–George Schwiers	2–John Friedrichsen, Petersen
5–Colbert	1–Andy Forman, Hughes

Cox–Bob Bult

1940
Varsity

8–Walt Casey	4–John Hansen
7–Ray Talcott	3–Chet Gibson
6–Stan Freeborn	2–John Schroepfer
5–Bill Blevins	1–Stan Backlund

Cox–Jim Dieterich

Junior Varsity

8–Les Still	4–Bill Beal
7–Harry Dubois	3–Bill Fulton
6–Forrest Dubois	2–John Friedrichsen
5–Al Daggett	1–Harry Connolly

Cox–Art Gassaway

Freshmen Pacific Coast Champions

8–Bob Schaeffer	4–John Kearns
7–Jim Lemmon	3–Marshall Robinson
6–Harold Flesher	2–Parker Sedgwick
5–Jim Moore	1–Ray Mortensen

Cox–Dunny Woodbury

1941
Varsity

8–Jack Kearns   4–John Friedrichsen
7–Jim Lemmon   3–Bill Blevins
6–Harold Flesher   2–Bill Rawn
5–Jim Moore   1–Ray Mortensen
                  Cox–Art Gassaway
                  Bill Lamoreaux

Junior Varsity IRA Champions

8–Les Still   4–Bill Lamoreaux
7–Bob Olson   3–Frank Nicol
6–Howard Holmes   2–Walt Casey
5–George Misch   1–Dave M. Turner
                  Cox–Bob Johnson
                  Marshall Robinson

Freshmen Pacific Coast Champions

8–Roy Johnson   4–George Wendell
7–Henry Penner   3–Bob Olson
6–Putnam Livermore   2–Jack Pabst
5–Francis Bauer   1–Chester Murray
                  Cox–Bob Cocke

1942
Varsity

8–Jack Kearns   4–George Wendell
7–Jim Lemmon   3–George Misch
6–Putnam Livermore   2–Frank Nicol
5–Jim Moore   1–Ray Mortensen
                  Cox–Dunny Woodbury

Junior Varsity

8–Bob Schaeffer   4–Jack Pabst
7–Bob Berry   3–Marshall Robinson
6–Howard Holmes   2–Walt Casey
5–Norm Hennessy   1–David M. Turner
                  Cox–David Bradfield

Freshmen

8–Bill Noack   4–Don Ewing
7–David L. Turner   3–Don Richardson
6–Bill Fleharty   2–Jim Hardy
5–Pertti Lindfors   1–John Robinson
                  Cox–Richard Hyams

1943
Varsity Pacific Coast Champions

8–Bob Schaeffer   4–George Wendell
7–David L. Turner   3–Marsh Robinson
6–Putnam Livermore   2–Frank Nicol
5–Jim Moore   1–Clyde Rockwell
                  Cox–Dunny Woodbury

Junior Varsity

8–Bob Watson   4–Jack Hoffman
7–John Goerl   3–Bob Edmund
6–Tom Mulcahy   2–Warren Wolff
5–Ben Sawtelle   1–John Robinson
                  Cox–Norm Sinsheimer

Freshmen

8–Bill Scherer   4–Adolph Kiesil
7–Charles Stevenson   3–Ward Brand
6–Dave Wright   2–Clayton Houston
5–Eric Peterson   1–Hans Jensen
          Cox–Don McNary, Harvey Wannamaker

1944 and 1945

World War II

1946
Varsity

8–Bill Noack   4–Bob Hughes
7–Jim Lemmon   3–Jack Stack
6–Allen Smith   2–Bob Spanger
5–Paul Chamberlain   1–Clyde Rockwell
                  Cox–Vincent Cullinane

1947
Varsity Pacific Coast Champions

8–Bill Noack   4–Faber Peek
7–David L. Turner   3–Ernest Gunther
6–Jim Hardy   2–Bob Spenger
5–Jack Stack   1–Ray Mortensen
                  Cox–Ralph Purchase

Junior Varsity IRA Champions

8–Ian Turner*   4–Lloyd Butler*
7–Dave Brown*   3–John Goerl
6–Darrell Welch*   2–Bill Scherer
5–George Ahlgren*   1–Dave M. Turner
                  Cox–Bob White*

(*freshmen)

          Other Freshmen:
          3–Art Sueltz
          2–Roger Thompson
          1–Warren Deverel

1948
Varsity Olympic Champions

8–Ian Turner   4–Lloyd Butler
7–David L. Turner   3–Dave Brown
6–Jim Hardy   2–Justus Smith
5–George Ahlgren   1–Jack Stack
                  Cox–Ralph Purchase
             Walter Deets, Hans Jensen

Junior Varsity

8–Walter Deets   4–Darrell Welch
7–Hans Jensen   3–Dick Larsen
6–Foster Murphy   2–Bill Scherer
5–George Bauman   1–Bart Ely
                  Cox–Bob White

Freshmen

8–Ron Reuther   4–John Davidson
7–Dave Draves   3–Phil Compton
6–Ken Cusick   2–Bill Durland
5–Carroll Whitney   1–Charles Hornbeck
                  Cox–Don Glusker

1949
Varsity IRA and Pacific Coast Champions

8–Ian Turner   4–Lloyd Butler
7–Dave Draves   3–George Bauman
6–Bob Livermore   2–Justus Smith
5–Dick Larsen   1–Bob Spenger
                  Cox–Ralph Purchase
        George Ahlgren, Dave Brown, Jim Hardy

Junior Varsity Pacific Coast Champions

8–Walter Deets	4–Darrell Welch
7–Carroll Whitney	3–Francis Baronovich
6–Jim Hardy	2–Bob Sumner
5–Art Seultz	1–Bart Ely
	Cox–Ed Fogerty

Freshmen

8–Bill Loorz	4–Tom Adams
7–Bill Hull	3–Tom Johnson
6–Paul Henriksen	2–Clark Gallaway
5–Fred Avilez	1–Martin Jennings
	Cox–Bob McEuen

1950
Varsity

8–Ian Turner	4–Lloyd Butler
7–Dave Draves	3–Art Sueltz
6–Bob Sumner	2–Justus Smith
5–Fred Avilez	1–Lester Berryman
	Cox–Ed Fogerty
	Bill Hull, Tom Johnson

Junior Varsity Pacific Coast Champions

8–Bill Loorz	4–Tom Adams
7–Bill Hull	3–Tom Johnson
6–Bob Livermore	2–Harry Gardiser
5–George Bauman	1–Bob Spenger
	Cox–Earl Baird

Freshmen

8–John Lamon	4–John Class
7–Glenn Miller	3–Bruce Coombs
6–Bill Owen	2–Charles Newman
5–Bill Lawrence	1–Pete Scott
	Cox–Bob Misrach

1951
Varsity

8–Bill Loorz	4–Ken Cusick
7–Bill Hull	3–Dave Draves
6–Paul Henriksen	2–Tom Adams
5–Terry Grew	1–Harry Gardiser
	Cox–Bob McConnell
	Bill Durland, Bill Schnack

Junior Varsity IRA Champions

8–Ron Reuther	4–Merritt Robinson
7–Conway Peterson	3–Al Lorenz
6–Bill Durland	2–Bill Schnack
5–Fred Avilez	1–John Lowe
	Cox–Don Glusker

Freshmen

8–Pete Dolliver	4–Howard Morrow
7–Walter Schilpp	3–Hal Wollenberg
6–Mark Levy	2–Dan Power
5–Phil Cordes	1–Tom Walsh
	Cox–Armand Maggenti

1952
Varsity Pacific Coast Champions

8–Bill Loorz	4–Paul Henriksen
7–Bill Hull	3–Allen Samson
6–Merritt Robinson	2–Tom Adams
5–Fred Avilez	1–Bob Johnson
	Cox–Bob McConnell

Junior Varsity Pacific Coast Champions

8–Ken Noack	4–Beau Breck
7–Marty Rotto	3–Bruce Coombs
6–Howard Morrow	2–Pete Dolliver
5–Willis Andersen	1–Pete Scott
	Cox–Bob McEuen

Freshmen Pacific Coast Champions

8–Marshall Leve	4–Norm Parsons
7–Charles Fraser	3–Jacques de Lorimer
6–Don Keene	2–Carl Thoresen
5–Tom Fellner	1–Tom Light
	Cox–Nelson

1953
Varsity

8–Beau Breck	4–John Class
7–Glenn Miller	3–Larry Marshall
6–Dick Rahl	2–Marshall Leve
5–Willis Andersen	1–Jacques de Lorimer
	Cox–Bob Misrach

Bill Owen, Chuck Harrington, Bob Johnson, Howard Ducker, Bruce Coombs

Junior Varsity

8–Cliff Fagin	4–Reg Rhein Jr.
7–Frank Robbin	3–Martin Rotto
6–Bill Owen	2–Don Abbott
5–Tom Fellner	1–Bob Johnson
	Cox–Armond Maggenti

Freshmen

8–Carlos Andrade	4–Dick Doyas
7–Bill Walker	3–Bob Hutchins
6–John Russell	2–Pell Voorhies
5–Ron Klinge	1–Steve de Voto
	Cox–Lowell Shifley

1954
Varsity

8–Dick Gaffery	4–Beau Breck
7–Jacques de Lorimer	3–Bill Walker
6–Dick Rahl	2–Reg Rhein Jr.
5–Glenn Miller	1–Tom Light
	Cox–Armand Maggenti
	Tom Fellner

Junior Varsity

8–Marshall Leve	4–Dick Steyer
7–Martin Roto	3–Steve de Voto
6–Norm Parsons	2–John Jones
5–Ron Klinge	1–Walt Grens
	Cox–Desmond Coffelt

Freshmen

8–Norm Tuttle	4–Vic Unruh
7–Dave Reese	3–John Petersen
6–Andy Farrer	2–Doug Schmidt
5–John Hardy	1–Mike Meyers
	Cox–Gene Hessel

1955
Varsity

8–Norm Tuttle	4–Mark Tuft
7–Jacques de Lorimer	3–Ramon Riggs
6–John Hardy	2–Norm Parsons
5–Dick Dobbins	1–Tom Light
	Cox–Brooks Key

Junior Varsity

8–Carter Swensen	4–Marshall Leve
7–Bill Walker	3–Steve de Voto
6–Dick Rahl	2–Reg Rhein Jr.
5–Tom Fellner	1–Roger Lowe
	Cox–Gene Ross

Freshmen

8–Rich Bartke	4–Lee Kerin
7–Garry Weyand	3–Rudy Kuhn
6–John Dieterich	2–Bob Swanson
5–Steve Chapman	1–John Dowdell
	Cox–Joe Kitterman

1956
Varsity

8–Gordon Raub	4–Joe Fornier
7–Garry Weyand	3–Dick Dobbins
6–John Dieterich	2–Tom Grady
5–John Petersen	1–Dick Howard
	Cox–Gene Hessel

Junior Varsity

8–Norm Tuttle	4–John Hardy
7–Bill Walker	3–Steve Whisenand
6–Mark Tuft	2–Lee Kerin
5–Ramon Riggs	1–Roger Lowe
	Cox–Gene Ross, Donn Stevens

Freshmen

8–Dave White	4–George DeLong
7–Don Bishop	3–Paul Arrasmith
6–Dave Allen	2–John Miller
5–John Bengston	1–Don Kearns
	Cox–Rod Rose

1957
Varsity

8–Rich Bartke	4–George DeLong
7–Don Bishop	3–Claude Hutchison
6–John Dieterich	2–Bob Swanson
5–Frank Stevenson	1–Dick Howard
	Cox–Gene Hessel

Junior Varsity

8–Don Anderson	4–Norm Tuttle
7–Garry Weyand	3–Paul Arrasmith
6–Dick Jordan	2–Tom Grady
5–John Petersen	1–Bob Santee
	Cox–Joe Kitterman

Freshmen

8–Dave Flinn	4–Ray Hertel
7–Elmore Chilton	3–Jim Demsey
6–Don Wiesner	2–Joe Neil
5–Gary Yancey	1–John Petrick
	Cox–Arlen Lackey

1958
Varsity

8–Don Martin	4–Ray Hertel
7–Elmore Chilton	3–Jim Demsey
6–Milos Terzich	2–Dave Flinn
5–Gary Yancey	1–Tom Wittingslow
	Cox–Bruce Horwitz

Junior Varsity

8–Bob Brooke	4–George DeLong
7–Gary Anderson	3–Claude Hutchison
6–John Dieterich	2–Bruce Hansen
5–Don Bishop	1–Joe Neil
	Cox–Joe Kitterman

Freshmen

8–Martin McNair	4–Rich Costello
7–Lucien Miller	3–Bob Berry
6–Tim Lyman	2–Chris Barnes
5–Joe Newman	1–Wally Adams
	Cox–Chuck Orman

1959
Varsity

8–Martin McNair	4–Ray Hertel
7–Elmore Chilton	3–Bob Berry
6–Milos Terzich	2–Dave Totten
5–Jack Matkin	1–Joe Neil
	Cox–Ralph Udick

Junior Varsity IRA Champions

8–Don Martin	4–Chris Barnes
7–Gary Anderson	3–John Christensen
6–Dave Flinn	2–Tim Scofield
5–Gary Yancey	1–Dick McKinnon
	Cox–Arlen Lackey

Freshmen

8–Tom Dunlap	4–Larry Bacon
7–Ray Brown	3–Steve Harvey
6–Bill Parker	2–Tony Diamond
5–Allan Brown	1–Jim Cobb
	Cox–Rick Blunden

1960
Varsity IRA and Western Sprint Champions

8–Don Martin	4–Martin McNair
7–Elmore Chilton	3–Bob Berry
6–Chris Barnes	2–Bruce Hansen
5–Jack Matkin	1–Gary Yancey
	Cox–Arlen Lackey
	Ray Hertel, Joe Neil

Junior Varsity Pacific Coast and Western Sprint Champions

8–Dave Totten	4–Doug Muirhead
7–Gary Anderson	3–Lucien Miller
6–Tim Lyman	2–Ray Hertel
5–John Christensen	1–Joe Neil
	Cox–Ralph Udick
	Bob Santee, Dave Flinn

Freshmen

8–Gary Rogers	4–Don Berger
7–Ed Faridany	3–Roger Adams
6–John Cory	2–Sam Speake
5–Steve Brandt	1–Dick Bass
	Cox–Bob Shimasaki
	Tom Palmer, John Bayless

1961
Varsity IRA and Pacific Coast Dual Race Champions

8–Martin McNair	4–Rich Costello
7–Kent Fleming	3–Bob Berry
6–Chris Barnes	2–Tim Lyman
5–Steve Brandt	1–Jack Matkin
	Cox–Chuck Orman

Junior Varsity Pacific Coast Dual Race and Western Sprint Champions

8–Dave Totten	4–Gary Rogers
7–Lucien Miller	3–Ed Faridany
6–Bob Curley	2–Tim Scofield
5–Roger Adams	1–Ron Gridley
	Cox–Steve Horn

Freshmen

8–John King	4–Al Stewart
7–Dan Hatch	3–Ron Sellers
6–Ed Bradbury	2–Tom Grimes
5–Gus Schilling	1–Norm Stanley
	Cox–Jim Libien

1962
Varsity

8–Steve Johnson	4–Don Wiesner
7–Gus Schilling	3–Roger Adams
6–Tim Lyman	2–Rich Costello
5–Steve Brandt	1–Ed Faridany
	Cox–Steve Horn

Junior Varsity

8–Tim Scofield	4–Gary Rogers
7–John Gotshall	3–Eric Van de Water
6–Don Berger	2–Al Stewart
5–Ron Sellers	1–Ed Bradbury
	Cox–Bob Shimasaki
	Tom Dunlap

Freshmen

8–Dave Berg	4–John Boudett
7–Jack Gregory	3–Cliff Rhodes
6–Walt Brown	2–Pete Summers
5–Tom Howard	1–John Sellers
	Cox–Gary Orton

1963
Varsity Pacific Coast Dual Race Co–Champions

8–Steve Johnson	4–Don Wiesner
7–Kent Fleming	3–John Sellers
6–Eric Van de Water	2–Gary Rogers
5–Steve Brandt	1–Gus Schilling
	Cox–Bob Shimasaki

Junior Varsity

8–Ronn Kaiser	4–Frank Brown
7–Ed Faridany	3–Ed Bradbury
6–John McConnell	2–Alan Mooers
5–Malcolm Thornley	1–Tom Palmer
	Cox–Jim Libien
	Walt Brown

Freshmen

8–Mike Page	4–Jay Jacobus
7–Jack Reding	3–Hal Eastman
6–Scott Gregg	2–Jim VanHoften
5–Russ Fisher	1–Jeff Brennan
	Cox–Rick Karon

1964
Varsity IRA, Pacific Coast Dual Race, and Pacific Coast Sprint Champions

8–Steve Johnson	4–Mike Page
7–Gus Schilling	3–John Sellers
6–Scott Gregg	2–Alan Mooers
5–Malcolm Thornley	1–Ed Bradbury
	Cox–Jim Libien
	Don Wiesner, Ron Sellers

Junior Varsity

8–Bob Cross	4–Eric Van de Water
7–Jack Gregory	3–Frank Brown
6–John McConnell	2–Don Wiesner
5–Roy Romey	1–Ron Sellers
	Cox–Dan Phillips
	Ronn Kaiser

Freshmen

8–Denny Lane	4–Rich McLellan
7–John Drew	3–Jeff Palmer
6–John Hoefer	2–Dave Parrish
5–Mike Hoagland	1–Hardy Jones
	Cox–Bob Arbios
	Pete Noyes

1965
Varsity Pacific Coast Dual Race Champions

8–Denny Lane	4–Mike Page
7–Malcolm Thornley	3–Roy Romey
6–John King	2–Norm Bliss
5–Frank Brown	1–John Sellers
	Cox–Bob Arbios, Reg Watt Jr.
	Bob Cross, Scott Gregg, Ron Sellers, John McConnell

Junior Varsity Pacific Coast Dual Race Champions

8–Bob Cross	4–Rich McLellan
7–Dan Hatch	3–Hardy Jones
6–Scott Gregg	2–Russ Medevic
5–Ron Sellers	1–Norm Stanley
	Cox–Doug Shirachi

Freshmen Pacific Coast Dual Race Champions

8–Stan Taylor	4–Jerry Richardson
7–George Gibbs	3–Tom Van Meter
6–Bruce Robertson	2–Dave Crockett
5–Pat Stanton	1–Tom Tryon
	Cox–Russ Takei

1966
Varsity

8–Bob Cross
7–Rich Tietz
6–Bruce Robertson
5–Hardy Jones

4–Mike Page
3–Roy Romey
2–Norm Bliss
1–Rich McLellan

Cox–Bob Arbois
Denny Lane

Junior Varsity

8–Doug Thure
7–Jack Reding
6–Norm Bliss
5–Jeff Palmer

4–Jerry Richardson
3–Pat Stanton
2–John Hoefer
1–Hal Eastman

Cox–Doug Shirachi

Freshmen

8–Gary Stacey
7–Dave Lafferty
6–Ray Brown
5–Jim Richards

4–Bob Ellsberg
3–Greg Lee
2–Dick Riegels
1–Steve Pierce

Cox–Mike Shinoda

1967
Varsity

8–Scott Gregg
7–Steve Pierce
6–John Hoefer
5–Jim Richards

4–Dave Parrish
3–Jim Gage
2–Stan Taylor
1–Pat Stanton

Cox–Russ Takei, Bob Arbios
Rich McLellan, Dave Crockett, Hardy Jones, Norm Bliss,
Denny Lane

Junior Varsity

8–Bob Peoples
7–Dwight Morgan
6–Denny Lane
5–Jeff Palmer

4–Bob Ellsberg
3–Tom Tryon
2–Norm Bliss
1–Tom Veblen

Cox–Ken Kubota
Bruce Robertson, Jerry Richardson

Freshmen

8–Larry Baker
7–Garry Newgard
6–Willis Boyce
5–Inman Rouce

4–Frank Graetch
3–Mike Schelp
2–Mike Fletcher
1–Hal Bobrow

Cox–Hank Delevaiti

1968
Varsity

8–Stan Taylor
7–Steve Pierce
6–Bruce Robertson
5–Jim Richards

4–Jerry Richardson
3–Pat Stanton
2–John Hoefer
1–Tom Tryon

Cox–Russ Takei

Junior Varsity

8–Bob Peoples
7–Tom Veblen
6–Rich Liebman
5–Dwight Morgan

4–Bob Ellsberg
3–Mike Schelp
2–David Williamson
1–Don Costello

Cox–Ken Kubota
Gary Shean

Freshmen

8–Manning Moore
7–Warren Fine
6–Jim Elliott
5–Paul Knight

4–Mike Johnson
3–Tom Lindberg
2–Jeff Lawrence
1–John Greene

Cox–Jerry Harris
Tom Wilson

1969
Varsity

8–Dwight Morgan
7–Warren Fine
6–Rich Liebman
5–Paul Knight

4–Mike Johnson
3–Jim Richards
2–Mike Fletcher
1–Jim Rogers

Cox–Russ Takei

Junior Varsity

8–Bob Peoples
7–Tom Veblen
6–Frank Graetch
5–Mike Schelp

4–Roger Claypool
3–Larry Vaughn
2–Jim Elliott
1–Steve Pierce

Cox–Joselito Yujuico

Freshmen

8–Scott Henderson
7–Pat Lickess
6–Sam Bacon
5–Bill Caneo

4–Jeff Halliday
3–Tom Bain
2–Walt Hallinan
1–Kent Johnson

Cox–Byron Lee

1970
Varsity

8–Manning Moore
7–Paul Knight
6–Mike Johnson
5–Joe Flynn

4–Mike Fletcher
3–Mike Schelp
2–Roger Claypool
1–Warren Fine

Cox–Bob Dave

Junior Varsity

8–Mark Jones
7–Pat Hayes
6–Doug McEachern
5–Tom Bain

4–Jim Rogers
3–Dave Brown
2–Jim Elliott
1–Gary Marks

Cox–Byron Lee

Freshmen

8–Brian Rodriguez
7–Eddie Young
6–Ivar Highberg
5–Phil Peterson

4–Mark McCall
3–Kim Rotchford
2–Greg Bortolussi
1–Jeff Storbeck

Cox–Kern Trembath

1971
Varsity

8–Mike Johnson
7–Pat Hayes
6–Doug McEachern
5–Joe Flynn

4–Kelly Moore
3–Paul Knight
2–Dage O'Connell
1–Warren Fine

Cox–Bob Dave
Gary Marks

Junior Varsity

8–Jim Elliot
7–Ed Young
6–Dave Brown
5–Tom Bain

4–Greg Bortolussi
3–Gary Marks
2–Walt Hallahan
1–Jim Rogers

Cox–Byron Lee

Freshmen

8–Richard Dorn	4–Kevin Donovan
7–Steve Marks	3–Steve Imsen
6–Bruce Kreider	2–Hague
5–David Petry	1–Joel Sturm
	Cox–Bob Martinez

1972
Varsity

8–Kelly Moore	4–Bruce Kreider
7–Pat Hayes	3–Steve Marks
6–Doug McEachern	2–Dage O'Connell
5–Tom Bain	1–Gary Marks
	Cox–Bob Dave

Junior Varsity

8–Greg Bortolussi	4–Mark McCall
7–Mark Wilber	3–Phil Wilson
6–Walt Hallanan	2–Dennis Erickson
5–Scott Hollingsworth	1–Jeff Williams
	Cox–Bryan Lee

Freshmen

8–Jim Stewart	4–Bill Wikander
7–Fred Hummel	3–Steve Roach
6–Mike Bennett	2–Jim Scardino
5–Matt Fishel	1–Kirk Russell
	Cox–Tony Hamamoto

1973
Varsity

8–Steve Roach	4–Steve Marks
7–Pat Hayes	3–Fred Hummel
6–Greg Bortolussi	2–Mike Bennett
5–Matt Fishel	1–Bruce Kreider
	Cox–Bob Dave

Junior Varsity

8–Dage O'Connell	4–Mark Jones
7–Gary Marks	3–John Duhring
6–Mark McCall	2–Kirk Russell
5–Jim Scardino	1–Jeff Williams
	Cox–Bill Glazier

Freshmen

8–Bob Snyder	4–Bob Cunningham
7–Craig Huntington	3–Dan Cotton
6–Bob Guthrie	2–Bob Hayes
5–Kent Cary	1–John Bacon
	Cox–Marco Meniketti

1974
Varsity Pacific Coast Dual Race Champions

8–Tim Hodges	4–Scott Hollingsworth
7–Jim Scardino	3–Craig Huntington
6–Jeff Walker	2–Bruce Kreider
5–Mike Bennett	1–Steve Marks
	Cox–Marco Meniketti

Junior Varsity

8–Steve Roach	4–Bob Guthrie
7–Matt Fishel	3–John Duhring
6–Dan Cotton	2–John Bacon, Kirk Russell
5–Jim Stewart	1–Dean Wright
	Cox–Sue Bassett

Freshmen

8–John Walker	4–Walt Holtz
7–Karl Brandes	3–Ulrich Lemke
6–Dick Clark	2–Chuck Drew, Steve Sundberg
5–Keith Jackson	1–Mark Sutro
	Cox–Tom Bradfield

1975
Varsity

8–Tim Hodges	4–Scott Hollingsworth, Bob Guthrie
7–Jim Scardino	3–Ulrich Lemke
6–Jeff Walker	2–Keith Jackson
5–Mike Bennett	1–Dick Clark
	Cox–Marco Meniketti

Junior Varsity

8–Dean Wright	4–Dan Cotton
7–Craig Huntington	3–George Piperis
6–Sandy Parkman	2–Joel Turner
5–Karl Brandes	1–Mark Sutro
	Cox–Bradley

Freshmen

8–Walter Stern	4–Mike Savage
7–Stewart Otte	3–Schnack
6–Gregg Bailey	2–Scott Loorz
5–Neal Hoffman	1–Duke Burnham
	Cox–Bob Mon

1976
Varsity IRA Champions

8–Dean Wright	4–Joel Turner
7–Ulrich Lemke	3–Mark Sutro
6–Bob Guthrie	2–Jeff Walker
5–Neal Hoffman	1–Keith Jackson
	Cox–Marco Meniketti

John Bacon, Jeff Harris, Fred Hummel, Bob Whitford

Junior Varsity Pacific Coast Sprint and Pacific Coast Dual Race
Champions

8–Bob Whitford	4–Gregg Bailey
7–Matt Fishel	3–Craig Huntington
6–John Bacon	2–Rich Clark
5–Steve Fry	1–Jeff Harris
	Cox–Bob Mon

Freshmen

8–Robert Waggener	4–Dan Pitcock
7–Myles Raphael	3–Stewart Lenz
6–Paul Prioleau	2–Kirk Goddard
5–Pete Taylor	1–John Gabler
	Cox–Bill Pratt

1977
Varsity

8–Bob Whitford	4–Fred Hummel
7–Ulrich Lemke	3–Mark Sutro
6–Paul Prioleau	2–Jeff Walker
5–Tyler Gaisford	1–Keith Jackson
	Cox–Bob Mon

Junior Varsity

8–Scott Loorz	4–John Bacon
7–Joel Kew	3–Stewart Lenz
6–Gregg Bailey	2–Robert Waggener
5–Karl Brandes	1–Jeff Harris
	Cox–Pete Anderson

Freshmen

8–Matts Wickmann	4–Peter Muelener
7–Eric Bailey	3–Jack Sholl
6–Rick Nichelman	2–Eric Lenz
5–Don Dutcher	1–William Hull
	Cox–Dan Akagi

1978
Varsity

8–Paul Prioleau	4–Gregg Bailey
7–Jack Sholl	3–Don Dutcher
6–Ross Brunson	2–Chris Brown
5–David Reddick	1–Stewart Lenz
	Cox–Bob Mon

Junior Varsity

8–Scott Loorz	4–David Goerss
7–Miles Raphael	3–Chuck Hansen
6–Robert Waggener	2–Charles Perry
5–Joel Kew	1–Brad Kaderabeck
	Cox–Pete Anderson

Freshmen

8–D. Crouse	4–Brad Stine
7–P. Richardson	3–Eric Fuller
6–Greg Aplet	2–Dale Emery
5–Peter Mattiessen	1–John Caton
	Cox–Mark Zembsch

1979
Varsity Pac–10 Sprint and Pacific Coast Dual Race Champions

8–Vince Horpel	4–Brad Stine
7–Don Dutcher	3–Stewart Lenz
6–Paul Prioleau	2–Craig Amerkhanian
5–Dave Reddick	1–Miles Raphael
	Cox–Valerie McClain

Junior Varsity Pacific Coast Dual Race Champions

8–Robert Waggener	4–Greg Aplet
7–Eric Bailey	3–John Caton
6–David Goerss	2–Charles Perry
5–Peter Mattiessen	1–Dale Emery
	Cox–Pete Anderson

Freshmen

8–Hagen Hottman	4–J. Devany
7–Brewer Stone	3–Paul Carson
6–P. Bryant	2–Randy Thomas
5–George Livingston	1–D. Harvey
	Cox–Jim Anderson

1980
Varsity Pacific Coast Dual Race Champions

8–Dan Louis	4–Randy Thomas
7–Don Dutcher	3–Peter Mattiessen
6–Brad Stine	2–Craig Amerkhanian
5–Dave Reddick	1–Dale Emery
	Cox–Mark Zembsch

Junior Varsity Pac–10 Sprint and Pacific Coast Dual Race Champions

8–Kevin Rogers	4–Hagen Hottman
7–George Livingston	3–Brad Hubler
6–H. Watkins	2–Eric Lenz
5–John Caton	1–Brewer Stone
	Cox–Jim Anderson

Freshmen

8–Tim Devaney	4–C. Ferguson
7–Dave DeRuff	3–T. Gaegler
6–Chris Huntington	2–C. Mattiessen
5–J. Pfluke	1–S. Lamon
	Cox–J. Coulter

1981
Varsity

8–Dan Louis	4–Chris Huntington
7–Dave DeRuff	3–Paul Marron
6–Brad Stine	2–Randy Thomas
5–George Livingston	1–Paul Carson
	Cox–Mark Zembsch

Junior Varsity Pac–10 Sprint and Pacific Coast Dual Race Champions

8–Kevin Rogers	4–Dave Kurka
7–John Caton	3–Peter Mattiessen
6–Hagen Hottman	2–Tim Devaney
5–Brad Hubler	1–Brewer Stone
	Cox–Jim Anderson
	Bruce Neilson

Freshmen Pac–10 Sprint and Pacific Coast Dual Race Champions

8–Mike Kuhn	4–Ben Swan
7–John Santucci	3–Phil Moore
6–Tom O'Toole	2–Alistair Black
5–Henry Mattiessen	1–Dave Moore
	Cox–Jeff Rubin

1982
Varsity Pac–10 Sprint and Pacific Coast Dual Race Champions

8–Dan Louis	4–Chris Huntington
7–Dave DeRuff	3–Brewer Stone
6–Chris Clark	2–Henry Mattiessen
5–George Livingston	1–Paul Carson
	Cox–Mark Zembsch

Junior Varsity Pac–10 Sprint Champions

8–Hagen Hottman	4–John Santucci
7–Alistair Black	3–Ben Swan
6–Randy Thomas	2–Dave Kurka
5–Bruce Neilson	1–Mike Kuhn
	Cox–Rich Mukai, Jeff Goshay

Freshmen IRA, Pac–10 Sprint, and Pacific Coast Dual Race Champions

8–Eric Cohn	4–Brian Cuneo
7–Sean Seward	3–Tony Matan
6–Matt Pribyl	2–Davis Bales
5–Pat Graffis	1–Matt Anacker
	Cox–Mike Shinn

1983
Varsity

8–Dan Louis	4–Brian Cuneo
7–Charlie Reed	3–Tony Matan
6–Dave DeRuff	2–Henry Mattiessen
5–Chris Huntington	1–Paul Carson
	Cox–Mike Shinn

Junior Varsity

8–Ted Swinford	4–Jack Devaney
7–Eric Klug	3–Pat Graffis
6–Eric Cohn	2–Davis Bales
5–Dave Kurka	1–Jimi Gleason
	Cox–Tony Venegas

Freshmen

8–Andy Hewitt	4–Greg Diaz
7–Tom Rosskopf	3–Tom Cahart
6–Bob Mathewson	2–Jim Smith
5–Karl Johsens	1–Stewert Huntington
	Cox–Craig Henderson

1984

Varsity

8–Henry Mattiessen	4–Brian Cuneo
7–Karl Johsens	3–Fred Adam
6–Charlie Reed	2–Bob Mathewson
5–Tony Matan	1–Eric Klug
	Cox–Mike Shinn

Junior Varsity

8–Matt Anacker	4–Pat Graffis
7–Andy Hewitt	3–John Santucci
6–Jimi Gleason	2–Mike Kuhn
5–Matt Pribyl	1–Dave Browstein
	Cox–Pat Slavin

Freshmen Pacific Coast Sprint, Pac–10, and Pacific Coast Dual
Race Champions

8–Greg Anastas	4–Boston Heller
7–Paul Duryea	3–George McNitt
6–Bruce Appleyard	2–Mike Eisenstat
5–John Cutting	1–Dave Rouda
	Cox–Amy DeFiebre

1985

Varsity Pacific Coast Dual Race Champions

8–Eric Cohn	4–Boston Heller
7–Jim Harding	3–Daemon Anastas
6–Andrew Hewitt	2–Steve Esslinger
5–Tony Matan	1–Fred Adam
	Cox–Tony Venegas

Junior Varsity Pacific Coast Dual Race Champions

8–Bruce Appleyard	4–Brian Cuneo
7–Tom O'Toole	3–Karl Johsens
6–Davis Bales	2–Jim Smith
5–Pat Graffis	1–Stewert Huntington
	Cox–Rob Adams

Freshmen

8–George Ballaseux	4–Sam Swan
7–Karl Ullman	3–Joaquin Sufuentes
6–Sam Hobbs	2–Barry King
5–Brett Hughs	1–Dave Cannon
	Cox–James Hopenfeld

1986

Varsity Pacific Coast Dual Race and Pacific Coast Sprint
Champions

8–Chip McKibbon	4–Tom McKinney
7–Jim Harding	3–Jim Smith
6–Daemon Anastas	2–Stewert Huntington
5–Brock Grunt	1–Steve Esslinger
	Cox–Tony Venegas

Junior Varsity

8–Kevin O'Brien	4–Ken Muller
7–Andy Hewitt	3–Steve Dettlinger
6–Sam Hobbs	2–Joe Krafka
5–Karl Johsens	1–Bob Knapp
	Cox–James Hopenfeld

Freshmen

8–Mike Howells	4–Doug McClary
7–Mike Schoback	3–Brian Milder
6–Forest Patterson	2–John Starett
5–Kanus Ulrichs	1–Mike Miller
	Cox–Gary Tan

1987

Varsity Pacific Coast Dual Race Champions

8–John McKibben	4–Tom McKinney
7–Jim Harding	3–Jim Smith
6–Daemon Anastas	2–Stewert Huntington
5–Brock Grunt	1–Ross Flemer
	Cox–Tony Venegas

Junior Varsity

8–Kevin O'Brien	4–Kelly Brosnan
7–Karl Ullman	3–Ken Muller
6–Bob Mathewson	2–Steve Dettlinger
5–Eric Lutter	1–Joe Krafka
	Cox–Gary Tan

Freshmen

8–Tim Ryan	4–Scott Wilson
7–Scott Hamilton	3–John Camagna
6–Bill Carstanjen	2–Rick Crabb
5–Andy McCappin	1–Mike Markman
	Cox–Aaron Browning

APPENDIX B
LIST OF COACHES

Ky Ebright. (Sketch by Howard Brodie.)

///

Varsity Coaches

1893–1896	*E. M. Garnett, Harvard '87*
1897–1900	*None listed: probably season's captain*
1901–1903	*W. B. Goodwin, Yale '90*
1904–1908	*E. M. Garnett, Harvard '87*
1909	*Dean Witter, Cal '09*
1910–1911	*None listed: probably season's captain*
1912	*T. A. Davidson, Cal '11*
1913	*None listed: probably season's captain*
1914–1915	*Charles Stevenson*
1916–1923	*Ben Wallis, Yale '10*
1924–1959	*Ky Ebright, Washington '17*
1960–1966	*Jim Lemmon, Cal '43*
1967–1972	*Marty McNair, Cal '61*
1973–1980	*Steve Gladstone, Syracuse '65*
1981–1983	*Mike Livingston, Harvard '70*
1984–1987	*Tim Hodges, Cal '75*
1988–	*Bruce Beall, Washington '73*

Freshmen Coaches

1893–1922	*None listed*
1923	*Heinie De Roulet, Cal '22*
1924–1943	*Russ Nagler, Washington '20*
1947–1951	*Russ Nagler, Washington '20*
1952	*David L. Turner, Cal '48*
1953	*Ron Reuther, Cal '52*
1954–1959	*Jim Lemmon, Cal '43*
1960	*John Halberg, Washington '58*
1961	*Joe R. Neal, Cal '60*
1962	*Stan Shawl, Cal '59*
1963	*Rich Costello, Cal '61*
1964–1965	*Tom Dunlap, Cal '62*
1966–1967	*John McConnell, Cal '65*
1968–1979	*Kent Fleming, Cal '63*
1980	*Roy Eisenhardt, Dartmouth '60*
1981–1983	*Tim Hodges, Cal '75*
1984–1986	*Paul Prioleau, Cal '79*
1987–	*Bob Newman, UCLA '68*

/ /

Shells by Name and Year of Purchase

1893–1922	No record
1923	*Bear*
1924	*Blue and Gold*
1925	*Berkeleyan, Poppy*
1926	*Jonah, Wiskie*
1927	*Forty-Niner, Argonaut*
1928	*Golden Gate*, Sierra*
1929	*Shasta, Yosemite*
1930	*Sequoia*
1931	*California II, Golden Bear*
1932	*Franciscan**
1935	*Spirit of '28*
1936	*California Clipper*
1938	*Treasure Island*
1939	*Pacifica*
1942	*George Blair*, Banner Blue*
1948	*El Dorado*
1949	*Bear Marauder, Pacific Pride*
1950	*Berkeley Belle, Miss Italy*
1952	*Argonaut II*
1953	*El Capitan*

1956	*Gold Rush, Virginia*
1958	*To Be*
1961	*A-OK**, Turn Blue* (four)
1962	*Californian**, Amador*
1964	*City of Vallejo, Monterey*
1965	*Golden Bear*
1967	*Japanese* (four)
1968	*ARC, Spirit of '28 II*
1970	*Dean Witter, Golden Bear II*
1973	*Franciscan, Yosemite*
1974	*Mariposa*
1976	*Sierra, Siskiyou, Modoc*
1977	*Tehema*
1979	*Matt Franich, Lou Penney*
1981	*Dean Witter II*
1982	*Trinity*
1983	*Tuolomne*
1984	*Allan H. Trant*
1986	*Dirty Dozen, Warrior*
1987	*Porter Sesnon*

*Olympic shell
**Stored at Syracuse

APPENDIX D
LIST OF SENIOR MANAGERS

///

1893–1906	*No record*		1950	*Howard Middleton*
1907	*John Tyssowski*		1951	*Milton Robinson*
1908	*John Tyssowski*		1952	*Richard Sallanger*
1909	*None listed*		1953	*Bob Young*
1910	*R. D. Montgomery*		1954	*Jim Matthews*
1911–1912	*None listed*		1955	*Dick Byrnes*
1914	*M. P. Griffiths*		1956	*John Robertson*
1915–1912	*None listed*		1957	*Bob Ulrich*
1919	*John Burns*		1958	*Bob Ekdahl*
1920	*John Burns*		1959	*Chauncey Yano*
1921	*John Mage*		1960	*Bob Patton*
1922	*Costello*		1961	*Dave Tavernetti*
1923	*Oscar Hinsdale*		1962	*Gil Walker*
1924	*Elliot Seymour*		1963	*Bill Stein*
1925	*Wayne Thomas*		1964	*Lee Johnson*
1926	*Kenny Bridges*		1965	*Charles Julian*
1927	*H. Allen Thompson*		1966	*Dennis Seguine*
1928	*Blake Wharton*		1967	*Everett Mathews*
1929	*Sidney Thaxter*		1968	*David Miller*
1930	*Thomas Robb*		1969	*Kevin Tom*
1931	*Fred Witzel*		1970	*Chip Stoner*
1932	*Dave White*		1971	*Bob Pomeroy*
1933	*Bob Ballachey*		1972	*Bob Pomeroy*
1934	*Edwin Cooper*		1973	*Mike Murphy*
1935	*Dale Kellogg*		1974	*Bob Mark*
1936	*Chet Ristenpart*		1975	*Jon Mauck*
1937	*Rex Jones Jr.*		1976–1977	*None listed*
1938	*Dick Gock*		1978	*Trip Betts*
1939	*Leland Scott*		1979	*Warren Fallat*
1940	*Sterling Roberts*		1980	*Warren Fallat*
1941	*Walt Cooley*		1981	*Warren Fallat, Duncan Fallat*
1942	*Bob Sproul Jr.*		1982	*Duncan Fallat*
1943	*Bob Evans*		1983	*Duncan Fallat*
1944	*Fran Allen*		1984	*Duncan Fallat*
1946	*Bob Lockhart*		1985	*Jim Mills*
1947	*Tom Tully*		1986	*Jim Mills*
1948	*Jim Yost*		1987	*None*
1949	*Linley Sales*			

LIST OF TROPHY
AWARD-WINNERS

///

FOUR TROPHIES ARE AWARDED TO members of the crew at the end of each season. The oldest is the Scholarship Cup, which was first awarded in 1926, recognizing the varsity member with the highest overall grade point average. The next oldest award is the Dean Witter Cup, which was initiated in 1927, and honors the outstanding

member of the varsity crew. The Ahlgren Award is for the most improved varsity oarsman, and it was first awarded in 1953. The Nagler Award, awarded to the most promising member of the freshmen crew, was initiated in 1954.

The Scholarship Cup

The donor of this cup is unknown; when the original cup was lost years ago, the California Alumni Club of New York took over sponsorhip and provided a substitute trophy, in gratitude to Cal's crews for the name recognition they provided for Berkeley athletics. It seemed that when their fellow New Yorkers heard about

a University of California team, they assumed it was either UCLA or USC in most sports; but through the Olympics and national championships, they were quite aware of the Cal crew from Berkeley. The recipients are as follows:

1926	Maynard J. Toll	1949	David P. Brown	1968	Larry Vaughn
1927	Peter D. Donlon	1950	Donald L. Glusker	1969	Thomas T. Veblen
1928	Francis H. Frederick	1951	Donald L. Glusker	1970	Paul L. Knight
1929	James T. Workman	1952	Thomas B. Adams	1971	Daig O'Connell
1930	David C. Dunlap	1953	Walter B. Grens	1972	Robert Dave
1931	David C. Dunlap	1954	Walter B. Grens	1973	Jim Scardino
1932	Charles R. Chandler	1955	Eugene H. Ross	1974	Jim Scardino
1933	Ward W. Klink	1956	Eugene A. Hessel	1975	Jeff Harris
1934	Ferd T. Elvin	1957	Eugene A. Hessel	1976	Joel Turner
1935	Raymond Andresen	1958	Ray Hertel	1977	Jeff Harris
1936	James Graves	1959	Ray Hertel	1978	John Fleming
1937	none listed	1960	Ray Hertel	1979	John Fleming
1938	Curtis M. Rocca	1961	John Kagel	1980	John Caton
1939	Benson B. Roe	1962	Tom Palmer	1981	Paul Carson, Dave DeRuff
1940	Arthur D. Gassaway	1963	Tom Palmer	1982	Alistair Black
1941	G. James Lemmon	1964	Eric Van de Water	1983	Alistair Black
1942	G. James Lemmon	1965	Richard Tietz	1984	David Brownstein
1943	James B. Moore	1966	Richard Tietz	1985	Tom O'Toole
1947	Robert E. Spenger	1967	Seth Alpert	1986	James Hopenfeld
1948	Robert E. Spenger			1987	Bob Mathewson

Dean Witter.

1948 Olympic Champion and #5 George Ahlgren.

The Dean Witter Trophy

Shortly after Ky Ebright started his career as the varsity coach at California, he decided a "most valuable player" award would be a morale booster for the squad. He approached Dean Witter '09, one of Cal's most powerful crew alumni, who was well on his way to becoming one of the leading stockbrokers in the West. Ky proposed that the trophy be named after Dean and that it be awarded for "loyalty, ability, and spirit." Dean was most agreeable and provided the very fine trophy still in use today. He stipulated that the award be given for "loyalty, proficiency, and spirit"—he believed that one is born with ability, whereas one develops proficiency. Those selected for this honor are as follows:

1927	*Hardy C. Hutchinson*	1960	*Gary T. Yancey*
1928	*Don Blessing*	1961	*Robert D. Berry*
1929	*Peter D. Donlon*	1962	*John P. Gotshall*
1930	*John M. Brinck*	1963	*T. Gary Rogers*
1931	*Harvey T. Granger*	1964	*Stephen C. Johnson,*
1932	*Norris J. Graham*		*August H. Schilling II*
1933	*Charles R. Chandler*	1965	*John K. Sellers*
1934	*Charles R. Chandler*	1966	*Myron E. Page*
1935	*Reginald M. Watt*	1967	*Norm Bliss*
1936	*Laurence Dodge*	1968	*Pat Stanton*
1937	*Laurence C. Arpin*	1969	*Dwight Morgan*
1938	*Curtis M. Rocca*	1970	*Paul Knight*
1939	*Jim Dieterich*	1971	*Mike Johnson*
1940	*Jim Dieterich*	1972	*Bob Dave*
1941	*Leslie E. Still Jr.*	1973	*Bruce Kreider*
1942	*Walter P. Casey*	1974	*Jim Scardino*
1943	*Thomas F. Mulcahy*	1975	*Mike Bennett,*
1947	*Ray K. Mortenson*		*Jim Scardino*
1948	*David L. Turner*	1976	*Fred Hummel*
1949	*Ralph K. Purchase*	1977	*Ulrich Lemke*
1950	*Justus K. Smith*	1978	*Robert Mon*
1951	*David S. Draves*	1979	*Paul Prioleau*
1952	*George W. Loorz*	1980	*Don Dutcher*
1953	*Willis U. Andersen*	1981	*Brad Stein*
1954	*Peter C. Dolliver*	1982	*George Livingston*
1955	*Richard H. Rahl*	1983	*Daniel Louis*
1956	*Ramon W. Riggs*	1984	*Henry Matthiessen*
1957	*John Peterson*	1985	*Tony Matan*
1958	*John Dieterich*	1986	*Steve Esslinger*
1959	*Milos Terzich*	1987	*Brock Grunt*

The Ahlgren Award

George L. Ahlgren '49, a member of the 1948 Olympic championship crew, was killed in an airplane crash December 31, 1951, while serving in the Navy. His fraternity, Sigma Alpha Epsilon, presented a trophy to the crew in his memory. It is awarded to the most improved varsity oarsman each year. The honorees are as follows:

1953	*Clifford Fagin*
1954	*John W. Jones*
1955	*Richard Dobbins*
1956	*Gordon A. Raub*
1957	*Frank A. Stevenson*
1958	*Donald W. Martin*
1959	*Timothy G. Scofield*
1960	*Bruce K. Hansen*
1961	*Richard H. Costello*
1962	*Stephen C. Johnson*
1963	*John W. McConnell*
1964	*Alan J. Moores*
1965	*Norman D. Stanley*
1966	*Richard E. Tietz*
1967	*Richard F. Liebman*
1968	*Donald O. Costello*
1969	*James D. Rogers*
1970	*Mike Schelp*

1971	*Daig O'Connell*
1972	*Greg Bortolussi*
1973	*Matt Fishel*
1974	*Joel Turner*
1975	*Scott Hollingsworth*
1976	*Jeff Harris*
1977	*Taylor Gaisford*
1978	*Charlie Perry*
1979	*Dave Goerss*
1980	*Eric Lenz*
1981	*Dave Kurka*
1982	*Jeff Goshay,*
	Brewer Stone
1983	*Ted Swinford*
1984	*Karl Johsens*
1985	*Daemon Anastas*
1986	*Kenneth Muller*
1987	*Steve Dettlinger*

Russ Nagler, Freshmen Coach 1924–1943 and 1947–1951.

Russ Nagler Memorial Award

Russ Nagler, Washington '20, was Cal's freshmen crew coach under Ky Ebright from 1924 to 1943 and from 1947 to 1951. He died in a fire December 28, 1952, after leaving coaching to become a full-time realtor. The many Cal crew alumni who had learned to row under Russ established a memorial award presented annually to the most promising freshman. Those who have received this honor are:

1954	*John P. Hardy*
1955	*Stephen R. Chapman*
1956	*George DeLong*
1957	*Gary T. Yancey*
1958	*Martin B. McNair*
1959	*William G. Parker*
1960	*Stephen R. Brandt*
1961	*Thomas A. Grimes*
1962	*John E. Gregory*
1963	*D. Scott Gregg*
1964	*Denison Lane*
1965	*Patrick J. Stanton*
1966	*James E. Richards*
1967	*Willis L. Boyce*
1968	*Michael B. Johnson*
1969	*William M. Cuneo*
1970	*Pat Hayes*

1971	*Bruce Kreider*
1972	*Fred Hummel*
1973	*Robert Guthrie*
1974	*Jeff Walker*
1975	*Duke Burnham*
1976	*Bob Waggener*
1977	*Jack Sholl*
1978	*Peter Mattiessen*
1979	*George Livingston*
1980	*Chris Huntington*
1981	*Ben Swan*
1982	*Brian Cuneo*
1983	*Greg Dias*
1984	*Bruce Appleyard*
1985	*Karl Ullman*
1986	*Mike Schoback*
1987	*Eric Lutter*

APPENDIX F
LIST OF IRA RESULTS

//

THE INTERCOLLEGIATE ROWING ASSOCIATION Regatta (IRA) started in 1895 with a varsity race of four miles on the Hudson River at Poughkeepsie, New York. The following year a two mile freshman race was added to the regatta. In 1914 a junior varsity race was also included, first at two miles, and later at three. There was no regatta from 1917 until 1920 due to World War I. It was again cancelled in 1933 due to the Depression. From 1942 through 1946 there was no regatta due to World War II. Starting again in 1947, the varsity distance was shortened to three miles. In 1950 it was moved to Marietta, Ohio. Because of flooding at this site for two years in a row, the races were moved in 1952 to Lake Onondaga in Syracuse, New York, where it has remained. In 1964 the races were shortened to 2,000 meters because it was an Olympic year. Following 1964 the regatta went back to the longer distances, but in 1968 it was agreed to concentrate on the international distance of 2,000 meters. Practically all races nationwide are now rowed at that distance, including the IRA. From its inception through at least the late 1960s the IRA victor was acknowledged to be the National Champion.

The IRA Regatta now covers three days. The winners of three opening heats on Thursday qualify for the finals. On Friday there are three repechage (second chance) heats among those who lost the day before, and the winners qualify for the finals. On Saturday the championship finals are held for the winners of the opening heats and the repechage heats. A petite final is provided for those who don't qualify for the championship event. In the results below the notation "didn't qualify" indicates that crew, although entered, failed to make the championship final.

Varsity

1921	Second
1926	Sixth
1927	Third
1928	First
1929	Swamped
1930	Fourth
1931	Fourth
1932	First
1934	First
1935	First
1936	Second
1937	Fifth
1938	Second
1939	First
1940	Fifth
1941	Second
1947	Fourth
1948	Second
1949	First
1950	Second
1951	Fourth
1952	Fifth
1953	Sixth
1954	Fifth
1955	Sixth
1956	Tenth
1958	Fifth
1959	Fourth
1960	First
1961	First
1962	Third
1963	Fourth
1964	First
1965	Seventh
1966	Eighth
1967	Eleventh
1976	First
1977	Third
1978	Sixth
1980	Didn't qualify
1984	Third
1985	Sixth
1987	Sixth

Junior Varsity

1926	Third
1927	Third
1931	Second
1932	Second
1934	Fourth
1938	Second
1939	Third
1940	Third
1941	First
1947	First
1948	Second
1949	Third
1950	Second
1951	First
1952	Third
1953	Sixth
1954	Third
1955	Sixth
1956	Sixth
1958	Third
1959	First
1960	Second
1961	Second
1963	Third
1964	Second
1965	Sixth
1967	Seventh
1976	Fourth
1977	Second
1980	Second
1983	Fourth

Freshmen

1926	Second
1927	Sixth
1928	Seventh
1929	Second
1930	Seventh
1932	Fourth
1935	Second
1936	Second
1937	Second
1938	First
1939	Fifth
1970	Didn't qualify
1973	Didn't qualify
1975	Fifth
1976	Didn't qualify
1981	Third
1982	First
1983	Didn't qualify
1984	Didn't qualify

WASHINGTON, STANFORD, AND WISCONSIN DUAL RACE RESULTS

//

California versus Washington Varsity

The 1903, 1904, and 1905 races were in fours with cox at approximately a two-mile distance. Races from 1908 through 1948 were at three miles. In 1949 the Washington course was modified to two-and-three-quarter miles and then to two-and-one-half miles in 1951. All races on the Oakland Estuary through 1967 were at three miles, with the exception of 1964 when it was 2,000 meters for the Olympic year. In 1968 all national races were set at 2,000 meters in conjunction with Olympic and international competition. All races from 1970 have been at 2,000 meters. Note that prior to 1920 some triangular races occurred.

1903	Washington 1½ lengths
1904	California, Stanford, Washington 10 lengths
1905	California 2 lengths
1907	All three crews swamped
1908	Washington 5 lengths
1911	Washington 7 lengths
1912	Stanford, Washington, California 1 length
1913	Washington, Stanford, California 12 lengths
1913	Washington 7 lengths
1914	Washington, Stanford, California 5 lengths
1914	Washington 4 lengths
1915	Stanford, Washington, California 1 length
1916	Washington 16 lengths
1917	Washington, California, Stanford 4 lengths
1919	Washington, California, Stanford 4 feet
1920	Washington 5 feet
1921	California 5 feet
1922	Washington 10 lengths
1923	Washington 3½ lengths
1924	Washington 10 lengths
1925	Washington 8 lengths
1926	Washington 5 lengths
1927	California 4 lengths
1928	California ½ length
1929	California 5½ lengths
1930	Washington ¼ length
1931	Washington 1 length
1932	California 18 lengths
1933	Washington 7 lengths
1934	Washington ¼ length
1935	Washington 6 feet
1936	Washington 3 lengths
1937	Washington 5 lengths
1938	Washington 1½ lengths
1939	California 12 lengths
1940	Washington 2 lengths
1941	Washington 3½ lengths
1942	Washington 3 lengths
1943	California 7½ lengths
1947	California 2 lengths
1948	Washington 2½ lengths
1949	California 10 feet
1950	Washington ¾ length
1951	Washington, California, Stanford 2 lengths
1952	California 4½ lengths
1953	Washington 7 lengths
1954	Washington 1¾ lengths
1955	Washington 6 lengths
1956	Washington 4¾ lengths
1957	Washington 6 lengths
1958	Washington 4¾ lengths
1959	Washington 2¾ lengths
1960	Washington ¾ length
1961	California 1 length
1962	Washington 1½ lengths
1963	Dead heat tie
1964	California 2 lengths
1965	California 1½ lengths
1966	Washington 3½ lengths
1967	Washington 5 lengths
1968	Washington 2 lengths
1969	Washington 8 lengths
1970	Washington 2¼ lengths
1971	Washington 2 lengths
1972	Washington 3 lengths
1973	Washington 1½ lengths

1974	California 1 length		1981	Washington 1¼ lengths
1975	Washington 3 lengths		1982	California ⅓ length
1976	Washington 10 feet		1983	Washington 2 lengths
1977	Washington ¾ length		1984	Washington 2 lengths
1978	Washington 1½ lengths		1985	California 1 length
1979	California 1¼ lengths		1986	California 1 length
1980	California 1½ lengths		1987	California 1½ lengths

California versus Stanford Varsity

Races from 1902 through 1904 were in fours with cox, and from 1907 through the present in eights.

1902	California		1958	California
1903	California		1959	California
1904	California, Stanford, Washington		1960	California
1905	California by default		1961	California
1907	Stanford		1962	California
1908	California		1963	California
1909	Stanford		1964	California
1910	Stanford		1965	California
1911	Stanford		1966	Stanford
1912	Stanford, Washington, California		1967	Stanford
1913	Washington, Stanford, California		1968	Stanford
1914	Washington, Stanford, California		1969	Stanford
1915	Stanford, Washington, California		1970	Stanford
1916	Stanford		1971	Stanford
1917	Washington, California, Stanford		1972	California
1919	Washington, California, Stanford		1973	California
1920	California		1974	California
1921	Stanford discontinued crew		1975	California
1943	California		1976	California
1947	California		1977	Stanford canceled
1948	California		1978	California
1949	California		1979	California
1950	California		1980	California
1951	California		1981	California
1952	California		1982	California
1953	California		1983	California
1954	California		1984	California
1955	Stanford		1985	California
1956	Stanford		1986	California
1957	Stanford		1987	California

California versus Wisconsin Varsity

Races usually were three miles at Cal and one-and-seven-eighths miles at Wisconsin.

1937	California		1954	Wisconsin
1947	California		1955	Wisconsin
1948	California		1956	Wisconsin
1949	California		1957	California
1950	California		1958	California
1951	California		1959	Dead heat tie
1952	Wisconsin		1960	California, Navy, Wisconsin
1953	Wisconsin		1982	California

MIKE LIVINGSTON'S REMARKS AT THE 1983 AWARDS BANQUET, THE FACULTY CLUB, BERKELEY

WE ARE GATHERED HERE TONIGHT to pay tribute to the members of the 1982–83 California crews. We call this an awards banquet, but that seems somehow inappropriate. To be sure, we will make awards, but crew never has been a sport rife with awards. I would suggest that the pursuit of the sport itself involves its own intrinsic rewards. I would ask you whom we honor tonight to reflect for a moment upon these rewards.

Obviously, competitive crew has been for you a discipline of the body. Your practice of crew has induced a sensitivity to and awareness of the physical body which has refined and animated virtually every bodily cell. You have watched your body grow and harden. You have become stronger. Your heart beats more powerfully. Your lungs and limbs are more elastic, more resilient. On a cellular level, you have facilitated and enhanced those metabolic processes which magically translate matter into energy against the pin. You have grooved neurological pathways and opened new capillaries. You have become attuned to the play of hormonal agents. You have searched for the thresholds of physical performance, and once you have found them, you have learned to dance on their edge: on the edge of balance and imbalance, rhythm and arhythm, momentum and inertia, control and abandonment, contraction and relaxation. You have, in short, probed the untamed regions of your own physical limits. . . . You have explored the ultimate frontier of your own living spaceship.

But crew has not been for you only a discipline of the body. Perhaps even more emphatically, it has been a discipline of the mind. Through this daily practice you have concentrated the mind with unwavering intensity. You have habitualized perseverance and honed the skills of disciplined commitment and focused application. Indeed, it is your will which has led you to the far reaches of your physical limits. Through the daily ritual of mindful practice you have forged a will of steel, and then you have turned that hardened will against your physical limits whenever they have arisen; and methodically, patiently, yet relentlessly you have pressed back those limits to reveal new worlds within your own being. And in doing so you have discovered more than the tremendous power of your body. . . . You have discovered the power of the will. It is a power which is infinite. It is the power of belief.

Finally, crew is a discipline of fellowship. Your commitment to rowing—which is as intimate a team sport as exists—has exposed you almost totally to your fellow oarsmen. You have stood naked before them in all your strength and weakness, in your security and your vulnerability. You have shared in victory and defeat. You have laughed together and even cried together. What has happened between you is something profound, and it goes beyond friendship. It is a bond of abiding respect forged in the fires of a common passion. It is incredibly powerful, and often it is for life. You have struggled for and won admission into an elite assembly of humanity, and we stand united by the majesty of our shared experiences.

The medals and trophies, the buffed physiques, and the low pulse rates, the letter jackets and trophy shirts are but superficial trappings of this sport. Its essence is embedded in the ritual of the daily practice, and now it is reflected in the spirits of each of you. You are not so much to be applauded, I feel, as envied. It has been a privilege to assist you in your practice. To the degree that you have known or felt the rewards of which I have spoken tonight, we have succeeded in our common enterprise. I believe there is no other meaningful measure of our success.

INDEX

Adams, Tom, 44, 45
Ahlgren, George, 37, 41, 42
Alameda Rowing Club, 1
Amador, 4, 5, 83
Anacker, Matt, 74, 75
Andersen, Willis, x, 99
Anderson, Gary, 48, 49
Anderson, Peter, 70–71
Andresen, Bob, 30, 31
Andresen, Ray, 28, 29, 30
Andrew, Dick, 30, 31
Anloff, 4
Aplet, Greg, 70–71
Archer, Pete, 50, 95
Ariel Rowing Club, 1
Ashley, Fred, 7
Ashley, Harold, 7
Avilez, Fred, 45, 46
Backlund, Stan, 31, 32
Bacon, John, 99, 114
Bailey, Eric, 70–71
Bales, Davis, 74, 75
Ball, Ivan, ix, 7
Bannister, E. A., 4, 5
Baptiste, Paul, 96
Barnes, Chris, 48, 49, 52, 53, 54
Bartke, Rich, x
Bauman, George, 43
Beall, Bruce, 82
Beekley, Del, 56, 65
Berg, Emil, 31, 32
Berkeley High School, 100
Berkenkamp, Gene, 29
Berry, Bob, 52, 53, 54
Big C Society, 7, 105
Blair, George, 39, 56
Blair, George, 39, 108
Blair, James, 26, 27
Blessing, Don, ix, 22, 23
Blevins, Bill, 30, 31, 35
"Blue Goose" (bus), 90, 91
Bradbury, Ed, 57–59
Brandt, Steve, 52, 54, 55
Brigham, Carroll, 28, 29
Brinck, Jack, 22, 23
Brown, Dave, 37, 39, 41, 42
Brown, L. A., 15
Bunnell, 4
Burnley, Dick, 28

Bush, Walt, 104
Butler, Lloyd, 37, 41–43
Caldwell, Hub, 22, 23
California Rowing Club, 68
Callow, Rusty, 18, 29, 72
Casey, Walt, 34
Caton, John, 70–71
Chandler, Charlie, 26, 27, 102
Chilton, Elmore, 52, 53
Christchurch Centennial Regatta, 44, 45
Christensen, John, 48, 49
Clark, Chris, 114
Cohn, Eric, 74, 75, 114
Collier, John L., 57
Columbia Rowing Club, 2
Condit, Phil, 22
Conibear, Hiram, 18, 84
Cory, C. L., 2
Costello, Rich, 54
Cuneo, Brian, 74, 75, 114
Cusick, Ken, 44, 45
Daggatt, Al, 30
Dally, Bill, 22, 23
Davidson, T. A., 7–9
DeFiebre, Amy, 79
DeRuff, Dave, 114
de Varona, Dave, 31, 32
Dieterich, Jim, ix, 31, 32, 111
Dignan, H. H., 7
Dodge, Ed, ix, 4, 5
Dodge, Larry, 4, 28, 29
Dolphin Rowing Club, 1
Donlon, Pete, 22, 23
Donnelly, Jack, 36, 103
Downs, R. C., 15
Draves, Dave, 43–45
Drlica, Karl, 96
Dunlap, Dave, 26, 27
Dunlap, Frank, 28
Dunlap, Tom, 110
Durland, Bill, 45, 46
Eastern Sprint Championships, 45
Easton, Stanley A., 2
Ebright, Carroll M. "Ky", ix, xi, 18–22,
    25–30, 32, 33, 36, 37, 39, 40, 44, 47,
    49, 50, 86, 88–90, 95–97, 99, 102,
    103, 107–111
Ebright, Kathryn, 36, 50, 75, 88
Eisenhardt, Roy, 72, 110

Elvin, Ferd, 28
Emerson, Linton, 31, 32
Emery, Dale, 70–71
Empacher, 84, 85
Evans, D. E., 4, 5
Fagin, Cliff, 96
Fennelly, Mike, 85, 104
Fleming, Kent, 54, 55, 67, 71
Flesher, Harold, 35
Flinn, Dave, 48, 49
Francis, Joe, 103
Franich, Matt, 91, 103, 104, 108
Frederick, Fran, 22, 23
Freeborn, Stan, 31, 32
Free Speech Movement, 60
Fremming, Harley, 29
Friedrichsen, John, 35
Friends of California Crew, ix, 9, 99,
    111, 112
Fryer, Roy, 3
Furth, Alan, 90
Gardiser, Harry, 44, 45
Garnett, E. M., xi, 2–7, 72
Gassaway, Art, 30, 31, 35
Gibbons, M. R., 2
Gibson, Chet, 31, 32
Gladstone, Steve, 62–64, 67–69, 72, 77,
    80, 99, 111, 112
Glusker, Don, 44, 45, 46
Goerl, John, 37
Goerss, Dave, 70–71
Goodwin, W. B., 4
Graffis, Pat, 74, 75
Graham, Norris, 26, 27
Gregg, Duncan, ix, 26, 27
Gregg, Scott, 58, 59
Grew, Terry, 44, 45
Grindley, 4
Guthrie, Bob, 67, 68
Hall, Winslow, 26, 27, 49
Hansen, Bruce, 50, 52, 53
Harbach, Ed, ix
Hardy, Jim, 41, 42
Hayes, Pat, 114
Henriksen, Paul, 44, 45
Hillen, Bob, 95, 96
Hodges, Tim, ix, x, 72–75, 78–82, 98,
    99, 110
Hoffman, Neal, 67, 68

Holman, Herm, 27
Holmes, Howard, 34
Hopper, Jimmy, 3
Houston, Bert, 10
Hull, Bill, 44, 45
Huntington, Chris, 114
Huntington, Craig, 99,
Huntington, Stewart, 114
Hutchison, Claude, 109, 112
Intercollegiate Rowing
   Association(IRA), ix, 15, 16, 21, 22,
   25, 27–32, 34, 35, 37, 39, 42, 43,
   45–47, 51, 52, 54–56, 58, 59, 61, 62,
   64, 66–71, 75, 77, 79–81, 89, 102
Jackson, Keith, 67, 68
Jacobus, Jay, 112
Jastram, Burt, 26, 27
Jensen, Hans, 39
Jewett, William D., xi, 2
Johnson, Bob, 34
Johnson, Steve, 55, 57–59
Jones, George C., 4, 5
Kaschper, 84
Kearns, Jack, 35
Kelly, Grace, 42
Kemp, T. J., 15
Kerr, Clark, xi, 50
Klug, Eric, 114
Klukkert, Jack, 30, 31
Knight, Paul, 62, 63
Lackey, Arlen, 48, 49, 52, 53
Lake Merritt Industrial League, 26
Lake Merritt Rowing Club, 99
Lamoreaux, Bill, 34
Larsen, Dick, 43
Larson, A. E., 15
Leader, Ed, 18, 21
Lemke, Ulrich, 67, 68
Lemmon, Jean, 45, 75, 88
Lemmon, Jim, ix, 32, 35, 36, 44, 50–52,
   57, 58, 60, 75, 88, 96, 99, 100, 102,
   109, 111
Libien, Jim, 57, 58, 59
Lindsey, Lou, 96
Livermore, Bob, 43
Livingston, George, 114
Livingston, Mike, x, 72, 73, 75–77, 83,
   98, 99, 112
Lockyer, Bill, 96
Loeb, J. P., 4, 5
Loorz, Bill, 44, 45
Lorenz, Al, 45, 46
Louis, Dan, 114
Lowe, John, 45, 46
Lyman, Tim, 50, 54
MacArthur, General Douglas, 22
Madson, Ernie, 36, 91, 103
Mage, John, 15
Maggard, Dave, 82
Marquardson, E. F., 15
Marsh, Professor Jerry, 88
Martin, Don, 48, 49, 52, 53, 111
Matan, Tony, 74, 75, 114

Matkin, Jack, 52, 53, 54
Mattiessen, Henry, 114
Mattiessen, Peter, 70–71
McClain, Valerie, 69
McConnell, John, 58
McGregor, Albert, 103
McKibbon, Chip, 114
McKinnon, Dick, 48, 49
McLellan, Hayes, 27
McMillan Jr., Dan A., 15, 16, 31
McNair, Marty, 52–54, 60–63, 100, 111
McNary, Don, 36
Mehan, F. G., 15
Meislahn, Findley, 70, 79
Meniketti, Marco, 67, 68
Merritt, Ralph E., 9
Misch, George, 34
Monahan, Bill, 18
Mooers, Alan, 58, 59
Moore, Jim, 35
Moore, Kelly, 62, 63
Morrow, W. G., 2
Mortensen, Ray, 35
Murray, Mike, 26
Myers, Paul, 7
Nagler, Russ, ix, 18, 19, 37, 50, 110,
   138
National Sprint Championships, 27, 29,
   37, 38, 45
Newell, Pete, 51
New Zealand National Championships,
   44, 45
Nicol, Frank, 34
Oberg, Conrad, 30, 31
Olson, Bob, 34
Olympics, ix, 16, 20–27, 30, 35, 38–43,
   46, 47, 50, 52, 55, 56, 61, 89, 90, 113
Orman, Chuck, 54
Oski I, 89
Oski II, 89, 90
Oski III, 22, 90
Pacific Coast Sprint Championships, 50,
   52, 55, 56, 58, 59, 79, 81
Page, Mike, 58, 59
Penney, Lou, ix, 9, 14, 111, 112
Perry, Charles, 70–71
Peterson, Conway, 45, 46
Phillips, R. J., 96
Pischel, Harold, ix, 10, 103
Pocock, George, 25, 32, 33, 44, 84, 108
Pocock, Stan, 84
Portland Rowing Club, 4
Pribyl, Matt, 74, 75
Prioleau, Paul, 114
Purchase, Ralph, 39, 41–43
Raney, Walt, 32, 33
Rawn, Bill, 35
Read, Frank, 96
Repath, K. H., 15
Reuther, Ron, 45, 46
Rice, Dave, 30, 31
Robertson, Oswald, 7
Robinson, Marshall, 34

Robinson, Merritt, 45, 46
Roe, Benson, 31, 32
Rogers, Gary, 55, 112
Rogers, J. M., 15
Rosenberg, Allen, 58
Royal Henley Regatta, 65, 68, 69, 75,
   76, 112
Ryan, Tim, 114
Salisbury, Alfred J., 4
Salisbury, Ed, 26, 27, 95
San Diego Crew Classic, 56, 66, 68–70,
   72, 73, 76, 78–81, 111
San Diego Rowing Club, 56
Sanford, Stork, 29, 32, 52, 58
San Francisco Rowing Club, 1
Schaeffer, Bob, 96
Scherer, Bill, 37
Schilling, Gus, 58, 59, 81
Schnack, Bill, 45, 46
Schoenbrod, 84
Schroeder, W. H., 7
Scofield, Tim, 48, 49
Sellers, John, 55, 58, 59
Serdahl, Earl, 30, 31
Seward, Sean, 74, 75
Shimasaki, Bob, 55
Shinn, Mike, 74, 75
Smith, Justus, 41–43
Smith, Kirk, 31, 32
Sonju, Norm, 32, 33
South End Rowing Club, 1
Spenger, Bob, 43
Sproul, President Robert Gordon, 28
Stack, Jack, 41, 42, 95
Stalder, Marvin, 22, 23
Steel, Malcolm, 1
Stevenson, Charles, 8, 9
Stiles, Bob, 44
Still, Les, 34
Sutro, Mark, 67, 68
Swanson, Evald, 28, 29
Swinford, Ted, 114
Talbott, George, 30, 31
Ten Eyck, Jim, 10
Tevis, Harry, 2
Thompson, Alex, 103
Thompson, Bill, 22, 23
Thompson, Tevis, 29
Thornley, Malcolm, 58, 59
Tilden, Charles Lee, 2
Titus, Bill, 84
Torrey, Harry Beal, ix, 2
Tower, Harold, 26, 27
Tracy, Clifton H., 3
Trant, Allen, 18
Turner, Dave L., 41, 42, 109, 110
Turner, Dave M., 34, 37, 39,
Turner, Ian, 37, 39, 41–43
Turner, Joel, 67, 68
Tyssowski, John, 6, 7
Udick, Ralph, 50
Ulbrickson, Al, 32, 33, 96
Van de Water, Eric, 55

Van Loo, Dick, 22
Vesper Rowing Club, 58, 113
Vespoli, 84, 85
Voorhees, Ed, 60
Waggener, Bob, 70–71
Waggerhouser, Roy, 3
Walker, Jeff, 67, 68
Wallis, Ben, ix, x, xi, 10, 14–16, 29, 89,
    103
Watt, Reg, 28, 29
Welch, Darrell, 37
Western Crew Coaches Association, 96
Western Intercollegiate Crew Coaches
    Association, 67, 78, 96
Western Sprint Championships, 47, 59,
    61, 62, 64–66
Wheeler, President Benjamin Ide, 6
White, Bob, 37
Wiesner, Don, 55
Wilder, Francis A., 3
Williams, Arleigh, 60
Witter, Dean, ix, xi, 6–8, 10, 18, 55,
    111, 137
Workman, Jim, 22, 23
Wright, Dean, 67, 68
Yancey, Gary, 48, 49, 52, 53
Yates, Jack, 28, 29
Yost, Jim, 89
Zembsch, Mark, 114

Designed and produced by David Comstock for
Western Heritage Press and The Friends of Cal Crew.
Text type is Galliard and display type is Venture Script,
composed by Robin Dellabough, David Comstock, and Dwan Typography.
Four thousand copies of the first edition were printed on
Lynx substance 60 white text paper and bound with
Roxite B 51545 pyroxylin impregnated fabric by
Thomson-Shore, Incorporated